T0272023

Unsettled Voices

From resurgent racisms to longstanding Islamophobia, from settler colonial refusals of First Nations voices to border politics and migration debates, 'free speech' has been weaponized to target racialized communities and bolster authoritarian rule. *Unsettled Voices* identifies the severe limitations and the violent consequences of 'free speech debates' typical of contemporary cultural politics, and explores the possibilities for combating racism when liberal values underpin emboldened white supremacy.

What kind of everyday racially motivated speech is protected by such an interpretation of liberal ideology? How do everyday forms of social expression that vilify and intimidate find shelter through an inflation of the notion of freedom of speech? Furthermore, how do such forms refuse the idea that language can be a performative act from which harm can be derived? Racialized speech has conjured and shaped the subjectivities of multiple intersecting participants, reproducing new and problematic forms of precarity. These vulnerabilities have been experienced from the sound of rubber bullets in the Occupied Palestinian Territories to UK hate speech legislation, to the spontaneous performance of a First Nations war dance on the Australian Rules football pitch.

This book identifies the deep limitations and the violent consequences of the longstanding and constantly developing 'free speech debates' typical of so many contexts in the West, and explores the possibilities for combating racism when liberal values are 'weaponized' to target racialized communities.

This book was originally published as a special issue of *Continuum: Journal of Media & Cultural Studies*.

Tanja Dreher is Scientia Associate Professor in Media at the University of New South Wales, Sydney, Australia. Tanja's research focuses on the politics of listening in the context of media and resurgent racisms, Indigenous sovereignties and intersectional feminism.

Michael R. Griffiths is Senior Lecturer in English and Writing at the University of Wollongong, Australia. He is the author of *The Distribution of Settlement: Appropriation and Refusal in Australian Literature and Culture* (2018). His essays have appeared in *Discourse, Postcolonial Studies, Australian Humanities Review* and many other venues. He is an active participant in the Jindaola Project—an initiative on decolonizing curriculum within the University of Wollongong.

Timothy Laurie is Lecturer in the School of Communication at the University of Technology Sydney, Australia. His core research interests include cultural theory, gender and sexuality studies, and philosophy, and he is Managing Editor of *Continuum: Journal of Media & Cultural Studies*. Currently, Timothy is co-authoring a book with Dr Hannah Stark on love and politics.

Unsettled Voices

Beyond Free Speech in the Late Liberal Era

Edited by
**Tanja Dreher, Michael R. Griffiths and
Timothy Laurie**

Routledge
Taylor & Francis Group

LONDON AND NEW YORK

First published 2021
by Routledge
2 Park Square, Milton Park, Abingdon, Oxon OX14 4RN

and by Routledge
52 Vanderbilt Avenue, New York, NY 10017

Routledge is an imprint of the Taylor & Francis Group, an informa business

Introduction, Chapters 1–7, 9–11 and Afterword © 2021 Taylor & Francis
Chapter 8 © 2018 Anshuman A. Mondal. Originally published as Open Access.

British Library Cataloguing in Publication Data
A catalogue record for this book is available from the British Library

ISBN: 978-0-367-48579-5 (hbk)
ISBN: 978-0-367-72252-4 (pbk)
ISBN: 978-1-003-04172-6 (ebk)

Typeset in Myriad Pro
by Newgen Publishing UK

Publisher's Note
The publisher accepts responsibility for any inconsistencies that may have arisen during the conversion of this book from journal articles to book chapters, namely the inclusion of journal terminology.

Disclaimer
Every effort has been made to contact copyright holders for their permission to reprint material in this book. The publishers would be grateful to hear from any copyright holder who is not here acknowledged and will undertake to rectify any errors or omissions in future editions of this book.

Contents

Citation Information   ix
Notes on Contributors   xi
Acknowledgements   xiv

Introduction: Unsettled voices: beyond free speech in the late liberal era   1
Tanja Dreher, Michael R. Griffiths and Timothy Laurie

1 Beyond denial: 'not racism' as racist violence   9
  Alana Lentin

2 'You cunts can do as you like': the obscenity and absurdity of free speech to
  Blackfullas   24
  Chelsea Bond, Bryan Mukandi and Shane Coghill

3 Off script and indefensible: the failure of the 'moderate Muslim'   38
  Randa Abdel-Fattah and Mehal Krayem

4 Inquiry mentality and occasional mourning in the settler colonial carceral   53
  Micaela Sahhar and Michael R. Griffiths

5 What does racial (in)justice sound like? On listening, acoustic violence and
  the booing of Adam Goodes   68
  Poppy de Souza

6 The 'free speech' of the (un)free   83
  Yassir Morsi

7 Silence and resistance: Aboriginal women working within and against
  the archive   96
  Evelyn Araluen Corr

8 The shape of free speech: rethinking liberal free speech theory   112
  Anshuman A. Mondal

9 In a different voice: 'a letter from Manus Island' as poetic manifesto   127
   Anne Surma

10 Manus prison poetics/our voice: revisiting 'A Letter From Manus Island', a
   reply to Anne Surma   136
   Behrouz Boochani

11 Behrouz Boochani and the Manus Prison narratives: merging translation with
   philosophical reading   140
   Omid Tofighian

   Afterword: Reconstructing voices and situated listening   149
   Timothy Laurie, Tanja Dreher, Michael R. Griffiths and Omid Tofighian

   Index   160

Citation Information

The chapters in this book were originally published in *Continuum: Journal of Media & Cultural Studies*, volume 32, issue 4 (2018). When citing this material, please use the original page numbering for each article, as follows:

Chapter 1
Beyond denial: 'not racism' as racist violence
Alana Lentin
Continuum: Journal of Media & Cultural Studies, volume 32, issue 4 (2018), pp. 400–414

Chapter 2
'You cunts can do as you like': the obscenity and absurdity of free speech to Blackfullas
Chelsea Bond, Bryan Mukandi and Shane Coghill
Continuum: Journal of Media & Cultural Studies, volume 32, issue 4 (2018), pp. 415–428

Chapter 3
Off script and indefensible: the failure of the 'moderate Muslim'
Randa Abdel-Fattah and Mehal Krayem
Continuum: Journal of Media & Cultural Studies, volume 32, issue 4 (2018), pp. 429–443

Chapter 4
Inquiry mentality and occasional mourning in the settler colonial carceral
Micaela Sahhar and Michael R. Griffiths
Continuum: Journal of Media & Cultural Studies, volume 32, issue 4 (2018), pp. 444–458

Chapter 5
What does racial (in)justice sound like? On listening, acoustic violence and the booing of Adam Goodes
Poppy de Souza
Continuum: Journal of Media & Cultural Studies, volume 32, issue 4 (2018), pp. 459–473

Chapter 6
The 'free speech' of the (un)free
Yassir Morsi
Continuum: Journal of Media & Cultural Studies, volume 32, issue 4 (2018), pp. 474–486

Chapter 7

Silence and resistance: Aboriginal women working within and against the archive
Evelyn Araluen Corr
Continuum: Journal of Media & Cultural Studies, volume 32, issue 4 (2018), pp. 487–502

Chapter 8

The shape of free speech: rethinking liberal free speech theory
Anshuman A. Mondal
Continuum: Journal of Media & Cultural Studies, volume 32, issue 4 (2018), pp. 503–517

Chapter 9

In a different voice: 'a letter from Manus Island' as poetic manifesto
Anne Surma
Continuum: Journal of Media & Cultural Studies, volume 32, issue 4 (2018), pp. 518–526

Chapter 10

Manus prison poetics/our voice: revisiting 'A Letter From Manus Island', a reply to Anne Surma
Behrouz Boochani
Continuum: Journal of Media & Cultural Studies, volume 32, issue 4 (2018), pp. 527–531

Chapter 11

Behrouz Boochani and the Manus Prison narratives: merging translation with philosophical reading
Omid Tofighian
Continuum: Journal of Media & Cultural Studies, volume 32, issue 4 (2018), pp. 532–540

For any permission-related enquiries please visit:
www.tandfonline.com/page/help/permissions

Notes on Contributors

Randa Abdel-Fattah is Discovery Early Career Researcher Award (DECRA) Research Fellow researching Islamophobia, race, youth and the war on terror in the Department of Sociology at Macquarie University, Australia. A long-time anti-racism activist, Randa is also the multi-award-winning author of 11 novels published and translated in over 20 countries. Her books include *Islamophobia and Everyday Multiculturalism* (Routledge, 2019) and the forthcoming *Coming of Age in the War on Terror* (NewSouth Publishing, 2021).

Evelyn Araluen Corr is a poet and teacher researching Indigenous literatures at the University of Sydney, Australia. She is a descendant of the Bundjalung nation but was born and raised in Dharug country and community.

Chelsea Bond is Senior Research Fellow at the Poche Centre for Indigenous Health at the University of Queensland, Australia. A Munanjahli and South Sea Islander woman, her work focuses on interpreting and privileging Indigenous knowledges and perspectives in relation to health, race, culture and identity. She has published a number of papers in relation to strength-based health promotion practice, Indigenous social capital and the conceptualization of Aboriginality within public health.

Behrouz Boochani is a journalist, scholar and filmmaker and has won numerous awards, including the Amnesty International Australia 2017 Media Award, the Liberty Victoria 2018 Empty Chair Award and the Anna Politkovskaya Award for journalism. Boochani co-directed (with Arash Kamali Sarvestani) the film *Chauka, Please Tell Us the Time* (2017) and won the Victorian Prize for Literature for his book *No Friend but the Mountains: Writing from Manus Prison* (Picador, 2018). Boochani is Senior Adjunct Research Fellow at the Ngāi Tahu Research Centre of the University of Canterbury, New Zealand, and Adjunct Associate Professor of Social Sciences at the University of South Wales, Sydney, Australia.

Shane Coghill is a Goenpul man from Quandamooka with a background in anthropology and archaeology. He is currently undertaking his PhD within the School of Historical and Philosophical Inquiry at the University of Queensland, Australia.

Tanja Dreher is Scientia Associate Professor in Media at the University of New South Wales, Sydney, Australia. Tanja's research focuses on the politics of listening in the context of media and resurgent racisms, Indigenous sovereignties and intersectional feminism.

Michael R. Griffiths is Senior Lecturer in English and Writing at the University of Wollongong, Australia. He is the author of *The Distribution of Settlement: Appropriation and Refusal in Australian Literature and Culture* (UWAP, 2018). His essays have appeared in *Discourse, Postcolonial Studies, Australian Humanities Review* and many other venues. He is an active participant in the Jindaola Project—an initiative on decolonizing curriculum within the University of Wollongong.

Mehal Krayem is Researcher in the Faculty of Arts and Social Science at the University of Technology Sydney, Australia.

Timothy Laurie is Lecturer in the School of Communication at the University of Technology Sydney, Australia. His core research interests include cultural theory, gender and sexuality studies, and philosophy, and he is Managing Editor of *Continuum: Journal of Media & Cultural Studies*. Currently, Timothy is co-authoring a book with Dr Hannah Stark on love and politics.

Alana Lentin is Associate Professor of Cultural and Social Analysis at Western Sydney University, Australia. She is a Jewish woman who is a settler on Gadigal land. She works on the critical theorization of race, racism and anti-racism. Her latest book is *Why Race Still Matters* (Polity, 2020) and she previously published *The Crises of Multiculturalism with Gavan Titley* (Zed, 2011). She co-edits the book series *Challenging Migration Studies*. Her academic and media articles as well as videos, podcasts and teaching materials can be found at www.alanalentin.net.

Anshuman A. Mondal is Professor of Modern Literature at the University of East Anglia (UEA), UK, and Chair of the Postcolonial Studies Association (PSA), UK. He is collaboratively leading a project with the English Association, University English (UK), the Institute of English Studies and the PSA on 'Decolonising the Discipline'. He is the author of four books and several essays and articles, including *Islam and Controversy: The Politics of Free Speech After Rushdie* (2014) and is co-editor, with Tanja Dreher, of *Ethical Responsiveness and the Politics of Difference* (2018). He is currently working on a book on anti-racism and 'free speech'.

Yassir Morsi is Lecturer in Politics at La Trobe University, Melbourne, Australia, and author of *Radical Skin, Moderate Masks* (2017). He is the Australian Critical Race and Whiteness Studies Association (ACRAWSA) Vice-President.

Bryan Mukandi is currently Lecturer in Medical Ethics at the University of Queensland, Australia. His background is in medicine, public health and philosophy, and his teaching and research revolve around the health and well-being of those described by Frantz Fanon as 'the damned of the Earth'. Bryan has published work philosophy and health publications and he is currently working on a monograph on Black consciousness.

Micaela Sahhar lectures on the history of ideas at Trinity College, University of Melbourne, Australia. Her current work focuses on narrative history, the settler–colonial paradigm and modes of resistance in the Israeli–Palestinian and Australian contexts.

Poppy de Souza (she/her) is an interdisciplinary researcher with a diverse portfolio career that leans across cultural, creative and critical research and practice. Recent scholarship has explored sound, race and the politics of voice/listening in the contexts of settler colonialism, offshore (and onshore) detention, community media and struggles for racial justice. Poppy is currently Research Fellow in the School of the Arts and Media at the University of New South Wales, Sydney, Australia, and is Adjunct Research Fellow with the Griffith Centre for Social and Cultural Research at Griffith University, Brisbane, Australia.

Anne Surma is Associate Professor in the English and Creative Arts programme at Murdoch University in Western Australia. She takes a literary approach to exploring the effects of language use in public and professional communications. She is author of *Public and Professional Writing: Ethics, Imagination and Rhetoric* (Palgrave Macmillan, 2005) and *Imagining the Cosmopolitan in Public and Professional Writing* (Palgrave Macmillan, 2013) and is currently completing a book-length project (with co-author Kristin Demetrious) which examines the shaping of contemporary social issues by neo-liberal narratives.

Omid Tofighian is an award-winning lecturer, researcher and community advocate, combining philosophy with interests in citizen media, popular culture, displacement and discrimination. He is Adjunct Lecturer in the School of the Arts and Media, University of South Wales (UNSW), Australia; Honorary Research Associate for the Department of Philosophy, University of Sydney, Australia; member of Border Criminologies, University of Oxford, UK; a faculty member at Iran Academia; and the Campaign Manager for 'Why Is My Curriculum White? – Australasia'. His published works include *Myth and Philosophy in Platonic Dialogues* (Palgrave Macmillan, 2016), and he is the translator of Behouz Boochani's multi-award-winning book *No Friend but the Mountains: Writing from Manus Prison* (Picador, 2018) and co-editor of *'Refugee Filmmaking', Alphaville: Journal of Film and Screen Media* (2019).

Acknowledgements

The editors would like to thank every contributor to this book: Behrouz Boochani for allowing us to reprint his work and for continuing to speak truth to power; Omid Tofighian for his manifest erudition; Anne Surma for her impassioned letter to Behrouz; Chelsea Bond, Bryan Mukandi and Shane Coghill for their theorized form of decolonial resistance; Alana Lentin for unfailing commitment to anti-racist research and pedagogy; Randa Abdel-Fattah and Mehal Krayem for breaking down the failure of the 'moderate Muslim' discourse, here and elsewhere; Poppy De Souza for teaching me that the sound of rubber bullets are discernable to some and that violence echoes worldwide; Yassir Morsi for his unflinching self-examination, and accompanying critique; Evelyn Araluen Corr for documenting the Aboriginal women's voices to whom Australia would not listen; Micaela Sahhar, my co-author in our article within this volume, for her commitment to decolonization everywhere and for the stories of Palestine we share; and Anshu Mondal for shaping the speech to come.

This book began with a colloquium on 'Free Speech and Religious Freedom after Charlie Hebdo and Section 18C' hosted by the Legal Intersections Research Centre (LIRC) at the University of Wollongong (UoW) in 2016, and co-convened by Tanja Dreher and Mike Griffiths. Thank you to LIRC for funding the colloquium, and to UoW for the Visiting International Scholar Award which brought Anshuman Mondal to Wollongong. Thank you to the Director of LIRC, Professor Nan Seuffert, for her inspiring leadership and support for the early conversations that began this book.

The editors also acknowledge the support of *Continuum: A Journal of Media and Cultural Studies* for first publishing these essays as a special issue (32, 4 [2018]), all the anonymous referees who contributed to that volume, and the editorial team – Panizza Allmark, John Tebbutt and Jessica Taylor – for their tireless efforts in collaborating with authors, reviewers and publishers to support research in cultural and media studies.

Tanja Dreher's work for this volume has been supported by an Australian Research Council Future Fellowship (FT140100515) and the Scientia Scheme at the University of New South Wales. Tanja's interest in the ethics, politics and practices of listening and speaking has developed over many years, and Tanja thanks Cate Thill, Justine Lloyd, Poppy de Souza, Penny O'Donnell, Susan Bickford, Leah Bassel, Bronwyn Carlson, Nick Couldry, Gerard Goggin, Sukhmani Khorana, Nicole Matthews, Lisa Slater, Gavan Titley and the many contributors to this volume for inspiration and vital conversations. Tanja would particularly like to thank Mike Griffiths for the exemplary collaboration and critical insights at every stage of developing this book, and Tim Laurie for vital contributions and expanding the scope in the most generative ways.

Michael Griffiths would like to thank every contributor once again, and acknowledge the incisive and invaluable writing, thought and advice of Tim Laurie and Tanja Dreher. There, my co-editors, Tim for coming on board the editorial team and contributing critically to the Afterword and Tanja Dreher for her patience and commitment to equity (particularly around editorial work-sharing)… and for listening… unwaveringly. Mike would also like to thank Micaela Sahhar once again for her critical and committed scholarship in our co-authored article in this volume and throughout her work.

Tim Laurie would like to thank again all the contributors, and Michael and Tanja for their attentiveness, patience and critical acuity both in the editorial process and in writing the Afterword. He would also like to add further gratitude to both Remy Low and Lucy Fiske, who have been sources of inspiration and advice in thinking through the importance of ethical issues within academic publishing practices.

Great thanks also to Faye Gardner at Newgen for shepherding us through the production process with a steady hand, and Caroline Church at Taylor and Francis for the opportunity to reprint and update this work.

This book is dedicated to all those subjects at the intersection of Indigenous, racialized and gendered experiences whose voices are ignored and suffocated, even as they raise those same voices to the sky, speaking truth to power.

Introduction

Unsettled voices: beyond free speech in the late liberal era

Tanja Dreher, Michael R. Griffiths and Timothy Laurie

When US President Donald Trump insisted on calling COVID-19 'the Chinese virus' just as the epicentre of the global pandemic was shifting from Wuhan to New York City in mid-March 2020, he mobilised racist speech in a mode that shows key features of the long-running 'free speech debates' that have increasingly come to shelter such speech from scrutiny. Challenged by a reporter as to why he continued to use the phrase even after documented racist incidents against Chinese-Americans, Trump replied: 'Because it comes from China. It's not racist at all. It comes from China, that's why. I want to be accurate'. In a move that sidelines those who warn of resurgent Sinophobia during the global corona-virus crisis, President Trump asserted the 'debatability' of claims of racism (Titley 2019) and a simple commitment to 'facts', shorn of any acknowledgement of the consequences of such racialised speech. For this US President, this marks not a break but a continuity between the pre- and post-coronavirus moment, a continuity that extends back to as early as Charlottesville. This book identifies the deep limitations and violent consequences of the longstanding and constantly developing 'free speech debates' typical of so many contexts in the West, and foregrounds decolonial and critical race possibilities when liberal values are 'weaponised' to target racialised communities.

Unsettled Voices provides a trenchant critique of absolutist free speech debates and centres situated knowledges and defiant voices beyond the racialised frame of late liberalism. The collection works against an absolutist framing of 'free speech' typical of trans-nationally mediated debates in the West since at least the publication of Salman Rushdie's *The Satanic Verses* in 1988, the Danish cartoons controversy of 2005 and, more recently, the murders at Charlie Hebdo in Paris. What kind of everyday racially motivated speech is protected by narrow interpretations of liberal ideology? How do everyday forms of social expression that vilify and intimidate find shelter through an inflation of the notion of freedom of speech and a refusal of the idea that language can be a performative act from which harm can be derived? What are the possibilities to combat racism when liberal values are 'weaponised' to target racialised communities? This critical account of 'free speech' opens space for a capacious account of voice and 'speaking differently' (Boochani, in this volume) beyond narrow assertive individualism and media focus on the claims to victim status of angry white men. While debate on the freedom to vilify is high on the media and public agenda, the policing of racialised voices raises far less concern. *Unsettled Voices* examines how these free speech controversies serve to silence the voices of those marked as other globally today, and foregrounds possibilities beyond this paradox. These issues are explored in transnational contexts with a particular focus on settler colonial Australia.

The paradoxes of free speech debates in Australia

From racist cartoons to booing at football matches, contemporary multicultures and settler colonies are characterised by recurring debates about the meaning of free speech and its limits. These mediated debates on freedom of expression are a flashpoint for wider processes of racialisation, nationalism and border policing. Here we sketch just a few of the high-profile 'controversies' that have characterised the long-running free speech 'debates' in Australia, all of which are analysed in detail in the chapters that follow.

Indigeneity and Islam have been at the centre of heated public debates about free speech in Australia, with conservative politicians and commentators asserting the absolute nature of freedom of speech over and against the everyday suffering it can cause. The 2016 federal election saw re-elected members of government call immediately for the repeal of legislation that regulates hate speech, Section 18C of the Racial Discrimination Act. This marked a renewal of the long-running '18C debate' triggered in 2011 by one of the rare rulings under this legislation, in which the conservative journalist Andrew Bolt was found in breach of anti-vilification provisions as two columns focused on a number of Indigenous Australians were, according to the court, not written in good faith and contained factual errors. The debate gained further momentum when the Human Rights Commission began an investigation of a cartoon by Bill Leak, a regular contributor to the national broadsheet *The Australian*, in which Leak depicted an Aboriginal father with a beer can in his hand and unable to recall his son's name. The cartoon appeared not long after the TV broadcast of footage of Dylan Voller, a First Nations teenager, shackled and in a spit hood in a juvenile detention centre. Described as 'Australia's Abu Ghraib', this footage also prompted claims that poor parenting was to blame for the massive over-incarceration of Indigenous children in Australia – an attitude that was inflated by Leak's cartoon.

As elsewhere, recent years have seen a resurgence of far-right political parties and movements in Australia. The return of One Nation's Pauline Hanson to the federal parliament prompted defence of a celebrity talk show host who advocated banning Muslim immigration. During 2015, star Australian Football League (AFL) player and former Australian of the Year, Adnyamathanha man Adam Goodes was subjected to a sustained campaign of booing by AFL crowds. Much of the public debate centred on the claim that this booing was 'not racist', but rather a benign sporting tradition. During the 18C controversy, the federal Attorney-General defended what he called 'the right to be a bigot'.

While debate on the freedom to vilify is high on the media and public agenda, the policing of racialised voices raises far less concern. First Nations leaders routinely call on governments to listen to Indigenous voices and expertise, to little avail. Most recently, the Uluru Statement from the Heart proposed an Indigenous Voice to Parliament, only to be rejected out of hand by the Turnbull federal government. In 2016, Warlpiri woman and Minister for Local Government Bess Nungarrayi Price was warned over disorderly conduct and told by the Speaker 'the language of the assembly is English' after she interjected in Warlpiri in a Northern Territory parliamentary debate. Kaurna elder Katrina Ngaityalya Power was criticised as 'insulting' and 'disrespectful' for a 2017 Anzac Day speech which referenced invasion and slavery.

A Facebook post by former ABC presenter Yassmin Abdel-Magied on Anzac Day 2017, the national public holiday commemorating the Australia New Zealand Army Corps (ANZAC) and Australian military forces generally, was also the catalyst for a vitriolic public debate. Like Goodes, Abdel-Magied was a former Young Queenslander of the Year and sat on numerous boards. After she posted 'Lest We Forget (Manus, Nauru, Syria, Palestine …)', the public broadcaster acquiesced to calls to end her contract and Abdel-Magied eventually left Australia. Later in 2017, a submission by the Islamic Council of Victoria that federal funding was urgently needed to create safe space for Muslim youth to meet and talk about a range of issues 'which in a public space would sound inflammatory' was dismissed as advocating for 'hate space' by the Victorian Premier.

This book examines how these free speech controversies serve to silence the voices of those marked as other globally today, and foregrounds possibilities to work beyond this paradox. Within late liberal political culture, the terms of debate by which difference is processed have risked subordinating considerations of equality to increasingly dominant and inflated conceptions of freedom. In the post 9/11 world globally, Muslim subjects are called upon to perform an ideal of the moderate, good, liberal subject that is nonetheless vulnerable to the label of 'radicalism'. First Nations in settler colonies are often called upon to perform such liberal subjectivity and silenced if they refuse political norms. For instance, Indigenous people calling to change or abolish 'Australia Day', a national public holiday celebrated on the anniversary of the arrival of the First Fleet on 26 January 1788, are labelled as divisive, uncivil or dangerous.

While the debates on Section 18C of the Racial Discrimination Act and racist cartoons have continued to make headlines for years, a range of laws that increasingly restrict free speech in broad ways are overlooked (Gelber 2017). For example, in 2015 a law was introduced prohibiting 'entrusted persons' employed in asylum-seeker detention centres from disclosing protected information. State governments have passed laws that increase police powers and curtail the right to peacefully protest. Recent laws also threaten the ability of journalists to expose government activities that are corrupt or illegal (Gelber 2017). A proposed Bill preventing the acceptance of international donations if the money goes towards advocacy has the potential to silence the vital advocacy role of charities and NGOs (Price 2017).

These restrictions on freedom of speech will be familiar in many contexts, including the United States where the Trump administration has extended anti-protest laws and issued the Centres for Disease Control and Prevention list of 'forbidden words', or France which has seen 'a steady creep towards ever more repressive state surveillance' since the *Charlie Hebdo* attacks (Titley et al. 2017). In both of these cases, the right uses speech and expression to its advantage but is far from reticent about restricting it where it suits agendas aligned to their political interest. In these contexts, as in Australia, public criticism of these restrictions is muted, while the 'free speech debates' centred on the right to vilify racialised communities rage on. Here we see the hypocrisy and the conservative agenda of so much high-profile and highly charged public 'debate' on the vital and very complex questions of speech, consequences and regulation. 'Free speech' has become a key battleground in long-running culture wars, played out in specific national and local contexts and deeply inflected by transnational mediation. Indeed, we see that liberal values such as 'free speech' have been 'weaponised' (Fekete in Titley et al. 2017), inextricably connected to the increased surveillance and over-policing of racialised communities in Europe, North America, Australia and beyond.

Shifting the terms of debate
Unsettled Voices is an opportunity to reframe the debate on speech and difference from outside liberal frameworks. The contributors not only critique, but also move beyond the racist and conservative agenda of free speech debates, suggesting possibilities to think outside the limitations of the liberal free speech paradigm.

Against the narrow conception of 'free speech' that dominates in the late liberal era, this book foregrounds an expansive conception of voice, resistance and refusal. Beyond the racist and conservative agenda of free speech debates, this collection focuses on the politics of voice, listening and receptivity, and the necessity to shift hierarchies of attention and value. The collection privileges knowledges, expertise and voices which are routinely marginalised or silenced in public discourse – including writing from detention, writing to avoid essentialisms and from unsettling and resisting Islamophobic and settler colonial structures. It also asks, what forms of solidarity, responsiveness or relationality are needed to meet writing from sovereignty and precarity? And how might close attention to unevenly shared vulnerabilities enable interdependent and defiant politics? In addressing these questions, the book marks out the limitations of so many contemporary 'free speech debates', highlights the violent consequences for racialised peoples, and suggests vital alternatives.

The book begins with a chapter by Alana Lentin, 'Beyond denial: "not racism" as racist violence', which shows that the excusing of racism is itself a reification and amplification of it – 'doubling down' on 'discursive violence' as she puts it. Building on an exhaustive survey of recent studies in critical consideration of racism, Lentin reminds us that racism is not an attitude but an action. What Lentin calls 'not racism' describes this 'denial and redefinition of racism'. The chapter draws out multiple forms of minimising racism, for instance, the claim that calling attention to racism is 'unhelpful'. The chapter usefully frames several key concerns that run through all the chapters in this volume. Most crucially, like a number of contributors, Lentin implicitly shows that while unconstrained free speech advocates accuse us anti-racist killjoys – we who point out the structural violence of the speech they would defend – of restricting free speech, the restriction and diminution of the value of speech is often covertly undertaken by these 'not racist' free speech advocates themselves. By delegitimising speech that takes umbrage with structural racism, a whole range of perspectives are refused a voice and platform for enunciation. 'Not racism', as Lentin names it, amplifies white fear of being labelled racist even as it diminishes the space within which people of colour and anti-racists might use speech to call attention to instances of their marginalisation and silencing.

The diminution of freedom (of speech and otherwise) from the experience of people of colour in the context of white supremacist societies is markedly drawn out in '"You cunts can do as you like": The obscenity and absurdity of free speech to Blackfullas' by Chelsea Bond, Bryan Mukandi and Shane Coghill. Bond, Mukandi and Coghill work from the example of Aboriginal songwoman Deborah Cheetham's refusal to sing the words 'we are young and free', on an invitation to publicly perform the Australian national anthem. Youth and freedom, here, signify values of Australia's settler population – the idea of Australia as a 'young' country founded on 200 years of settlement and not 40,000 years of Indigenous habitation as well as that of the freedom of the settler population, which First Nations experience to a highly diminished degree. Cheetham proposed, instead, the words 'in peace and harmony' as alternative lyrics for the anthem for her performance (and was refused).

That Cheetham would prefer to foreground the aspiration of her people to 'peace and harmony' over the fiction of Australia's 'youth and freedom' reveals the degree to which certain liberal values have come to privilege whiteness while others might contribute to conviviality (Gilroy 2005). Where liberty, equality and fraternity perhaps marked the founding values of modern liberalism, in many of the contributions in this volume we see that freedom is a value that can both emancipate and privilege. Equality – or 'peace and harmony' to use

Cheetham's formulation of it – might be seen as an equally important value that could restore some balance to the distribution of freedom and agency in societies where freedom of speech is often disproportionately allowed. As Bond, Mukandi and Coghill suggest, freedom in the phrase 'we are young and free' is not neutral but is predicated on the elimination or assimilation of 'Blackfullas'. This difference in application of standards for speech is drawn out further since, as Bond, Mukandi and Coghill survey, a disproportionate number of Aboriginal prisoners are incarcerated for charges linked to 'offensive language'. As they point out, there is a deep asymmetry between the Australian 'Attorney General's claim that Australians have the "right to be bigots" and say things that may cause offense, and the systematic over-surveillance and incarceration of Blackfullas on offensive language charges'. The ostensibly neutral right to speech is not equally distributed.

There is a similarly bitter irony in the way Australian broadcaster Yassmin Abdel-Magied was widely censured in media circles for what was seen as offensive speech by the very conservatives who claimed that free speech should remain unconstrained. What is revealed in this exchange is that free speech can be constrained but tends to be more so when it offends hegemonic values over and against when it is challenged in instances of harm to racialised minorities. That challenges to free speech from people of colour and their allies are seen as political incorrectness is then, often, counteracted by the hegemony of what some have called 'patriotic correctness'. Randa Abdel-Fattah and Mehal Krayem call attention to just this double bind in their chapter, which takes the case of Abdel Maggied as a starting point. They argue that the speech of the ideal 'moderate Muslim' is not a form of enunciation that can readily dissent from mainstream liberal views without facing the charge of radicalism. Thus, for Abdel-Fattah and Krayem, '[t]he ideal moderate' is 'simply a cosmetic addition to the multicultural display with no overt political inclinations and certainly no agenda to unsettle and destabilise the centrality of Whiteness'.

While Abdel-Fattah and Krayem focus on the discourse of the 'moderate Muslim' that is coaxed and rewarded in the public sphere, Micaela Sahhar and Michael R. Griffiths analyse how modes and manifestations of speech are managed and, at times, circumscribed, within the operations of settler colonial liberalism. These authors focus on forms of speech such as protest and government inquiries to unravel how forms of speech that critique or challenge settler colonial sovereignty are often restrained. Their chapter, 'Inquiry mentality and occasional mourning in the settler colonial carceral', focuses on the management of difference both internally in relation to First Nations bodies and externally in relation to refugees and asylum seekers by appropriating a late liberal language of 'protection'. The 'inquiry mentality' 'produces a din of discourse about the "tragic" violence to which First Nations subjects are subordinated without implementing the measures which might not only ameliorate such conditions but dismantle the settler colonial carceral as such'. Protests, vigils and public dissent in support of incarcerated refugees and asylum seekers are seen to be individualised and personalised – for example, the slogan 'not in my name' – and thus incapable of harnessing a collective force or the transformative impact required for the structural re-framing of discourse.

Poppy de Souza's contribution, 'What does racial (in)justice sound like?' centres on the booing of Adnyamathanha man Adam Goodes during the 2015 AFL season. Goodes drew sustained booing for weeks after performing a celebratory Indigenous dance on scoring a goal. De Souza suggests '[i]n the popular imagination at least, the roar of the crowd is the sonic barometer that measures who is accepted and who is rejected'. The chapter is an attempt to make sense of the popular refusal to accept that it was racism that led to the booing of Goodes. What, de Souza asks, prevents some from 'hearing racism in the crowd's booing?'. De Souza parses what she calls the 'acoustic violence' arising when 'those who are the targets of racialised violence become *attuned* to sonic qualities that are indistinct to untrained ears'. She identifies this acoustic violence by traversing multiple examples, from the US South under Jim Crow to the Occupied West Bank and back to the football stadiums of 2015 Australia, in order to show how often 'the white ear marks out the sonic boundary between belonging and non-belonging (or un-belonging), inclusion and exclusion; where words and sounds perform another kind of dispossession and displacement'.

Yassir Morsi's contribution to this book further develops the analysis developed by Krayem and Abdel-Fattah, calling attention to the inability of a Muslim to speak freely vested precisely in the context of contemporary liberal free speech debates. Morsi's chapter, 'The "free speech" of the (un)free', foregrounds his own position through an autoethnographic technique of writing; as he puts it, 'this research paper's nonlinear logic and its absence of sequence is my argument. I want in my discussion on free speech to embody my struggles as an "Islamist" to freely speak'. Through storytelling and confession, Morsi's chapter subtly articulates the degree to which a Muslim voice that wishes to depart from (and, indeed, challenge) the commonplace articulations of the apologist for Islam (the moderate) is always stifled and, indeed, stuttering. The chapter centres on an account of a television appearance during which Morsi struggled to find a way to critique Western colonialism without playing the role of the 'good Muslim' who must first denounce terrorist acts and movements of which he is not a part. The strength of Morsi's contribution comes above all in its method – revealing in a performative mode the degree to which challenges to the logic of liberalism will always, themselves, lack the cogency generated by liberalism's own self-generating logic. Morsi shows how, at least within liberal forms, the Muslim cannot speak. In speaking about this withholding of speech, Morsi's chapter speaks volumes.

Evelyn Araluen Corr's chapter, 'Silence and resistance: Aboriginal women working within and against the archive', acts to restore and record the history of Aboriginal women's self-representation as an explicit response to the silencing, specifically, of Aboriginal women's voices. Araluen Corr draws out the ambivalence of the colonial archive as simultaneously a site of the subordination of Aboriginal people to power (both material and symbolic) and also a space of reclamation – 'a repository of family history and thus also a site of recovery'. The chapter usefully surveys the work of multiple contributors to this critique of archive fever, from Larissa Behrendt to Natalie Harkin. The heart of her contribution comes in a sustained account of Maria Lock – a Dharug woman who, in the 1830s, was the first recorded writer to identify as Aboriginal. As Araluen Corr suggests,

> Engaging directly with Aboriginal expression in this period does not reveal a reconciled endorsement of Aboriginality as a relational primitivism of colonial authority, but rather a pluralism of the modes in which Aboriginal people resisted the material implications of their racial status.

Araluen Corr's chapter thus draws out the way Aboriginal women have, since contact, been articulating resistance in modes that are often in contention with stereotypical and reductive traces dominating the archive.

Anshuman A. Mondal contributes an exploration of the spatial metaphorics on which liberal ideas of freedom of expression are grounded (and how they might otherwise be). In 'The shape of free speech: Rethinking liberal free speech theory', Mondal anchors his discussion in a timely revisiting of one of the classic documents of liberalism, John Stuart Mill's 1859 *On Liberty*. In doing so, Mondal suggests two spatial metaphors: one that describes how Mill sees liberty functioning and one that describes how liberty might actually and more usefully be understood to function. The first is that of 'a single plane: smooth, continuous, homogeneous, indivisible and extendable without interruption until it reaches the outer limits'. This conception of liberty sees it as 'unidimensional', not possessing positive freedom but always being defined by an uninterrupted and uninterruptable negative freedom ('freedom from') that is never to be interrupted. For Mondal, Mill commits an error in suggesting that individual freedom of opinion is absolute and, in particular, in extending that absolutism to the external plane of social relations. These subtle deconstructions of the limits of Mill's classical assertions on liberty are accompanied by a constructive suggestion for possible future ways to construe freedom. Mondal suggests, following Talal Asad, that freedom, far from being a kind of homogeneous planar force, is a set of 'liquid' flows that are shaped by external social forces. Freedom is not an absolute irreducible value, then, but rather one which can be shaped to positive and negative ends; if freedom can be curtailed, then we can also debate the circumstances when it might (or might not) be appropriate for it to be curtailed.

The book concludes with three short chapters centred on the work of writer, journalist, scholar, cultural advocate and filmmaker Behrouz Boochani – a case study in the way expression should be extended and amplified from a position of vulnerability, precarity and detention that is normally silenced. Boochani produces work from Australian immigration detention on Manus Island, Papua New Guinea. On 9 December 2017, *The Saturday Paper* published 'A Letter from Manus Island', an essay and poetic manifesto 'for humanity and love' written by Boochani as a 'humanitarian message to Australia society and beyond' after a three-week protest in which he and 600 fellow refugee and asylum-seeker prisoners refused the Australian government's attempts to transfer them from immigration detention in Delta Camp and into 'transit centres' on Manus Island. To mark this piece, and Behrouz's contribution to public discourse while held on Manus, the essay was performed in the courtyard at the Malthouse Theatre in Melbourne by writer and poet Maxine Beneba Clarke (The Saturday Paper 2017). In the chapter, 'In a different voice: "a letter from Manus Island" as poetic manifesto', Anne Surma responds in the form of a letter, in direct reply to Boochani's own. Suma reflects on conventional responses to the ethical call to solidarity from vulnerable subjects, critiquing contemporary practices of humanitarianism under the influence of late liberal politics, the market and technology. Instead, Surma focuses on Boochani's 'different voices' – 'you instantiate another mode of writing and speaking' … 'you speak to us directly in an alternative register, so that we can stop, read and listen carefully, and perhaps learn to respond and relate to you otherwise'. In response to Boochani's writing, Surma discerns an alternative mode of humanitarianism, centred not on a trope of passive victimhood, but rather on the call to solidarity in response to defiant resistance.

Behrouz Boochani responds to Surma's chapter in 'Manus prison poetics/our voice: revisiting "A Letter From Manus Island", a reply to Anne Surma'. Throughout his work, Boochani has developed the concept of the Kyriarchal System: 'a complex set of structures that subject imprisoned refugees to relentless and pervasive practices of micro-control and macro-control'. In this chapter, Boochani emphasises that many of the key structures of Western societies participate, in their own ways, in this Kyriarchal System – universities, schools, army barracks, media, governments and human rights organisations. By using terminology and concepts devised by the system, discourses that legitimise borders and control of movement are replicated and reinforced. Instead, argues Boochani: 'In order to understand Australia's role in constructing prisons on Manus Island and Nauru, it is crucial to seek out perspectives that do not corroborate the dominant voices in Australian government and media'.

Finally, Omid Tofighian emphasises the situated nature of Boochani's writing and the interdependent way of knowing developed through his collaboration as translator of Boochani's work. Responding to both 'A Letter from Manus Island' and Boochani's award-winning book, *No Friend But The Mountains*, Tofighian draws out issues relating to the reception of the book and its philosophical underpinnings. In response to these 'revelations acquired from resisting', radically new sets of concepts, methods and criteria are required for interpretation – and also to avoid reinscribing stereotypes and tropes. To engage the epistemically privileged standpoint from Manus Prison requires responsibility and situated interpretation aiming for intimate and ethically transformative engagement.

Read together, the chapters in this book mark out the limitations of so many contemporary 'free speech debates', highlight the violent consequences for racialised and oppressed peoples, and suggest vital alternatives. We see here an important focus on the politics of voice and listening, receptivity and responsiveness and the necessity to shift hierarchies of attention and value. There is an urgent need to privilege the voices and stories which are routinely marginalised or silenced in public discourse – to amplify First Nations sovereign voices, dissenting voices, Muslim voices other than the 'moderate Muslim', incarcerated voices, asylum-seeker voices and more. The argument here is not 'anti-free speech', but rather works from a reckoning of the deep, racialised inequalities of speech that characterise contemporary liberalism, arguing instead for the amplification of disenfranchised voices. We also argue for a nuanced understanding of 'freedom' that is tempered with the values of solidarity and equality. These new understandings might include new modes by which speech is 'shaped' – the way context and ideology play a role in the way speech is constructed as protected (or, indeed, harmful) in contemporary liberalism. We need to call upon ourselves and others to remake a public culture that resists the claim that freedom of speech outstrips all other liberties.

References

Gelber, K. (2017). 'Free Speech is at risk in Australia and it's not from Section 18C'. *The Conversation*, https://theconversation.com/free-speech-is-at-risk-in-australia-and-its-not-from-section-18c-64800.

Gilroy, P. (2004). *After Empire: Melancholy or Convivial Culture*. London: Routledge.

Gilroy, P. (2005). Melancholia or conviviality: The politics of belonging in Britain. *Soundings*, 29(1), 35–46.

Price, J. (2017). 'Turnbull government's holiday plan to silence criticism from charities'. *Sydney Morning Herald*. www.smh.com.au/comment/turnbull-governments-holiday-plan-to-silence-criticism-from-charities-20171217-h06bzx.html.

The Saturday Paper (2017). 'Behrouz Boochani: A Letter From Manus Island'. *The Saturday Paper*. www.thesaturdaypaper.com.au/a-letter-from-manus-island

Titley, G., D. Freedman, G. Khiabany and A. Mondon (Eds) (2017). *After Charlie Hebdo: Terror, Racism and Free Speech*. London: Zed Books.

Titley, G. (2019). *Racism and Media*. Thousand Oaks, CA: SAGE Publications Ltd.

Beyond denial: 'not racism' as racist violence

Alana Lentin

ABSTRACT
While the idea that racism is accompanied by its denial is well established, this paper examines the widespread explicit advocacy of a stance of 'not racism'. The rejection of racism by proponents of positions that hinder the cause of racial justice is the discursive next step in 'postracial' racism. I examine the various ways in which racism has been proposed to be an 'unhelpful' framework. I make the case that the dominant position within philosophy of race that racism is, first and foremost, a moral failing has unwittingly contributed to the emergence of 'not racism' as a dominant expression in race thinking today. Following an examination of several key moral philosophical analyses of racism, I illustrate my argument that 'not racism' is a form of racist violence with reference to several recent and contemporary cases against the backdrop of the rise of 'Global Trumpism'.

12 August 2017, a white supremacist rally at the University of Virginia in Charlottesville resulted in the death of Heather D. Heyer and 19 injuries, as 'white nationalist', James Alex Fields Jr ploughed his car into counter-demonstrators. Anti-racist social media immediately noted the prevalent minimization that has accompanied the rise of the 'Alt-Right' since the election of Donald Trump. In one particularly favoured tweet, @kumailn noted,[1]

> 'We have swastikas.'

> 'They're not Nazis.'

> 'Our country should be white.'

> 'They're not Nazis.'

> 'We're actual Nazis.'

> 'They're not Nazis.'

The white supremacists who marched on Charlottesville themselves appeared to underscore the message. Peter Cvjetanovic, a white demonstrator whose picture was circulated online after the rally, appealed, 'I hope that the people sharing the photo are willing to listen that I'm not the angry racist they see in that photo' (Edwards 2017).

In the same weekend in Australia, businessman Dick Smith announced that he was funding 'a reimagined version of the iconic '80s "Grim Reaper" AIDS campaign' to warn of the dangers of too much immigration (Moran 2017). Asked if, in light of the events at Charlottesville, he didn't think that the ad risked scapegoating migrants and embolden-ing white supremacists, Dick Smith replied, 'No, the opposite will happen. It will bring the discussion into the open [...] [the ad] has nothing to do with racism, but that word is always used to stop any discussion' (Moran 2017). The prevalent view among white people, reflected by a large part of the media, is that we live at a time when purportedly commonsense views about race dare not be spoken. For those at the sharp end of racism, nothing could be further from the truth. The denial and redefinition of racism – that which I am calling 'not racism' – has become a central formulation for the expres-sion and legitimation of racism.

In another incident, in June 2017, a man, driving a van, rammed into members of the congregation outside the Finsbury Park Mosque, killing 1 and injuring 10. The attacker, Darren Osborne, was described by his family as troubled but 'not racist'. Osborne's actions, it was claimed, were not motivated by hate. He was a 'lone wolf' who was 'complex', according to *The Telegraph* newspaper's report, despite shouting, 'I'm going to kill all Muslims – I did my bit' after the attack (Ward, Evans, and Furness 2017). The portrait of Osborne as a troubled man accords with the image of the 2015 Charleston multiple murderer, Dylann Roof who, despite writing two white supremacist manifestos (Buncombe 2016), was assumed to have been motivated by mental instability rather than political ideology. In Australia, the repeat offenders of popular racism, seen for example in their apparently unending appreciation for blackface (Pearson n.d.), jostle with politicians to be the first to claim their 'non-racism' (Lentin 2016). It is thus commonplace for racism to be accompanied by its immediate denial.

As the editorial to this special issue correctly observes, purportedly neutral debates about freedom of speech predicated on a disingenuous liberal universalism constrain the boundaries of what can and cannot be named as racism. The one-sided demand for freedom of expression opens racism up to what Gavan Titley has called 'debatability': 'incessant, recursive attention *as to what counts as racism and who gets to define it*' (Titley 2016). The demand to be heard on matters racial has always been central to the flow of racist ideas. It is thus not novel to expose the extent to which racism, particularly in what are erroneously suggested to be 'postracial' times, relies on being dressed in the costume of neutrality and dialectics (Goldberg 2015). Gary Younge made the point in 2006 that the 'new and honest debate' about race proposed as necessary by then British Communities Secretary, Ruth Kelly, could not proceed as though it pertained only to Black and ethnic minority people and still be 'honest'. He suggested an equally open debate about white people that would encompass their failure to integrate in a multi-cultural society or 'choose moderate leaders' (Younge 2016). His point was clear: any attempt to couch suspicion of the actions and intentions of racialized people in the terms of 'debate' which does not at the same time submit the practices of majority white society to the same standards is racist. Attempts to preempt this criticism by explicitly prefacing any discussion of migration, integration, crime or terrorism with the well-worn formula, 'I am not racist, but ...' lays bare the speaker's knowledge of the ultimate inability to conduct such 'debates' on non-racial terms.

Some freedom of speech advocates, such as Dick Smith or the right-libertarian Australian senator David Leyonhjelm, are open about their demand to speak openly against 'the ethnic threat' to what are portrayed as deep-seated liberal–democratic values (Leyonhjelm 2017). Such actors do not shield their disregard for non-white people and support for their views is growing both in and outside government in Australia and elsewhere. Hence, their power should not be minimized. Nevertheless, it is significant that arguments for freedom of speech on matters racial are dominantly packaged in the terms of 'not racism'. My argument is that this is a rhetorical device borne of the primacy placed on distancing oneself from the accusation of racism (Ahmed 2016) in an age when racism is rendered universal, ahistorical and reduced to a question of individual morality. But more than that, contained within the demand to speak freely and thus to determine the direction of the 'debate' on race is also the determination to control the definition of racism itself. This is a white demand, even when it is made at times by people of colour (see, for example, D'Souza 1996), for it is a demand that folds its insistence on white supremacy within itself; just as whiteness presents itself as normality (Moreton-Robinson 2015), so too the debates white people call for are presented as neutral, thus doubling down on the discursive violence they enact.

'Not racism' can be witnessed in definitions of racism that either sideline or deny race both as an historical phenomenon and as experienced by racialized people. The determination of the racially dominant to define the referents of racism is not itself new, and indeed has been central both to the inception of the term and to its discussion in a variety of contexts (Hesse 2011). However, the emphatic nature with which 'not racism' is declared today can be seen as the culmination of a protracted period of debate and denial. The current period, during which we are witnessing a deepening and expansion of systemic, state and popular racism against migrants and asylum seekers, the undocumented, Indigenous people, Muslims and Black people is, I suggest, accompanied by an ever more vigorous denial that these phenomena are racist. My main contention in this paper is that the assertion of 'not racism' that accompanies many structurally white discussions of and pronouncements on matters of race is itself a key form of racist violence.

I track the trajectory that has led here by assessing the contribution of academic and political discussions over the definition of racism, arguing that a singularly moral perspective on racism that divorces it from the politically systemic has partly contributed to the primacy of 'not racism'.

Defining racism

Miri Song (2014) asks us to consider what becomes permitted when 'almost any form of racial statement' is seen as racist. According to Song, increasingly in media representations, any mention of an individual racial attribute is portrayed as a case of racism. But do we have definitions of racism that are able to put paid to what Song calls the worrying 'trend toward a culture of racial equivalence' which trivializes and homogenizes 'quite different forms of racialized interactions' (107)? Song points at the problem when she indicates that 'the concept of racism cannot be understood in a wholly abstract, formulaic way, divorced from the lengthy history in which beliefs and practices about racial inferiority and superiority emerged and were consolidated' (124). But looking at the use of racism both in popular discourse and in philosophical discussions raises concerns that available definitions are not always sufficiently grounded in the actual history of race. The dominant interpretation of racism has been a moral one which sutures it to assessments of individual character. This view elides the performative function of race, in what Hesse calls 'raceocracies', as a key form of governmentality that is elaborated upon in racial–colonial contexts and accompanies the growth of the modern European nation state (Hesse 2013).

Debates in moral philosophy focus on the question of whether racism should be assessed in terms of beliefs or actions and effects. In contemporary popular interpretations, all three elements may be present, but a purported lack of intention to cause harm is mobilized to excuse racism. Moreover, racism is seen as a measure of individual character and incidents of racism are presented as isolated and atypical. Lastly, racism is proposed to be an unhelpful frame for interpreting events, thus reverting blame for racism onto the victim (Ahmed 2012).

Racism as morality

Some of the more compelling debates about how to define racism recognize that the view of racism as primarily a structural problem or an ideological one miss an important dimension, namely how the one informs and is informed by the other (Garcia 1999). Garcia cites Omi and Winant (1994) as proponents of this consolidating view. However, for Garcia this does not answer the question of 'which is it that constitutes racism and which is merely one of its effects?' (Garcia 1999, 2). For example, Nelson, Dunn, and Paradies' (2011, 263) definition – that racism is about the maintenance and exacerbation of 'avoidable and unfair inequalities in power, resources or opportunities across racial, ethnic, cultural or religious groups in society' – would be open to criticism by Garcia. The definition does not engage the question of who instigates and sustains the inequalities adversely affecting racialized groups and, relatedly, who benefits from their existence. For Garcia, slightly differently, the problem in such a definition is that it opens the possibility for racists to disappear in the absence of the existence of systemic inequalities, thus discounting the realm of ideology. As he puts it, in some accounts of racism that see it as wholly reliant on what Omi and Winant call 'social projects', racism can be said never to be the fault of individuals.

> On the other it allows, with almost equal absurdity, that even if all my beliefs concerning, actions toward, and feelings about people of another race remain the same, they (and I along with them) can change from racist to not racist (or vice versa) simply because a system of racial domination disappears from society surrounding me (or arises within it). (Garcia 1999, 12)

In contrast, Garcia (1999) proposes a 'volitional' theory of racism in which racism is about 'racially informed disregard' for those of another racial group. Garcia claims that his view helps explain why racism consists of such a diverse range of 'actions, beliefs, projects, hopes, wishes, institutions and institutional practices, remarks, and so on' (1999). He also says that racism always constitutes ill will towards the other and thus is always pejorative. This explains why there is such effort made by individuals to distance themselves from being labelled as racist. In other words, it is one possible way for making sense of the prevalence of 'not racism'.

However, Garcia (1999), while recognizing that racism has individual manifestations in thoughts and feelings, beliefs and actions as well as institutional ones, allows for racism to be seen as a universal phenomenon that is not confined to the historically racially dominant. In fact, he considers that 'institutions may sometimes continue to operate on what were originally racist restrictions even at a later time when no one any longer administers them in pursuit of those racist ends' (17). In other words, he places primacy on intent. Indeed, for Garcia, the direction is from the individual to the institutional: 'Racism can move from individual hearts to infect institutions' (1999) Therefore, while he concedes that the lingering effect of past racism may continue to infect institutional practice, he does not believe that elements of racist history that still exist are in themselves racism. In other words, for Garcia, it is necessary to be able to identify a volitional racist acting on the basis of ill will towards others to call an act or situation racist.

What Garcia is attempting to do in developing his account of volitional racism is not without merit in that it insists on the inability to hide behind misinterpreted intentions, so often the refuge of racists when caught in the act of what I have called 'racism in public' (Lentin 2016). However, the theory also permits the possibility of 'reverse' or 'anti-white' racism, because every act of racism must be judged on its own merits and not associated with an historical trajectory. Thus, while Garcia disagrees with Dinesh D'Souza's contention that Black anti-white racism in the United States is now more dangerous than white antiblackness because it is not an adequate reflection of the current balance of power, he does not reject 'reverse racism' entirely. On the contrary, he discounts provocation as a spur for what he calls 'Black racism', believing it an 'ugly phenomenon' whose presence is detrimental to the cause of racial justice.

Garcia's (1999) summation of racism is that it is a form of 'moral viciousness'. He claims that it is not trivial to see racism as primarily a personal rather than a political matter. Essentially rejecting race critical analyses that argue that racism of both a personal and an institutional nature is always political and that only systemic transformation can bring about an end to racism, he suggests that 'racism can be eliminated only by a change of heart' (19). He gets to this conclusion by separating between racism and race. Racism is not the only problem faced by Black people in the United States who are confronted with myriad other 'social difficulties', he claims. What is apparent is that Garcia sees racism as separable from these social difficulties because they can exist without a volitional 'moral viciousness'. However, what remains unclear is just what he thinks race to be. He states that 'eliminating racism may not solve all our problems of race' (20). But is race, for Garcia, a way of categorizing people, a form of self-identity, or the systemic level which exists independently of racist beliefs and acts? While this remains unclear, the way in which Garcia frames racism, while not completely relative, and certainly not, as is clear in his criticism of D'Souza, utterly universalized and disconnected from its history, still allows for racism to float free from the embedding anchors of racial rule (Goldberg 2002).

In contrast to Garcia, another philosopher of racism, Tommie Shelby (2014) proposes that a political philosophical account of racism serves us better than one from moral philosophy. Shelby engages Blum's 'narrow scope conception of racism' (2014, 59; Blum 2002). According to Shelby, Blum argues, echoing Song, that far too many 'lesser moral infractions' are labelled racist and that this leads to racism losing all meaning (Shelby 2014, 59). Moreover, including too many behaviours or attitudes under the heading of racism might lead to individuals becoming 'socially anxious' about being judged racist that they may become unwilling to 'productively engage in open dialogue' (Shelby 2014).

For Blum, then, 'this overly expansive use of "racism" intensifies group antagonism, inhibits interracial cooperation, and hence retards our progress toward racial conciliation' (Shelby 2014, 59). Shelby correctly argues that the problem with Blum's approach is that the only rationale for favouring a narrow conception of racism is that people today do not like to be labelled racist. Shelby asks how much of this is to do with a moral opposition to racism and how much is it rather an expression of individual avoidance of the potential dangers of being associated with racism. We may well think that if an individual is curtailing her speech due to a fear of being seen as racist, she would otherwise engage in this speech if she thought it safe to do so.[2] As Shelby (2014, 60) points out, the avoidance of being seen to hold racist views is not necessarily the same as having a deeply held moral opposition to racism:

> If racial minorities are to believe that racism is generally thought to constitute a particularly serious moral wrong, one warranting strong condemnation, then they will naturally want a convincing explanation for why so many people oppose policies that would likely reduce its incidence or mitigate its negative effects.

Moreover, Shelby contends that Blum overplays the reticence of whites to be seen as racist. In contrast, many white people in the United States simply claim that racism is no longer a significant phenomenon and that Black people and other racialized minorities who claim racial disadvantage are merely 'playing the race card'. This is particularly salient given, as I am suggesting, that racism has mainly been understood as a moral mater, a view backed by both Garcia and Blum. Racism, may thus be seen by whites as a matter of morality that cuts both ways – the morality of being non-racist, or at least to be seen as such, and the matter by the same token for Blacks not to identify racism where it is said not to exist ('playing the race card'). If we accept that this is descriptive of the commonsense view of racism, then it becomes problematic to consider racism as first and foremost a matter of morality.

Shelby is less sceptical about the utility of a moral frame, but he suggests that the emphasis that Blum places on restricting our definition of racism in the interests of achieving racial justice is to put the cart before the horse. He rightly says that we cannot suggest a resolution to racism before explaining what racism is. Therefore, we should not foreclose a discussion of the terms of reference around racism because it might alienate white people coming in good faith to interracial dialogue. Declarations of good faith are as much at the heart of 'not racism' arguments as they are at the heart of anti-racist ones. Often, as we shall see, deeming a situation not to be racist is done in the interests of 'not making everything about race' and thus, it is suggested, not aggravating a given situation 'needlessly'. Of course, what is not asked is *for whom* the discussion of racism is needless or aggressive and for whom it is simply an understanding they have come to based on well-founded experience (Lorde 1981; Eddo-Lodge 2017).

The discussion of definitions engaged in by Garcia, Blum, Shelby and others is relevant for my purposes for two reasons. Firstly, these authors have pinpointed some of the concerns that anti-racists have or should have concerning the ways in which racism is discussed in mainstream western societies including the postracial dimension and the dominance of what I have called the three Ds of racial management: deflection, distancing and denial (Lentin 2016). But secondly, the participation of these authors in a *moral* discussion around racism, provides intellectual fortification for the dominant view of racism as primarily a matter of individual morality. While each of them admirably, though insufficiently, engages the fundamental question of how to bridge a focus on individual action and the structuring conditions undergirding them, all but Shelby ultimately fail in meeting Song's demand for precision and historicity in definitions of racism (Song 2014).

Seeing 'not racism'

Objections raised to the inclusion of race in political debates often denounce the perceived moralism of doing so. From this perspective, it is seen as unstrategic to include race in discussions of migration for example, because to do so would be to alienate 'ordinary people'. For example, in an article on Australian voters' attitudes to asylum seekers, Tietze (2014) writes,

> By posing ordinary Australians as the cause of the brutal treatment of asylum seekers, refugee advocates are reduced to making moral exhortations rather than trying to find ways to link ordinary people's and asylum seekers' struggles against the politicians on the basis of shared interests.

Viewing calling attention to racism as moralistic browbeating is based on a narrow view of race (mainly as 'racial science') which fails to fully consider how racial taxonomies became embedded in systems of rule and continue to be reproduced culturally. It has become accepted to see ideological racism as responsible for the production of the race idea (Fields and Fields 2012), but such an approach relies on race being viewed only as 'a physical fact' (Fields, Fields, and Farbman 2015) and not predominantly as a governmentality (Hesse 2007). Views such as those exemplified by Tietze, while paradoxically decrying moralism, are thus based on an ahistorical view of racism as a matter of questionable beliefs. As the previous discussion has shown, the approach taken by moral philosophers is one example of the overemphasis on morals. However, the engagement of Garcia, Blum and others in such discussions is derived from the generalized political confinement of racism to the moral realm, to the detriment of a deep discussion of the structuring effects of race thinking for individual actions. As Fields, Fields and Farbman (2015) say, correctly, racism is not an 'attitude or a state of mind, like bigotry: it's an action'.

The primacy of the moral view of racism as well as the general lack of knowledge or interest in race critical scholarship and Black and otherwise racialized scholars in academia, politics and the media establishes 'not racism' as the major discursive filter through which race matters are sifted. 'Not racism' is predicated on the idea that racism is a moral wrong. A separation is thus established between the properly racist and the purportedly commonsensical, honest, and practical views of the 'non-racist' majority. 'Not racism' takes the right to define racism away from those affected by it and, in this way, is a form of racist violence. I discuss two key dimensions of 'not racism': firstly, the suggestion that racism is 'unhelpful' and, secondly, that anti-racism is a hegemonic moral orthodoxy that strangles freedom of expression.

Racism as 'unhelpful'

Centering race in debates on pressing social, economic and political issues is often proposed to be unhelpful. This view is expressed by Eric Kaufman in his study, 'Racial Self-Interest is Not Racism' (Kaufman 2017). Kaufman conducted research with Trump and Clinton voters in the United States and 'leave' and 'remain' voters in the UK Brexit referendum on the extent to which their choices were framed by issues of immigration and race. He claims that 'accusations of racism levelled at anti-immigration parties and voters contribute to conservatives' mistrust of elites' (2). The study aims to couch discussions of voters' preoccupations around race in less polarizing terms and worries that 'reasonable' debate about the social impact of migration in particular is hampered by individual self-censorship. For Kaufman, people 'worry about violating social norms against racism, not just in front of others, but even in their private thoughts' (6).

Kaufman claims anti-racism has become the norm since the civil rights era in the United States. Norms 'engage emotions of guilt, shame and disgust' in those who may not completely believe in them (2017). He interrogates whether it is in fact 'disgusting to want less immigration to help maintain the size of an ethnic majority?' (Kaufman 2017). His discussion departs from two main contentions: Firstly, that anti-racist moralism is dominant and, secondly, that we must distinguish between racism and what he calls 'racial self-interest'. He argues that,

> White conservatives whose immigration stance is influenced by a desire to slow decline in their group's share of the population rather than due to an irrational fear of outgroups, feel accused of racism. This breeds resentment. (Kaufman 2017)

Like Blum, but for different political ends, Kaufman wants narrower definitions of racism in the aim of loosening what he sees as a stranglehold on debates about multiculturality in the United Kingdom and the United States. What Kaufman wishes to exclude from the definition of racism is very different from the type of attention to historical detail Song calls for. In fact, it is precisely the lack of anti-racist hegemony that motivates Song and the slippage, in the absence of real knowledge about racism, into the culture of 'racial equivalence' that she warns against.

The trope of unhelpfulness is wrapped in apparent concern for identifying real racism as opposed to, presumably, false or exaggerated claims of racism. The quest to identify 'real' racism is based on the emphasis placed on what I have called 'frozen racisms'; examples from the past, particularly the Holocaust, Apartheid and Jim Crow, against which all other manifestations may be judged (Lentin 2014). It is curious, however, how often contemporary anti-Black or anti-Muslim racism, for example, are minimized by comparison with these past exemplars, while the case for recognizing 'anti-white' racism is concomitantly advanced (cf. D'Souza 1996). David Goodhart, for example, in his support for Kaufman's research claims that, as a term, racism 'has been subject to mission creep' (Kaufman 2017, 2). This has led in his estimation to a situation in which 'those in public debate cannot draw a distinction between group partiality and a racism based on the fear, hatred or disparagement of outgroups' (Kaufman 2017). While the first, that which Kaufman calls 'racial self-interest', may be rational, the latter is unacceptable, their mutual dependency precluded.

The problem in Kaufman and Goodhart is twofold. Firstly, racism is confined to a morally contestable expression of hatred, similar to Garcia's notion of volitional ill will. Secondly, racism is disconnected from race. The 'greater comfort people often feel among familiar people and places' is an expression of the filiality and familiarity that race reproduces positively for whites (Weinbaum 2004). For the white opponents to migration interviewed by Kaufman, this sense of comfort is not dissociable from the fact that whiteness is not only a 'privileged identity' but also a 'vested interest' (Harris 1993, 1725). Kaufman confuses racial self-interest expressed as white opposition to immigration with the sense of ethnic belonging, especially that of minority ethnicities, whose interests are not pandered to by parties and governments in the quest of (re)election. Goodhart (2014, 255), in particular, performs a guileful reappropriation of anti-racist criticisms of race colourblindness by claiming,

> [...] the well-meaning attempt to override the human instinct to notice difference creates much greater sensitivity to and self-consciousness about race. Surely, rather than making strenuous efforts to avoid noticing difference, it is better to notice it and feel at ease with it.

By mobilizing an equalizing definition of racism in which all groups, whites included, are proportionately affected by it, Kaufman and Goodhart construct each as having an anti-racist interest. The interest of white people concerned by immigration is to shield themselves from cultural, social and economic incursion. This is 'not racism'. Rather it is suggested to be on a par with minority groups' interests in preserving their cultures and traditions.[3] However, because the primary mechanism of protection for these 'not racist' white groups is through the 'bolster[ing of] the demographic position of their ethnic group', there are significant problems with arguing that these are the same. White anxieties about their number are a major mobilizing facet of racial rule. Being outnumbered by Black and Native peoples is at the heart of the concern of occupying regimes with white settlement in North America, Australia and Israel (Harris 1993; Tuck and Yang 2012; Dunbar-Ortiz 2015; Moreton-Robinson 2015; Wolfe 2016). Moral panic about demographic tipping points are major themes in contemporary race management in post-immigration societies as debates about impending 'majority–minority' cities can attest (Finney and Simpson 2009). If concern for white futures is the mobilizing factor in what Kaufman wishes to present as neutral 'racial self-interest' debates, there is no way, based on our knowledge of the history of race, for these not to be an expression of racism. The maintenance of white superiority in both numbers and power is at its core.

Cutting anti-racism down to size

A major concern for all proponents of 'not racism' is that the rush to dub a situation racist is an imposition on 'ordinary citizens' of an elitist world view which reprimands them for their beliefs (Goodhart 2014, 251). Construing anti-racism as morally hegemonic and disruptive to debate has a long legacy. Paul Gilroy noted the effects 30 years ago of British head teacher, Ray Honeyford's objections to anti-racist education at his Bradford school (Gilroy 1987). For Honeyford, those who promoted anti-racism in schools were either liberals 'suffering from a rapidly dating postimperial guilt' or 'teachers building a career by jumping onto the latest educational bandwagon' as well as Black 'professional intellectuals' and a 'hardcore' of left-wing academics (Honeyford

1984, 13). As Gilroy (1987, 68) notes, the elevation of Honeyford as a martyred victim of the anti-racist establishment meant that it mattered little that he had been employed to teach at a school with mainly Black pupils. His attack was not seen as racist because it was countered with the apparently rational culturalist argument that not to give Black children an education on British history and tradition was to 'privilege their attachment to non-British cultures' and to thwart their integration.[4]

Ben Pitcher (2006) assesses the 2005 British Conservative Party's publicity campaign which asked 'are you thinking what we're thinking?' under a pseudo-handwritten, lower-case: 'it's not racist to impose limits on immigration.' As Pitcher correctly notes, the present continuous 'thinking' is used knowingly in the place of the alternative 'believe'. The billboard thus cannot be said to be an expression of the belief system of the Conservative Party. Rather, it sends the message that the party is in tune with the thoughts of the ordinary voter who is a good person despite having doubts about the benefits of immigration. The phrase 'are you thinking what we're thinking?' contains within it a logic of disavowal similar to 'I'm not racist but …' Pitcher cites Billig who says that this formulation allows the racist thought to be construed as part of the external world rather than as part of the individual's own belief system (Billig 1988; cited in Pitcher 2006, 6). Pitcher identifies the primacy placed on 'not racism' in this campaign remarking that, in this disavowal, 'the object "racism" must be rejected, and its content is therefore reappropriated as "not racism"' (7). Those who the billboard addresses are being comforted that their innermost, unspoken thoughts are not immoral, and are even rational.

Where I disagree with Pitcher is that the threat of anti-racist social censure is so strong that it has precipitated new formulations of racism. I agree with him that 'not racism' constitutes a new framing of racism that is presented as a means of overcoming censorship, including self-censorship. However, rather than this suppression of racist thought and speech being real, what is being mobilized by the 'not racism' formulation is the *idea* of censorship rather than its reality. To be sure, there have been some significant instances of sanctions being imposed on those who have publically expressed racism, such as the 2014 case of basketball team owner, Donald Sterling (Lentin 2016). However, there are many other cases in which racism is denied or excused. Indeed, some racisms more than others are called to attention, as was evident in the opposition to Irish journalist Kevin Myers for an anti-Semitic article in a British newspaper which overlooked his long history of anti-Traveller, anti-Black and anti-migrant racism and related misogyny on the pages of Irish newspapers for many years (Titley 2011). As can be seen in the renewed respect for figures such as Powell and Honeyford, there is always the possibility for reinstatement with the passage of time and the dissipation of outrage. After all, the current President of the United States was said to have been 'only joking' when he praised aggressive police tactics which lead yearly to the loss of thousands of Black lives (Cobb 2017). The only way in which anti-racism can be construed as dominant, therefore, is through a negation of the struggles around race, class and gender in which Black, Brown and otherwise racialized people have been engaged for generations (Virdee 2014). While I agree unequivocally with Sara Ahmed that the primary response to the accusation of racism is one which distances the accused from the racist thought or act (Ahmed 2012), this is not because anti-racism is actually hegemonic. Rather, what is hegemonic is the moral interpretation of racism that, by individualizing it, fails to engage with the structuring conditions of race of which racism is an expression.

Cutting anti-racism down to size involves setting it up as an elite enterprise. Like Honeyford's attack on Black professionals and left-wing academics, more recently British sociologist and anti-austerity campaigner, Lisa McKenzie (2015) mobilized similar tropes. In a *Guardian* article, she argued that 'white working-class women', in some areas of the United Kingdom already facing harsh austerity policies, feared greater hardship as a result of asylum seekers being housed there. The women claimed to have been asked by Iraqi asylum seekers for 'business' (sex) but were reticent to complain about sexual harassment due to the fear of being seen as racist by elites. McKenzie's argument collapses together several key themes of anti-immigrationism: sexualized racism, and the fear of being usurped by less-deserving outsiders. She claims 'not racism' because a number of the women have biracial children with African-Caribbean men, as she herself does. In her work on women in the Nottingham St Anns estate, McKenzie claims that many of the women with Black partners describe white men as 'boring', pretending to be Black but not being 'the real thing'. They also talk about Caribbean food as more interesting and about multicultural schools as better for their children (McKenzie 2013). McKenzie thus relies on the trope of multiculturalism as a supplement to the dominant culture (Hage 1998) to support the 'not racism' of her interviewees.

The debate following McKenzie's article reveals the emphasis placed on the two key facets of 'not racism': the unhelpfulness of racism and the elitism of anti-racism. Katie Beswick (2015) argued in McKenzie's defence that she was right to point out that to 'uncritically dismiss these women's fears as "racism" was unhelpful'. It is not clear what speaking about racism is unhelpful *for*. On the one hand, McKenzie claims to privilege the voices of unheard white working-class women because as she claimed on Twitter, 'I also don't think race is central I think class is.'[5] On the other hand, her 'not racism' is predicated on the fact that St Anns is predominantly an Irish and Black neighbourhood. Echoing the Conservative party campaign, McKenzie suggests, 'it is not racist' to raise concerns about new migrations at a time of economic depression. However, this reasoning assumes that austerity has not in fact worse affected Black people and ethnic minorities in Britain on average than the population as a whole and that racialized people are somehow excised from the working class.[6] The fact that some of the criticism of her failure to connect race and class came from academics discounts them as elitist. Racism, again is presented as the moralizing stick used to beat the unsophisticated. Rather than examine how the whole working class is subjugated by economic austerity, McKenzie chooses to portray class and race interests as diametrically opposed.

Conclusion

To speak of racism is to be excessive just as to be racialized is to be deemed in excess. There is thus no clear way of separating the demand to speak less about racism from the demand to speak less, or indeed to *be* less. That which Du Bois (1903) named 'the real question, How does it feel to be a problem?' is still at the core of what are euphemistically referred to as 'race relations'. The demand to not be reminded of racism is what drives 'not racism'. 'Not racism' goes beyond denial, recognized as being a central dynamic of racism post-race (Dunn and Nelson 2011), by claiming ownership over the definition of racism. To define 'not racism', racism must first be defined, and so the proponents of 'not racism' establish grounds for defining racism which rely on a singularly moral and individualized account of racism and an ahistorical excision of race. So, David Goodhart (2017), explaining why 'racial self-interest is not racism', claims,

> The challenge here is to distinguish between white racism and white identity politics. The latter may be clannish and insular, but it is not the same as irrational hatred, fear or contempt for another group – the normal definition of racism .

The normal definition, according to Goodhart, performs the separation between rationality and irrationality which is itself central to a racial epistemology. In a wide-ranging discussion of racism and rationality, David Goldberg (1990) rejects the thesis that racism is always irrational on both logical and moral grounds. To determine the morality of racism, he argues, 'we cannot, on pain of circularity, simply claim its immorality a priori and infer its irrationality from this'. Indeed, racism may very well be rational especially because, historically, 'racially discriminatory laws and practices have enabled the profit ratio to be maintained or increased both on the micro- and on macrolevels and, indeed, have been intentionally introduced at times with this end in view' (333). This view accords due weight to the predominance of racial capitalism as central to the understanding of both the emergence and longevity of race and, consequently, racism. It supports the argument against McKenzie that excising Black people and ethnic minorities from the working class for the purposes of making an argument about the predominance of class over race refutes the history of the codependency of race and class (Robinson 1983). For Goodhart's separation of racism and racial self-interest to work, he must bracket racial capitalism as beyond the realms of 'real' racism.

Goldberg (1990) uses the precise example of immigration restrictions to prove that 'some racist beliefs will be strongly rational, for they satisfy widely accepted formal criteria of rationality'. Just as Goodhart does, many argue that preserving cultural tradition is a rational aim that can be reached through the restriction of immigration. It can only be argued that this is 'not racism' by adhering to a strict biological account of what racism is. Goldberg advances a 'rationality-neutral definition of racism' that necessitates only that racists ascribe racial characteristics to others and that this can be either biological or social. Moreover, it does not necessarily imply ascribing hierarchy. Its overriding feature is 'exclusion on the basis of (purported) racial membership' whether 'intended, actual or (implicitly) rationalized' (319). As Goldberg shows, a key way in which immigration restrictions in particular are claimed to be 'not racist' is through universalizing the claim to cultural preservation by equating state immigration policies with the multiculturalist demands of minority ethnic and religious groups. To follow this logic would be to equate the violent carcerality of state migration regimes with the recognition appeals of community groups.

Three elements – the predominance of individualist moralism; the reliance on an overly narrow, strictly biological and hierarchical account of racism; and the universalization of racism as equally practiced by all groups independent of status and power – contribute to the dominance of 'not racism'. To counter 'not racism' as a key mode in which racism is expressed, the 'noise' produced by racism's debatability (Titley 2016) has to be silenced with the systematic reconstruction of racism's effects through, as Goldberg puts it, 'structural transformation and discursive displacement' rather than more 'moral education' which only contributes to the rejection of racism as 'unhelpful' and anti-racism as elitist, beliefs that justify the further denial of racial justice (Goldberg 1990, 345).

Notes

1. https://twitter.com/kumailn/status/896459965832896512. Accessed 13 August 2017.
2. One is reminded here of Donald Trump's invocation of 'locker room talk' when recordings of violently misogynistic statements he made emerged on the 2016 Presidential election campaign trail.
3. In defence of his participation in the white supremacist rally at Charlottesville, Peter Cvjetanovic, claimed, 'I came to this march for the message that white European culture has a right to be here just like every other culture' (Edwards 2017).
4. In the last few years, a number of articles have appeared in the British press calling for a reassessment of Honeyford's views in the light of Muslim radicalization (Parkinson 2012; Jack 2014) echoing others which gave a similar treatment to the anti-immigrationism of conservative British politician, Enoch Powell (cf. Kundnani 2007).
5. Tweet by Lisa McKenzie @redrumlisa archived by the author on 17 September 2015.
6. Research by Black Activists Rising Against Cuts supports this http://blackactivistsrisinga gainstcuts.blogspot.com.au. Accessed 3 August 2017.

Disclosure statement

No potential conflict of interest was reported by the author.

References

Ahmed, S. 2012. *On Being Included: Racism and Diversity in Institutional Life*. Durham NC: Duke UP.

Ahmed, S. 2016. "Evidence", *Feminist Killjoys*, July 12. https://feministkilljoys.com/2016/07/12/evi dence/.

Beswick, K. 2015. "On Refugees, Lisa McKenzie and the Problem with Writing" *katiebeswick.com*, 20 September. https://katiebeswick.com/2015/09/20/

Billig, M. 1988. "Prejudice and Tolerance." In *Ideological Dilemmas: A Social Psychology of Everyday Thinking*, edited by M. Billig, S. Condor, D. Edwards, M. Gane, D. Middleton, and A. Ridley, 100–123. London: Sage.

Blum, L. 2002. *I'm Not a Racist, But...": The Moral Quandary of Race*. Ithaca, NY: Cornell University Press.

Buncombe, A. 2016. "Dylann Roof 'Wrote Second Racist Manifesto' While Awaiting Trial for Charleston Church Shooting," *The Independent*, 23 August. http://www.independent.co.uk/ news/people/dylann-roof-wrote-second-racist-manifesto-text-note-white-supremacist-while-awaiting-trial-for-a7205351.html.

Cobb, J. 2017. "Donald Trump Is Serious When He Jokes about Police Brutality," *The New Yorker*, Accessed 1 August 2017. http://www.newyorker.com/news/news-desk/donald-trump-is-serious-when-he-jokes-about-police-brutality.

D'Souza, D. 1996. *The End of Racism*. New York: Free Press.

Du Bois, W. E. B. 1903. "Of Our Spiritual Strivings." In *The Souls of Black Folk: Essays and Sketches*. Chicago: A. C. McClurg.

Dunbar-Ortiz, R. 2015. *An Indigenous Peoples' History of the United States*. Boston MS: Beacon Press.

Eddo-Lodge, R. 2017. *Why I'm No Longer Talking to White People about Race*. London: Bloomsbury.

Edwards, D. 2017. '"I'm Not the Angry Racist They See": Alt-Righter Became Viral Face of Hate in Virginia — And Now Regrets It,' *Rawstory*, 13 August.

Fields, B., K. Fields, and J. Farbman. 2015. "How Race Is Conjured", *Jacobin*, 29 June. https://www.jacobinmag.com/2015/06/karen-barbara-fields-racecraft-dolezal-racism/.

Fields, K., and B. Fields. 2012. *Racecraft: The Soul of Inequality in American Life*. London: Verso.

Finney, N., and L. Simpson. 2009. *'Sleepwalking into Segregation'? Challenging the Myths about Race and Migration*. Bristol: Policy Press.

Garcia, J. 1999. "Philosophical Analysis and the Moral Concept of Racism." *Philosophy and Social Criticism* 25 (5): 1–32. doi:10.1177/0191453799025005001.

Gilroy, P. 1987. *'There Ain't No Black in the Union Jack': The Cultural Politics of Race and Nation*. London: Unwin Hyman.

Goldberg, D. 1990. "Racism and Rationality: The Need for a New Critique." *Philosophy of Science* 20 (2): 317–350. doi:10.1177/004839319002000303.

Goldberg, D. 2002. *The Racial State*. Malden, Mass. and Oxford: Blackwell.

Goldberg, D. 2015. *Are We All Postracial Yet?* London: Polity (e-book).

Goodhart, D. 2014. "Racism: Less Is More." *The Political Quarterly* 85 (3): 251–258. doi:10.1111/1467-923X.12097.

Goodhart, D. 2017. "White Self-Interest Is Not the Same Thing as Racism." *The Financial Times*, 2 March. https://www.ft.com/content/220090e0-efc1-11e6-ba01-119a44939bb6?mhq5j=e1

Hage, G. 1998. *White Nation: Fantasies of White Supremacy in a Multicultural Society*. New York: Routledge.

Harris, C. 1993. "Whiteness as Property." *Harvard Law Review* 106 (8): 1710–1791. doi:10.2307/1341787.

Hesse, B. 2007. "Racialized Modernity. An Analytics of White Mythologies." *Ethnic and Racial Studies* 30 (4): 643–663. doi:10.1080/01419870701356064.

Hesse, B. 2011. "Self-Fulfilling Prophecy. The Postracial Horizon." *South Atlantic Quarterly* 110 (1): 155–178. doi:10.1215/00382876-2010-027.

Hesse, B. 2013. "Raceocracy: How the Racial Exception Proves the Racial Rule." *YouTube*. https://www.youtube.com/watch?v=QCAyQNWteUA.

Honeyford, R. 1984. "Education and Race: An Alternative View" *The Salisbury Review*, Winter: 30–32.

Jack, I. 2014. "Was the 1980s Bradford Head Teacher Who Criticised Multiculturalism Right?" *The Guardian*, June 14. https://www.theguardian.com/commentisfree/2014/jun/13/was-1980s-headteacher-who-criticised-multiculturism-right.

Kaufman, E. 2017. *Racial Self Interest Is Not Racism: Ethno-Demographic Interests and the Immigration Debate*. March: Policy Exchange report.

Kevin, D., and J. Nelson. 2011. "Challenging the Public Denial of Racism for a Deeper Multiculturalism." *Journal of Intercultural Studies* 32 (6): 587–602. doi:10.1080/07256868.2011.618105.

Kundnani, A. 2007. "Rights Not Rhetoric." *The Guardian*, 2 November. https://www.theguardian.com/commentisfree/2007/nov/02/rightsnotrhetoric.

Lentin, A. 2014. "Post-Race, Post-Politics: The Paradoxical Rise of Culture after Multiculturalism." *Ethnic and Racial Studies* 37 (8): 1268–1285. doi:10.1080/01419870.2012.664278.

Lentin, A. 2016. "Racism in Public or Public Racism: Doing Antiracism in Postracial Times." *Ethnic and Racial Studies* 39 (1): 33–48. doi:10.1080/01419870.2016.1096409.

Leyonhjelm, D. 2017. "18C Debate Highlights the Ethnic Threat to Free Speech." *Australian Financial Review*, March 30. https://www.afr.com/opinion/columnists/18c-debate-highlights-the-ethnic-threat-to-free-speech-20170330-gv9n4q

Lorde, A. 1981. "The Uses of Anger: Women Responding to Racism." Keynote presentation, National Women's Studies Association Conference, Storrs, Connecticut. http://www.blackpast.org/1981-audre-lorde-uses-anger-women-responding-racism.

McKenzie, L. 2013. "Narratives from A Nottingham Council Estate: A Story of White Working Class Mothers with Mixed-Race Children." *Ethnic and Racial Studies* 36 (8): 1342–1358. doi:10.1080/01419870.2013.776698.

McKenzie, L. 2015. "The Refugee Crisis Will Hit the UK's Working Class Areas Hardest." *The Guardian*, 16 September. https://www.theguardian.com/society/2015/sep/16/refugee-crisis-hit-uk-working-class-powerless.

Moran, R. 2017. "Dick Smith Revives 'Grim Reaper' Ad in Bid to Curb Immigration Numbers." *Sydney Morning Herald*, 13 August. http://www.smh.com.au/entertainment/tv-and-radio/dick-smith-revives-grim-reaper-ad-in-bid-to-curb-immigration-numbers-20170814-gxvjj8.html.

Moreton-Robinson, A. 2015. *The White Possessive: Property, Power, and Indigenous Sovereignty*. Minnesota: University of Minnesota Press.

Nelson, J., K. Dunn, and Y. Paradies. 2011. "Bystander Anti-Racism: A Review of the Literature." *Analyses of Social Issues and Public Policy* 11 (1): 263–284. doi:10.1111/j.1530-2415.2011.01274.x.

Omi, M., and H. Winant. 1986. *Racial Formation in the United States*. 1st ed. New York: Routledge.

Parkinson, J. 2012. "Ray Honeyford: Racist or Right?" *BBC News*, 10 February. http://www.bbc.com/news/uk-politics-16968930.

Pearson, L. n.d. "Blackface and Whitewashing." *Indigenous X*. http://indigenousx.com.au/blackface-and-whitewashing/.

Pitcher, B. 2006. "Are You Thinking What We're Thinking? Immigration, Multiculturalism and the Disavowal of Racism in the Run-Up to the 2005 British General Election." *Social Semiotics* 16 (4): 545–551. doi:10.1080/10350330601019892.

Robinson, C. 1983. *Black Marxism. The Making of the Black Radical Tradition*. London: Zed Books.

Shelby, T. 2014. "Racism, Moralism and Social Criticism." *Du Bois Review* 11 (1): 57–74. doi:10.1017/S1742058X14000010.

Song, M. 2014. "Challenging a Culture of Racial Equivalence." *British Journal of Sociology* 65 (1): 107–129. doi:10.1111/1468-4446.12054.

Tietze, T. 2014. "Why We Shouldn't Blame Voters For Our Appalling Asylum Policies" *New Matilda*, 15 July. https://newmatilda.com/2014/07/15/why-we-shouldnt-blame-voters-our-appalling-asylum-policies.

Titley, G. 2011. "Are Gypsies Having Sex with Britain's Swans? Or, the Meaning of Myers." *Politico*, 7 April. http://politico.ie/archive/are-gypsies-having-sex-britain's-swans-or-meaning-myers.

Titley, G. 2016. 'The Debatability of Racism: Networked Participative Media and Racism', *Rasismista Ja Rajoista*. Accessed June 8, 2016 https://raster.fi/2016/02/17/the-debatability-of-racism-networked-participative-media-and-postracialism/.

Tuck, E., and W. Yang. 2012. "Decolonization Is Not a Metaphor." *Decolonization: Indigeneity, Education & Society* 1 (1): 1–40.

Virdee, S. 2014. *Racism, Class and the Racialized Outsider*. London: Palgrave.

Ward, V., M. Evans, and H. Furness. 2017. "Who Is Darren Osborne? Everything We Know about the Finsbury Park Mosque Suspect." *The Daily Telegraph*, 21 June. http://www.telegraph.co.uk/news/0/darren-osborne-everything-know-finsbury-park-mosque-suspect/.

Weinbaum, A. E. 2004. *Wayward Reproductions: Genealogies of Race and Nation in Transatlantic Modern Thought*. Durham: Duke University Press.

Wolfe, P. 2016. *Traces of History: Elementary Structures of Race*. London: Verso.

Younge, G. 2016. "For 50 Years Voters have been Denied a Genuine Debate on Immigration. Now We're Paying the Price." *The Guardian*, June 16. https://www.theguardian.com/commentisfree/2016/jun/15/honest-debate-immigration

'You cunts can do as you like': the obscenity and absurdity of free speech to Blackfullas

Chelsea Bond(iD), Bryan Mukandi(iD) and Shane Coghill

ABSTRACT

In the same year that Adam Goodes quit the game of AFL, soprano and composer Deborah Cheetham refused to sing the Australian National Anthem at the AFL Grand Final because she could not bear to sing the words 'for we are young and free'. In this article, we examine why the act of singing about being 'free' would be both absurd and obscene for Blackfullas in Australia. Engaging with the songs of Black people, locally and globally, we reveal the fiction of free speech and freedom for all and the interests those fictions serve.

Abbreviations: AFL: Australian Football League; AO: Officer of the Order of Australia; CMC: Crime and Misconduct Commission; RCIADIC: The Royal Commission into Aboriginal Deaths in Custody

Introduction

> The history of Black literature provides, in my opinion, a much more illuminating account of the nature of freedom, its extents, and limits, than all the philosophical discourses on this theme in the history of Western society. Why? ... Black literature in this country and throughout the world projects the consciousness of a people who have been denied entrance into the real world of freedom. Black people have exposed, by their very existence, the inadequacies not only of the practice of freedom, but of its very theoretical formulation (Davis 2010, 46).

At the end of 2015, Yorta Yorta song woman,[1] Deborah Cheetham, AO, turned down the opportunity to sing the Australian national anthem in front of what would have been one of her largest audiences ever, the Australian Football League (AFL) Grand Final. This was the same year that AFL player Adam Goodes, an Adnyamathanha and Narungga man, announced his retirement from the game. No longer willing to subject himself to the sustained booing from AFL spectators, Goodes also refused to participate in the usual Grand Final fanfare afforded retiring players. The absence of Goodes and Cheetham from the 2015 AFL Grand Final celebrations was a powerful, yet silent statement to a game and to a nation about the irreconcilable tensions that Blackfullas experience.

The treatment of Adam Goodes in his final playing years in the AFL is well documented and has inspired this special issue. Cheetham's less well-documented refusal to sing the national anthem's proclamation of freedom has similarly inspired us to consider the obscenity and absurdity of free speech to Blackfullas.[2] It prompted us as Black scholars[3] to consider more deeply the acts of speech and song of Black peoples, here and abroad. We, like Davis, assert that it is from the testimony of Blackfullas and Black folk more broadly,[4] that we can understand freedom, practically and theoretically. Drawing upon Mills (1997) racial contract, we testify from our varying cultural and disciplinary positions as Black scholars to the fiction that is 'free speech' and 'freedom for all'. We expose how these fictions seek to mask a deeper and more sinister fabrication – the fundamental lie upon which the white colonial settler state was built: *Terra Nullius*, while at the same time, illuminating the truths to which Blackfullas are prepared to give voice.

'Don't sing me your anthem'

The act of refusing to sing or stand for a national anthem is not a particularly new or novel form of resistance for Black folk. Interestingly, Cheetham had been prepared to sing 'Advance Australia Fair' at the AFL Grand Final. There was one condition; she wanted to alter the opening line. The offending lyrics, according to Cheetham (2015), were the words, 'for we are young and free', and she requested to sing instead 'in peace and harmony' (See Table 1).

Given Australia's violent treatment of Blackfullas, Cheetham's refusal to rejoice in a fictitious youth and freedom is understandable. Almost 20 years earlier, Aboriginal female folk trio, Tiddas, released their song *Anthem* (Tiddas 1996), in which they sing about the absurdity of that same line within the anthem:

> Don't sing me your Anthem, when your Anthem's absurd.

> We might have been born here, but we're not young and free

It is worth pausing here and paying close attention to the compromise Cheetham was willing to make. Table 1 shows the political fabrication, the fiction, the lie to which Blackfullas are asked to assent in the national anthem, alongside the adjustment and political negotiation to which Cheetham was willing to give voice. The former calls for obliteration.[5] The latter tells a forward-looking story; it is a song woman's articulation of a more just future to come, one worthy of Blackfullas' voices. That too may be a fiction, but it is one in which Cheetham could rejoice. This is in keeping with Derrida's (2009) remark, regarding political organization and the nation-state, that some fictions are better than others; some are more 'honest' and some more 'dishonest' than others.

The expectation that Blackfullas in Australia 'rejoice' in being 'young and free' goes further than calling for universal participation in a white-washed mythic narrative around the birth of a nation. It is tantamount to demanding that Blackfullas be complicit in, and celebrate, the effacement of those who were here prior to 1788. That effacement is foundational to Australia. The fable or narrative myth of the founding of the nation is anchored in place by the legal fabrication that is *Terra*

Table 1. Cheetham's proposed modification to the opening lines of the national anthem.

Original	Modification
Australians all let us rejoice, For we are young and free	Australians all let us rejoice, In peace and harmony.

Nullius – that those Blackfullas who were here prior to and at the landing of the First Fleet, were not. Yet, as Goenpul scholar Moreton-Robinson (2017) points out '[t]he Indigenous body signifies our title to land and our death reintegrates our body with that of our mother earth'. The presence of Indigenous bodies, both in life and in death, testifies to the lie that is *Terra Nullius*.

What the story of a 'young' Australia 'gives [...] to be known', what it 'makes known' (Derrida 2009, 34–5), is the absence of Blackfullas.[6] The telling of the story of this country as though the landmass upon which it stands was uninhabited when the 'First Fleet' landed, serves as alibi for white Australia.[7] Cheetham's refusal to sing of a 'young' nation, was a refusal to bear false witness and a refusal to sing herself out of place. In fact, as early as 1938, Blackfullas were contesting the fiction of a young or new nation. It was on 26 January 1938, on 'Australia Day',[8] that Ferguson, Cooper and Patten circulated the pamphlet, 'Aborigines Claim Citizen Rights' (Aborigines Progressive Association 1938), in which they stated:

> You are the New Australians, but we are the Old Australians. We have in our arteries the blood of the Original Australians, who have lived in this land for many thousands of years. You came here only recently, and you took our land away from us by force. You have almost exterminated our people, but there are enough of us remaining to expose the humbug of your claim, as white Australians, to be a civilised, progressive, kindly and humane nation. By your cruelty and callousness towards the Aborigines you stand condemned in the eyes of the civilised world.

As with the gesture of return of the Caribbean Islander, poet Aimé Césaire ([1956] 1995), Cheetham's stance should be understood as the conjuring of 'pasts that [will] not pass and futures that [are] already emerging'; an act of 'radical remembrance through which [...] commemoration's will to domesticate' is thwarted (Wilder 2009, 123).[9] The emerging future that Cheetham is willing to countenance is one where there is peace and perhaps harmony, yet neither she, nor Tiddas are willing to indulge even an aspirational declaration of freedom. What are we to make of this, given that across the world, the aspiration of freedom is a prominent theme in the music of the marginalized?

'I know why the caged bird sings'

Chikowero (2015, 2) has written about the significance of song to anti-colonial liberation struggles. He notes, for instance, that during the period of settler colonial rule, 'song was key to how Africans conceptualized their changing world [...] Through embodied song and oral history, they touched each other's hearts and summoned the spirits of their martyred ancestor-leaders to guide the agenda of self-liberation'. Bob Marley's *Redemption Song* (2002) does this. So too African American writer Dunbar 1993 poem, *Sympathy*, which casts Black folk as caged birds yearning for freedom.

Decades later, Maya Angelou ([1969] 2015) takes up this theme of the caged bird that sings as a means of framing the telling of her story: the prospect of freedom is all that the caged bird can sing of; this unknown freedom; and with wings clipped and feet tied, all the bird can do is open its throat to sing. And in that same American civil rights cauldron, Nina Simone – who sang *Why?* ([1968] 2010), in response to the assassination of Martin Luther King Jr.; *Mississippi Goddam* ([1964] 2010); and like Billie Holiday before her, *Strange Fruit* ([1954] 2006), that lament of the racist mutilation of black bodies by white supremacists – also sang 'I wish I could break/All the chains holding me' ([1967] 2010), in which she wishes that she were a bird flying in the sky.

In that song, Nina Simone dreams of one day breaking the chains incarcerating Black Americans in the United States. Meanwhile, here in Australia, Blackfullas, Cheetham, the Tiddas, and many others (Gorrie 2016; Liddle 2017; McQuire 2016), assert that singing about freedom is absurd and offensive; that it is tantamount to demanding that the caged bird pretend that its wings aren't bruised from beating against bars, or demanding that it sing a joyful carol.[10] What is the meaning of this freedom, for which Black folk elsewhere can aspire but of which Blackfullas refuse to sing?

In *Black Skin, White Masks*, Fanon (2008) makes the distinction between the freedom that was gradually being won by Black Americans through struggle, and that 'given' to some Black people in lands controlled by France. The freedom of the latter, for Fanon, was no freedom at all, but merely a pretense. It is domestication rather than freedom.[11] While Fanon's views regarding the situation of Black people in 1952 America may have been an idealized one, it is noteworthy that freedom manifests in movement. Freedom is cast as the desire to return to Africa, and later mitigated into the desire to escape North – North of the Mason-Dixie line; North of the US-Canada border; North in the bodily escape heavenward if need be. The spirituals, the blues, Bob Marley's *Redemption Song* – these reflect this conception of freedom as movement; freedom as that which is found elsewhere.[12] Yet if one considers Marsalis (1997) *Blood on the Fields*, Native Americans figure as sources of knowledge about survival on and off the land, and as crucial allies in the project of enslaved Black folks' escape towards freedom in the north. For these Black folk, Marsalis' repeated refrain, 'freedom is in the trying', means that the path to freedom can only be won by an unrelenting drive towards an elsewhere. The oratorio ends with *Due North*, a piece of music which itself drives the listener forward. However, it is important to not lose sight of the situation of Native Americans; the First Nations peoples from whom Black folk may seek help in escaping, are on their land. Fleeing north does not lead to freedom for First Nations peoples in a colonial settler society; but displacement. Freedom for First Nations people cannot be countenanced so long as the setters maintain power and remain in place. The difference between Blackfullas and Black folk is that Blackfullas are First Nations peoples too. It is Australia, not slavery, that is the cage from within which Blackfullas sing.

In Australia today, therefore, the notion of being free is as fictitious to Blackfullas as the notion of being young. That is, while the Black folk in France described by Fanon were subject to the fiction that freedom bestowed by another is freedom – that one can somehow be forced into a manner of being and knowing and operating by another and that is called freedom – even that oppressive pretense is generally denied Blackfullas in Australia today. Blackfullas aren't for the most part forcefully 'invited in'. That assimilatory path is reserved for later arrivals. The fiction into which Blackfullas are consigned is the idea that Blackfullas are simply not there. It is an elegant, if horrifying equation. The longstanding means by which Australia has attempted, in earnest, to 'close the gap' between First Nations peoples and other inhabitants, is to follow the path laid by the nation-state's 'founding fathers', and do away with Blackfullas altogether. If Blackfullas are not, if Blackfullas are imagined to no longer be there, then the realm of freedom that prevails for Whitefellas must be all there is.

As Fanon (2001, 29) explains, '[t]he colonial world is a world cut in two' – it is a world in black and white. Not only black and white, Fanon goes so far as to claim that 'this world cut in two is inhabited by two different species' (30). Decolonisation, on this account, entails 'no more and no less than the abolition of one zone, its burial in the depths of the earth or *its expulsion from the country*' (31, emphasis ours). The reverse holds in the colonial state. Whitefellas, for the most part (enough Whitefellas for the status quo to persist), partake in the make believe that Blackfullas are no longer. For the most part, white Australia wills First Nations peoples into anachronisms belonging to a bygone era, or anachronisms left behind by time. This fiction serves Whitefellas well.[13]

The imagined absence of Blackfullas enables what Afro-Caribbean social and political philosopher, Mills (1997, 1–2), describes as 'the system of domination by which white people have historically ruled over and, in certain important ways, continue to rule over nonwhite people': the 'Racial Contract'.[14] That is, the liberal democratic Social Contract applies in the Western world between people – specifically, adult human beings. The fable of an Australia born in 1788 is one in which citizenship is, by definition, white. The Federation that was proclaimed in 1901 was one in which participation as citizen was predicated on whiteness. Mills' argument has to do with the persistence of that state of affairs, such that those of us who are 'subpersons – niggers, injuns, chinks, wogs, greasers, blackfellows, kaffirs, coolies, abos, dinks, googoos, gooks' (17), those of us who were not the intended beneficiaries of the Social Contract, remain bound to the Racial Contract. Deemed not quite human, non-whites do not enjoy the full spectrum of rights and privileges guaranteed to those whose humanity the Western world has never questioned. And while one can imagine most white Australians protesting loudly that they would never allow themselves to be signatories to such a state of affairs, Mills (1997) cautions that 'the Racial Contract prescribes for its signatories an inverted epistemology, an epistemology of ignorance [...] producing the ironic outcome that whites will in general be unable to understand the world that they themselves have made' (18). As a result, white people, to 'a significant extent, [...] will live in *an invented delusional world, a racial fantasyland*, a "consensual hallucination"' (18, emphasis ours).

In this racial fantasyland that is Australia, the Prime Minister Malcolm Turnbull will support an inquiry into the weakening of Section 18C of the Racial Discrimination Act in response to fears that Bill Leak, a cartoonist who on multiple occasions used his right of free speech to offend, demean and dehumanize Blackfullas, was hounded to his death (Kelly 2017). Section 18C, which imposes limits on free speech to protect individuals of 'diverse racial, national or ethnic origins' from 'insult', 'offence', 'humiliation' or 'intimidation', is concerned with and acts to protect 'minorities' (Tate 2016). To weaken it is to weaken the protection afforded to Blackfullas. And yet, as part of the process of safeguarding the right of Whitefellas to offend Blackfullas and other non-white Australians, a 2017 parliamentary committee

> 'canvassed a range of reform options including the creation of a "reasonable persons" test – aimed at establishing a tougher test for what constitutes conduct that "insults" and "offends" – as well as the replacement of these terms with a stricter definition such as "harass"' (Kelly 2017, 1).

That is, in order to ensure that a Whitefella need never suffer harm as a consequence of racially offending or insulting a person of colour in Australia, a group of the nation's leading lawmakers worked towards creating legal structures that allow Whitefellas the right to all but verbally harass Blackfullas.

Worse, this was the second attempt to accomplish what the government failed to do following 'the Bolt affair' – a case brought by Pat Eatock and others to the Federal Court of Australia in which Section 18C was successfully deployed. In his judgement, Justice Bromberg (2011) observed that two articles written by the columnist Andrew Bolt

> conveyed *offensive* messages about fair-skinned Aboriginal people, by saying that they were not genuinely Aboriginal and were pretending to be Aboriginal so they could access benefits that are available to Aboriginal people.

There was an ironic offence taken by many Whitefellas that the law protects Blackfullas from offence on the basis of one's race. Australia is a land of rights and laws – but should Blackfullas attempt to call upon those laws as a shield against the perpetuation of offensive, white supremacists lies, commentators, legal scholars, parliamentarians and even Prime Ministers are galvanized in the effort to reduce the potency of those laws … all in the name of freedom.

The inventiveness of white bad faith extends as far as the nation's Attorney General, George Brandis, a white man, complaining of racial discrimination for being called a 'white man'. To be clear, this powerful white man's contribution to parliamentary debate in favour of stripping the legal protections afforded to Blackfullas subject to the lies being told about their ancestry and identity, told of the times he was 'deeply offended and insulted' when he was referred to as a 'white man'. The simple statement of fact – that he is a white man – when deployed in support of those subject to the Racial Contract, is interpreted, in the Australian parliament, by the white man responsible for upholding the nation's law, as vilification for having white skin. Another sad irony[15] is that this white man, George Brandis, is the same white man who proclaimed the following: 'People do have a right to be bigots, you know. In a free country, people do have rights to say things that other people find offensive, insulting or bigoted' (cited in Tate 2016).

'Who let the dog's out?'[16]

On 19 November 2004, Mulrunji,[17] an Aboriginal man on Palm Island[18] in North Queensland was arrested on a public nuisance charge. That morning he was intoxicated to a level, which had been described as 'happy drunk'.[19] It was in this state, that he encountered Queensland Police Officer Sergeant Chris Hurley and Community Police Liaison Officer Lloyd Bengaroo who were in the process of arresting a local Aboriginal man. Mulrunji is reported as having chided Bengaroo for locking up a fellow Blackfulla. Bengaroo instructs Mulrunji to move along so as to avoid being arrested himself. Having complied, Mulrunji is reported to have sung the song *Who let the dogs out?* which prompted Officer Hurley to climb into his vehicle, and reverse back to Mulrunji to ask 'What's your problem with police?'. Without waiting for a reply, he arrests Mulrunji on the charge of public nuisance. Within 45 min of his arrest Mulrunji was found dead in a police cell; his liver almost cleaved in two, with four broken ribs, ruptured portal vein and a haemorrhaging pancreas. It is little wonder that Blackfullas might not sing about freedom; singing can get you killed.

The public nuisance offense that Mulrunji was charged with had been introduced in the state of Queensland in 2003, and took effect on the 1 April 2004; just 7 months before he was killed. According to the Crime and Misconduct Commission (CMC), this new offence 'was first introduced in the context of public interest over an extended period in relation to the behaviour of intoxicated Indigenous homeless people, particularly in Cairns, Townsville and Mt Isa'. The public nuisance offense represented a broadening of the old 'offensive language and behaviour provision, allowing police to "arrest virtually anyone"' (Crime and Misconduct Commission 2008). Yet, evidence suggests that police do not regulate the behaviours of everyone, and in fact, offensive language charges have long been 'selectively enforced' upon Blackfullas across the country.

Over a decade earlier, The Royal Commission into Aboriginal Deaths in Custody (RCIADIC) (Johnston 1991) found that Blackfullas were disproportionately arrested and detaining in custody for trivial offences, most typically via charges of offensive language (accompanied alongside resisting arrest and assaulting police). They found Blackfullas were more likely to be arrested for assault occasioning no actual bodily harm, were twice as likely to be arrested in circumstances where assault occasioning no harm is the most serious offence, and three times more likely to be imprisoned for these offenses. Langton (1988) demonstrated how many of these offenses come about solely through interactions with police officers; the offence being the temerity to speak back to agents of the state (see Table 2).

As a result, The RCIADIC (1991) made the recommendation that:

(a) The use of offensive language in circumstances of interventions initiated by police should not normally be occasion for arrest or charge; and
(b) Police Services should examine and monitor the use of offensive language charges.

Yet over two decades on from the RCIADIC, Anthony (2016) claims that public order offences continued to be punished, with police powers extended rather than reduced. And certainly, in the state of Queensland that rings true. The introduction of the new 'public nuisance' offense of which Mulrunji was charged, enabled a broader definition of the type of misconduct people could be charged for, and contravened the recommendation of the RCIADIC which required specific monitoring of obscene language offences. A review undertaken by the Crime and Misconduct Commission (CMC) (2008) into the introduction of the public nuisance charge found that Blackfullas were 12.6 times more likely to be charged than Whitefellas, and were more likely to be arrested and issued with a notice to appear than receiving a caution, conferencing or other counselling.

Table 2. Blackfullas, Free Speech and The Offences in Public Places Act 1980.

Case 1 Two police officers on a routine patrol entered a public bar and allegedly heard the offender say in a loud tone of voice: 'Here are those fucking coppers again to lock up us black fellows'. There were no other customers in the bar at the time and no staff. The offender pleaded not guilty. She was convicted, fined $100, in default 4 days hard labour, with 3 months to pay.
Case 2 The offender allegedly called out in the main street: 'You can get fucked you bastards, and you coppers can get fucked too. The offender pleaded guilty. She was convicted and fined $50. In default 48 h Imprisonment with hard labour, with 1 month to pay.
Case 3 The offender was approached by police officers in a private residence on an Aboriginal settlement after his de facto wife complained about his throwing articles of furniture from the house. On being approached, it was alleged that he said: 'You cunts can do as you like, you won't prove anything'. He pleaded guilty, was convicted and fined $100, in default 4 days with hard labour, with one month to pay.

Table 3. Police Narratives Around the Arrest of Blackfullas for 'Public Nuisance' Offences: An Example.

P1: Police have attended the offence location and observed a large group of ATSI persons. Offender has been aggressive towards police and stated to police 'get fucked you cunts why don't you leave us alone'. Offender has also attempted to walk away from police and continued to yell abuse at police from a distance. Offender was arrested for disorderly. (43)

Blackfullas are also more likely to have a conviction recorded for the offense and more likely to be imprisoned, than receive a fine. The review found that one out of three offensive languages only charges involved Indigenous offenders and almost half related to language directed at police (see Table 3).

The CMC concluded:

It appears police often respond to offensive language used by Indigenous people where it could not be suggested that there was any real 'interference' with the police carrying out their duties' and was suggestive of 'a tense and volatile relationship between police and Indigenous people.

The asymmetry between the Attorney General's claim that Australians have the 'right to be bigots' and say things that may cause offense, and the systematic over-surveillance and incarceration of Blackfullas on offensive language charges is glaring.

It is little wonder that Cheetham refused to rejoice in being 'young and free'. Free speech for all is a fiction, and a fiction, which Blackfullas refuse to testify to, much like the fiction of Terra Nullius. Indeed the two are inextricably linked. The presence of Blackfullas exposes the lie of unoccupied land, and offends white sensibilities. Consequently, it is the bodies, acts and speech of Blackfullas that must be regulated, curtailed and caged as a means to contain the lie, or at the very least, rationalize the imperative for lying. Mills' racial contract is evidenced in laws governing speech, which routinely 'over-emphasize(s) the seriousness of insults against majority (in particular, against enforcement agents themselves) and undervalues insults against disadvantaged minorities' (Sadurski 1994, 90). It is the reality that 'you cunts can do as you like' that Blackfullas are testifying to, and are being incarcerated for. The demands to be heard, the plea for inclusion are typically read as a threat and a foul attempt to silence, because free speech has functioned so well as a tool of domination for Whitefellas, So long as some may exercise their right to be bigots, while others don't have to right to walk home, debates about free speech are futile, and perhaps too, so is singing about freedom.

'The warrior in chains'

It was a cold and rainy summer night when I first heard his song
I was sitting in a prison cell wondering where my life had gone
As I heard his guitar playing low, I listened to the words
And the song he sang was soft and low and the saddest I have heard
When you're locked behind those cold grey walls, it's a long and lonely ride
After 6 long years in a prison cell, I guess the young man's dreams had died
I heard him crying late one night as I was lying in the dark
He started singing out his song and he sang it from the heart

Won't you play for me that song of thunder, bring to me a dream,
I left my youth behind me in other places I have been,
Let your black clouds open over me, oh cleanse me with your rain
Let your four winds bring some freedom, to the warrior in chains.
There's two things that don't go together well, that's a black man and prison cell
The cold remorse, the agitation, and not even missed on a mission station
And the guilty ones are those who blame the black man who hangs his head in shame
Instead of letting him build his pride before some other senseless suicide
When they tried to wake him in the morning, they found that he was dead
But I knew his spirit was flying free, in those dark clouds overhead
When we gathered in the chapel, I swore I heard him sing his song
And as the rains poured from those thunder clouds, I just had to sing along
Won't you play for me that song of thunder, bring to me a dream,
I left my youth behind me in other places I have been,
Let your black clouds open over me, oh cleanse me with your rain
Let your four winds bring some freedom, to the warrior in chains.
Lyrics, *Warrior in Chains.*

Given the words of Davis (2010) at the beginning of this article, it is fitting that we conclude with the lyrics to *Warrior in Chains* a song written[20] and performed by Gomeroi man Roger Knox (2014). Affectionately referred to as 'Black Elvis', Knox is a proud country singer who regularly tours prisons in Australia, Canada and the United States. His song *Warrior in Chains* bears similarities to the 'Caged Bird'. The song the warrior sings from his prison cell, much like the caged bird is 'not a carol of joy or glee'. It too is an aspirational plea for freedom, however on the surface, it offers us a most disturbing proposition; that it was only in death that the Warrior's spirit was able to fly free. Perhaps this was Knox's way of making sense of the tragic and senseless suicides within his community. However, perhaps, this song tells us not of suicide, but instead provides an 'illuminating account of the nature of freedom' (Davis 2010, 46).

Perhaps this song is not a song commemorating the death of the warrior, but instead the death of freedom for Blackfullas. It is from his chains that the Warrior sings to us about the possibility of freedom, wishing for it to wash over him, for it to return in a dream. The warrior's song soft and low, is the saddest song Knox has heard, and it is at the chapel, in grieving in which Knox feels compelled to sing along. Together both Knox and the Warrior are mourning the loss of freedom. To sing of freedom from within the cage that is the Australian nation-state is an act of grieving for Blackfullas, and the insistence that we rejoice is most obscene and absurd. However, the resistance of Blackfullas to singing joyfully of the fiction of freedom is not a failing or weakness, rather, it testifies to the strength of the warrior to fight back.

Postscript

In writing this article, we had shared early iterations with an Indigenous postgraduate reading group within our institution. Included within that group is co-author and Senior Traditional Owner, Uncle Shane Coghill who is undertaking his PhD. It was with some apprehension that the draft article, with its confronting working title was disclosed to him. Chelsea Bond flagged apologetically with Uncle Shane that he might not like the language within the title. We collectively sat wincing in anticipation of his response. Uncle Shane looked up over the article, smirked and directed Bond to 'come over here'. As Bond walked over to him, he placed his forearms in front of his body, aligned but in opposite directions. Looking closer, Bond could see tattoo markings on his forearms each containing letters. On one arm were the letters 'c' and 'u' and on the other 'n' 't' and 's'. These random letters which had been etched in ink on his skin several decades earlier could not be read as a complete word until he placed his arms in this particular position; a pose of crossed arms which could be read as relaxed or defiant . We see on his body, not a tattoo of an obscene word, rather we see an example of a body speaking back, and speaking loud and clear about the experience of oppression, and to the oppressor; for there can be no doubting who the intended audience was. There is a recognition in this stance, of the surveillance of black bodies and silencing of black voices, yet at the same time, we see a steadfast refusal of that same body to be silent or compliant.

We dedicate this article to the Blackfullas who are no longer with us, but whose bodies remain as a stark reminder of the obscenity of rejoicing in freedom in a nation, which failed to recognize their existence, let alone their right to be free. Like Moreton-Robinson, we too recognize that in life and in death, the bodies of Blackfullas have and always will signify our title to this land.

Notes

1. The term 'song woman' is surprisingly difficult to explain. Aboriginal and Torres Strait Islander peoples use the term 'song woman' to refer to one engaged in more than performance, testimony, narration, or composition. We also note the relationship observed by Mackinlay (2000, 84) between 'Grandmother's Law' and *a-nguyulnguyul* performance, where 'the word *a-nguyulnguyul* is used by Yanyuwa to refer to a ... clever song or person'.
2. In this article, we use 'Blackfullas' to refer to Aboriginal and Torres Strait Islander peoples who are the First Peoples of Australia. Blackfulla is an Aboriginal English word typically used by Aboriginal and Torres Strait Islander Australians.
3. Chelsea Bond is an Aboriginal Australian Senior Lecturer and researcher in Public Health and Critical Indigenous Studies; Bryan Mukandi is an African Australian Philosopher and Health Policy and Systems researcher; Shane Coghill is an Aboriginal Elder and PhD candidate.
4. We use the term 'Black folk' deliberately, invoking Du Bois (1976) study. In so doing, we point to the prominence Du Bois gives to the songs of Black Folk. We also point to Du Bois' assembly of African Americans and Native Americans, for instance when he notes that '[w]e the darker ones come even now not altogether empty-handed ... the American fairy tales and folk-lore are Indian and African' (22). In referring to Blackfullas and Black folk, we affirm something of that assembly, without subsuming First Nations peoples, and the prior and specific relationship that Blackfullas have to country (Moreton-Robinson 2015), within the broader category of 'black peoples'.
5. Christopher Kelen (2003) offers a masterful reading of *Advance Australia Fair*, which replaced *God Save the Queen* as Australia's national anthem in 1984. Kelen interrogates the 'we' of the second line, and finds that '[w]e want to have always been here [...] This consciousness of an identity of pretended eternal rights is only achieved by multiple erasure [...] It is achieved by means of the *terra nullius* myth, the myth of a land empty prior to our coming' (169). He goes on to note that 'Aborigines are given no specific role in this song ... it is not their country or nationality being described here; rather the advance of *fair* Australia, an advance which takes place at the expense of an unmentionable non-polity' (170, emphasis in original).
6. Derrida (2009, 34) juxtaposes the violence undergirding the sovereign's power with power over (the ability to ordain) speech. He suggests a fabular grounding to political authority, where 'a fable is always and before all else speech [...] a fiction that claims to teach us

something, a fiction supposed to give something to be known, a fiction supposed to *make known [faire savoir], make so as to know* (emphasis and parentheses in original).

7. Derrida (2002, xvi), again helpful here, notes that 'although "alibi" means literally an *alleged* "elsewhere" in space, it extends beyond either topology or geography ... As an *allegation*, an alibi can *defer/differ* in time ... it can save itself by invoking another time' (emphasis in original). The fabrication of a young Australia provides an *elsewhere* – it displaces Blackfullas and overlays this time and place of colonial violence and dispossession with a fabled one in which white Australia is free to rejoice.

8. The commemoration as 'Australia Day' of the landing of the 'First Fleet' reinscribes annually the myth of this moment as the birth of Australia, prior to which the land, not spoken for by Europeans, is taken to have been 'empty', save for flora and fauna. Australia Day was first officially commemorated as 'Australia Day' in 1935. In 1936, William Cooper established the Australian Aborigines' League in Victoria; while Patten, Ferguson and Gibbs formed the Aborigines' Progressive Association in New South Wales in 1937. In 1938, these leaders declared Australia Day, a day of mourning.

9. Helen Ngo (2016), an Asian Australian philosopher, notes the following regarding holding a stance:

> [W]hen one holds a stance [...] this is an active endeavour [...] But while a horse stance can be held for the sake of training, it is also more: in the context of a form or routine, the stance serves as a foundation for transition, preparing and positioning the body for the next movement or strike. It is significant that in Chinese the word for stance, 步, can also be translated into English as 'step'. Holding is not only active, it also enables and prepares us for action and movement.

Ngo's work suggests that there are in Cheetham's stance lessons to be learnt, not only about the dispositions of Blackfullas, but also the forces to which Blackfullas are subjected and must respond on an habitual basis. Césaire's (1995) seminal *Notebook* can also be read as an articulation of the stance that he chooses to hold.

10. Despite the deployment of Judeo-Christian beliefs and narratives in the justification of the colonial project, particularly the invocation of that Judeo-Christian heritage by European settlers, the parallels between the author of Psalm 137 and Blackfullas is striking:

> By the rivers of Babylon we sat and wept
> when we remembered Zion.
> There on the poplars
> we hung our harps,
> for there our captors asked us for songs,
> our tormentors demanded songs of joy;
> they said, 'Sing us one of the songs of Zion!' (Psalm 137:1–3).

11. 'One day, a good white master, who exercised a lot of influence, said to his friends: 'Let's be kind to the niggers.'

> So the white masters grudgingly decided to raise the animal-machine man to the supreme rank of *man*, although it wasn't so easy [...] The black man was acted upon' (Fanon 2008, 194, emphasis in original).

12. See Davis (1999) *Blues Legacies and Black Feminism* for a thorough exploration of the relationship between freedom and movement or travel, particularly as regards the spirituals, the blues and jazz in African American life.

13. From the perspective of Blackfullas, as peoples subjected to colonial settlement, this fiction can be read in ways similar to Edward Said's (1986) 'Canaanite Reading' of Judeo(-Christian) expansion narratives:

Canaanites on the outside will resist and try to penetrate the walls banning them from the goods of what is, after all, partly their world too. The strength of the Canaanite [...] is that being defeated and 'outside', you can perhaps more easily feel compassion, more easily call injustice 'injustice', more easily speak directly and plainly of all oppression, and with less difficulty try to understand (rather than mystify or occlude) history and equality.

14. Mills (1997) understands the 'Racial Contract' as

That set of formal or informal agreements or meta-agreements [...] between members of one subset of humans, henceforth designated by (shifting) 'racial' (phenotypical/genea-logical/cultural) criteria [...] as 'white,' and coextensive with the class of full persons, to categorize the remaining subset of humans as 'nonwhite' and of a different and inferior moral status, subpersons, so that they have subordinate civil standing in the white or white-ruled polities [...] the general purpose of the Contract is always the differential privileging of whites as a group with respect to the nonwhites as a group, the exploita-tion of their bodies, land and resources, and the denial of equal socioeconomic oppor-tunities to them. All whites are *beneficiaries* of the Contract, though some whites are not *signatories* to it (11, emphasis in original).

15. There is something troubling about reducing a proclamation by the nation's Attorney General in favour of the right to bigotry, to a mere 'sad irony'. Perhaps it speaks to the unfortunate but unavoidable tolerance for violence developed by Blackfullas and Black folk. It is also worth bearing in mind that '[t]he "scene" of irony involves relations of power based in relations of communication' (Hutcheon 1995, 2). Perhaps therefore, what is troubling is not our recognition of irony, but the relations of power and relations of communication at the heart of Australia.

16. *Who Let The Dogs Out* is the title of a song released by Bahamian group Baha Men on 26 July 2000 which performed well in the music charts in Australia, New Zealand, the United Kingdom, and the United States of America.

17. In observance of Aboriginal custom, we use the name Mulrunji that is the traditional name of the deceased.

18. Established in 1914, Palm Island is a former government-run Aboriginal reserve, which operated as a prison camp for troublesome Aboriginal people from various parts of Queensland. Under the Restriction of the Sale of Opium and Protection of Aborigines Act (1897) representatives from over 40 different tribes were exiled on Palm Island.

19. Hooper (2009, 87) attributes this description to a community member who witnessed Mulrunji's arrest.

20. The lyrics to the song 'Warrior in Chains' were originally written by a Canadian Aboriginal man, Daniel Beattie. Mr Beattie was incarcerated in a Canadian prison which Roger Knox and others had performed in during the 1980s and during this tour, he gifted him two songs, one of which was 'Warrior in Chains'. The lyrics today have been amended slightly, but the song of freedom shared between two Aboriginal men in two different countries ultimately is unchanged.

Disclosure statement

No potential conflict of interest was reported by the authors.

ORCID

Chelsea Bond ⓘ http://orcid.org/0000-0002-5246-235X
Bryan Mukandi ⓘ http://orcid.org/0000-0002-0497-4166

References

Aborigines Progressive Association. 1938. "Aborigines Claim Citizen Rights!: A Statement of the Case for the Aborigines Progressive Association/By J.T. Patten and W. Ferguson." Sydney. Accessed 1 August 2017. http://nla.gov.au/nla.obj-241787110/view?partId=nla.obj-241788701.
Angelou, M. 2015. *I Know Why the Caged Bird Sings*. New York: Random House.
Anthony, T. 2016. "Deaths in Custody: 25 Years after the Royal Commission, We've Gone Backwards." *The Conversation*, April 13. https://theconversation.com/deaths-in-custody-25-years-after-the-royal-commission-weve-gone-backwards-57109
Bromberg, J. M. 2011. "Eatock V Bolt (2011) FCA 1103." http://www.abc.net.au/mediawatch/transcripts/1407_judgment.pdf.
Césaire, A. 1995. *Notebook of a Return to My Native Land: Cahier D'un Retour Au Pays Natal*. trans. by Mireille Rosello and Annie Pritchard. Hexham: Bloodaxe Books.
Cheetham, D. 2015. "Young and Free? Why I Declined to Sing the National Anthem at the 2015 AFL Grand Final." *The Conversation*, October 20. Accessed 8 July 2017. https://theconversation.com/young-and-free-why-i-declined-to-sing-the-national-anthem-at-the-2015-afl-grand-final-49234.
Chikowero, M. 2015. *African Music, Power, and Being in Colonial Zimbabwe*. Indiana: Indiana University Press.
Crime and Misconduct Commission. 2008. *Policing Public Order: A Review of the Public Nuisance Offence*. Brisbane: Crime and Misconduct Commission (Qld). Accessed July 27, 2017. http://www.cmc.qld.gov.au/data/portal/00000005/content/36703001211161906459.pdf.
Davis, A. 1999. *Blues Legacies and Black Feminism: Gertrude "Ma" Rainey, Bessie Smith and Billie Holiday*. New York: Vintage Books.
Davis, A. 2010. "Lectures on Liberation." In *Narrative of the Life of Frederick Douglas, an American Slave: Written by Himself*, edited by G. Ruggiero. San Fransisco, CA: Open Media Series.
Derrida, J. 2002. *Without Alibi*. ed. and trans. by Peggy Kamuf. Stanford: Stanford University Press.
Derrida, J. 2009. *The Beast and the Sovereign: Volume I*. trans. By Geoffrey Bennington. Chicago: University of Chicago Press.
Du Bois, W. E. B. 1976. *The Souls of Black Folk: Essays and Sketches*. New York: Buccaneer Books.
Dunbar, P. 1993. *The Collected Poetry of Paul Laurence Dunbar*. Charlottesville: University of Virginia Press.
Fanon, F. 2001. *Wretched of the Earth*. trans. by Constance Farrington. London: Penguin.
Fanon, F. 2008. *Black Skin, White Masks*. trans by Richard Philcox. New York: Grove Press.
Gorrie, N. 2016. "On Black Rage, New Funerals, And The Exhausting Resilience Of Our Mob", *Junkee*, September 1. http://junkee.com/black-rage-new-funerals-exhausting-resilience-mob/84230
Hooper, C. 2009. *Tall Man: A Death in Aboriginal Australia*. New York: Scribner.

Hutcheon, L. 1995. *Irony's Edge: The Theory and Politics of Irony*. London: Routledge.

Johnston, E. 1991. *National Report: Royal Commission into Aboriginal Deaths in Custody, Vols 2 and 5*. Royal Commission into Aboriginal Deaths in Custody. Canberra: AGPS.

Kelen, C. 2003. "Anthems of Australia: Singing Complicity." *National Identities* 5 (2): 161–177. doi:10.1080/1460894032000124402.

Kelly, J. 2017. "PM to Fast-Track 18C." *The Australian*, March 14. http://www.theaustralian.com.au/national-affairs/turnbull-to-fasttrack-18c-reforms-in-wake-of-bill-leaks-death/news-story/6d5a792ea13ce1ed46ce46c79f0d4eb2.

Knox, R. 2014. *Warrior in Chains: The Best of Roger Knox [CD]*. Alexandria: Undercover Music.

Langton, M. 1988. "Medicine Square." In *Being Black: Aboriginal Cultures in 'Settled' Australia*, edited by I. Keen. Canberra: Aboriginal Studies Press.

Liddle, C. 2017. "The Constitutional Recognition Debate Is Nothing like 1967", *ABC News*, May 27. http://www.abc.net.au/news/2017-05-27/constitutional-recognition-push-is-no-1967-referendum/8349872.

Mackinlay, E. 2000. "Maintaining Grandmothers' Law: Female Song Partners in Yanyuwa Culture." *Musicology Australia* 23 (1): 76–98. doi:10.1080/08145857.2000.10415915.

Marley, B. 2002. *Legend: The Best Of Bob Marley And The Wailers [CD]*. London: Island Records.

Marsalis, W. 1997. *Blood on the Fields [CD]*. New York: Columbia Records.

McQuire, A. 2016. "Amy McQuire on Don Dale: 200 Years of Trauma through A CCTV Lens", *New Matilda*, August 3. https://newmatilda.com/2016/08/03/amy-mcquire-on-don-dale-200-years-of-trauma-through-a-cctv-lens/

Mills, C. 1997. *The Racial Contract*. New York: Cornel University Press.

Moreton-Robinson, A. 2015. *The White Possessive: Property, Power, and Indigenous Sovereignty*. Minneapolis: University of Minnesota Press.

Moreton-Robinson, A. 2017. "Senses of Belonging: How Indigenous Sovereignty Unsettles White Australia" *ABC*, February 21. http://www.abc.net.au/religion/articles/2017/02/21/4623659.htm

Ngo, H. 2016. "Racist Habits: A Phenomenological Analysis of Racism and the Habitual Body." *Philosophy & Social Criticism* 42 (9): 847–872. doi:10.1177/0191453715623320.

Sadurski, W. 1994. "Racial Vilification, Psychic Harm, and Affirmative Action." In *Freedom of Communication*, edited by T. Campbell and W. Sadurski. Dartmouth: Aldershot.

Said, E. 1986. "Michael Walzer's 'Exodus and Revolution': A Canaanite Reading." *Grand Street* 5 (2): 86–106. doi:10.2307/25006845.

Simone, N. 2006. *Pastel Blues [CD]*. California: Verve.

Simone, N. 2010. *Forever Young, Gifted And Black: Songs Of Freedom And Spirit [CD]*. New York: Legacy Recordings.

Tate, J. 2016. "Free Speech, Toleration and Equal Respect: The Bolt Affair in Context." *Australian Journal of Political Science* 51 (1): 34–50. doi:10.1080/10361146.2015.1093092.

Tiddas. 1996. *Tiddas [CD]*. Baarn: Polygram.

Wilder, G. 2009. "Aimé Césaire: Contra Commemoration." *African and Black Diaspora: an International Journal* 2 (1): 121–123. doi:10.1080/17528630802513607.

Off script and indefensible: the failure of the 'moderate Muslim'

Randa Abdel-Fattah and Mehal Krayem

ABSTRACT
We have become increasingly aware of the importance of addressing diversity across media landscapes. Whilst we are still far from a genuine appreciation for difference, media outlets that view themselves as progressive understand the value of appearing diverse. This has meant that a number of Muslim voices have risen to prominence in recent years. Often these voices have attracted the title of 'moderate Muslim' as they are thought to represent a non-radical politics. This paper examines how the voice of this 'moderate Muslim' has been co-opted by the White mainstream as a sign of inclusion and commitment to multiculturalism but emphasizes that the moderate is never truly permitted to speak. In exploring how divergent voices have been publicly disciplined and how the right to speak has been positioned as a 'privilege', we show how Islamophobia permits a religious population to speak only via a select few voices, denying the spectrum of narratives, ideas and dissent. We argue that one troubling consequence of this dynamic is the chilling and marginalizing effect it has on dissenting Muslim voices who seek to destabilize efforts to produce and reproduce Islamophobia's good/bad, moderate/radical dichotomies.

Introduction

London-based journalist and author Eddo-Lodge (2017, xii) writes:

> The options are: speak your truth and face the reprisal, or bite your tongue and get ahead in life. It must be a strange life, always having permission to speak and feeling indignant when you're finally asked to listen. It stems from white people's never-questioned entitlement, I suppose..

Eddo-Lodge considers the difficulties of being heard when, as a person of colour, you attempt to speak of the structural effects that you experience as a result of the entrenched normality of Whiteness. She speaks openly of the feelings of hurt and frustration and the perceived futility of such an exercise, recognizing that a conversation about race goes nowhere without an acknowledgement of the power difference that accompanies conversations between 'Whites' and people of colour. Such an acknowledgement is noticeably absent in public discussions around Islam and Muslims, which inevitably become racialized. This creates the polarizing circumstances within which Muslims are expected to exist, forever floundering between categories of 'moderate' and 'extreme'.

Using a critical discourse analysis, this paper examines how the voice of the 'moderate Muslim' has been co-opted by the White mainstream as a sign of inclusion and commitment to multiculturalism but emphasizes that the moderate is never truly permitted to speak. Critical discourse analysis is useful for understanding how power manifests itself through language (Fairclough 1995). Van Dijk (2006, 115) makes clear the link between discourse and ideology. 'Since people acquire, express and reproduce their ideologies largely by text or talk', discourse analysis can expose underlying ideologies. This article stages a discourse analysis of newspaper articles, news stories and television interviews in order to reveal the ideological association of their authors/institutions and to make clear the way the 'moderate Muslim' is positioned in public discourse.

In exploring how divergent voices have been publicly disciplined and how the right to speak has been positioned as a 'privilege', we argue that a climate of heightened Islamophobia further polarizes the position of 'everyday' Muslims. The celebritization of the moderate Muslim becomes a perverse attempt at silencing dissenting voices and controlling the way acceptable forms of Islam are expressed and discussed. The celebritized moderate seldom speak on their own terms; instead, their very presence is a response to White anxiety. Their purpose is to assure the mainstream that the ostensible Muslim problem is under control. Below we observe the way youth ambassador Yassmin Abdel-Magied's speaking position has transitioned from that of an empowered young Australian to that of a 'public enemy' through a comparison of her *Q&A* appearance in 2015 and later in 2017. *Q&A* is a panel-style talk show on Australia's public broadcaster, the ABC, hosted by journalist Tony Jones. We then turn our attention to an incident at Sydney University Law School, where legal scholars, Associate Professor Salim Farrar and Dr Ghena Krayem, were embroiled in a 'shariah law' conspiracy, and finally we examine 'indefensible' Muslim voices via two examples in the media. We have chosen these examples as they represent a spectrum between the so-called 'moderate' and 'extreme' Muslim and highlight the invisibility of Whiteness by emphasizing the otherness of Islam in an Australian context.

Silence and the moderate

Whiteness functions as a political position in the Australian society. As Aileen Moreton-Robinson usefully frames it, Whiteness is constituted by the intersection of 'identity, institutional practices and discursive power which function as symbols of national belonging and nationhood' (Moreton-Robinson 2004, ix). At its core, Whiteness is the process of making invisible certain racial markers categorized as White. This invisibility then functions to normalize Whiteness, and through this normalization, 'other' categories are created. According to Frankenberg (1993, 1),

Whiteness is a location of structural advantage, of race privilege. Second, it is a 'standpoint', a place from which White people look at ourselves, at others, and at society. Third, 'Whiteness' refers to a set of cultural practices that are usually unmarked and unnamed.

In Australia, Whiteness plays a role in how the nation is organized. It is, as Hage (2002) argues, a 'mono-cultural Anglo-inspired orientation'. It dominates and patrols the borders of multicultural policy (Stratton 1998). It is around and through Whiteness that others are contained. Whiteness is not fixed and is always reproduced in relation to Others (Hage 1998, 58), meaning it can be accumulated to varying degrees. We argue here that the 'moderate Muslim', in particular the celebritized Moderate, has acquired a level of Whiteness that is deemed more broadly acceptable within this 'Anglo-inspired orientation'. This acceptability then functions structurally to further a 'cosmo-multicultural' agenda, where Whiteness remains centred and the concerns of 'others' exist only on the margins and only in relation to White concerns.

In March 2015, Yassmin Abdel-Magied appeared on ABC's *Q&A* programme. At that time, Abdel-Magied had a string of distinct and notable descriptors to her identity: young (24 years old), engineer, Sudanese-born, Australian (arriving at age 2), Muslim, hijabi, founder of a non-government organization, Youth Without Borders at age 16, Queensland's 2015 Young Australian of the Year, named one of the top 100 most influential engineers in Australia by Engineers Australia, member of the Australian government's G20 Youth Steering Committee, the Federal ANZAC Centenary Commemoration Youth Working Group and the Council for Australian-Arab Relations. Althpugh Abdel-Magied was a young rising Australian Muslim star, she was by no means a national household name.

The 2015 panel titled 'Bad Feminism: Contradictions and Careers' had Abdel-Magied appear alongside Julie Bishop, Minister for Foreign Affairs and Deputy Leader of the Liberal Party, academics/authors, Germaine Greer and Roxanne Gay, and Holly Kramer, CEO. In a discussion about feminism, Abdel-Magied said:

> I think Western feminism sees religion as a tool of oppression, whereas I see, and a lot of Muslim women see, our religion as a tool of liberation and as a basis to say, 'Hey, you know, we all agree that, you know, this book is divine, for example, and we've been given equal rights in this book, so you have to agree with it'.

These comments caused no media backlash, and her appearance passed rather uneventfully. In February 2017, Abdel-Magied then appeared alongside Tasmanian Senator, Jacquie Lambie, saying 'Islam to me is the most feminist religion'. This comment and the subsequent confrontation between Abdel-Magied and Lambie were the catalyst for countless media headlines in the aftermath. In the week that followed, Australia's broadsheet paper *The Australian* published an article with the headline 'Activist Yassmin Abdel-Magied "blind" to Islam's Treatment of Women', whereas the *Daily Telegraph* wrote 'What really happens when the "wrong" kind of guest appears on Q and A' and proceeded to explain why a flurry of people 'with too much time on their hands' were demanding the ABC issue a formal apology to Abdel-Magied for the way she was treated during her appearance.

Media interest in Abdel-Magied did not cease once the Q&A saga had passed. Instead, this led to heightened scrutiny of her every public statement. On ANZAC Day, 25 April 2017, Abdel-Magied posted 'Lest we forget. Nauru. Manus. Palestine'.[1] The post, which articulates a critique of the relation between Australia's regime of incarceration and detention and the ongoing occupation of the Palestinian Territories, generated national media outrage. *The Herald Sun* condemned Abdel-Magied for 'hijacking the sacred "Lest We Forget" tribute' and quoted a number of high-profile politicians, including Immigration Minister Peter Dutton, who called her post a 'disgrace', and Tasmanian Senator Eric Abetz, who called the post 'disrespectful' and 'deeply reprehensible'(Loussikian and Rawthorne 2017). Meanwhile, Federal MP George Christensen called for Abdel-Magied to be sacked from her position at the ABC hosting the news and current affairs programme *Australia Wide* (Loussikian and Rawthorne 2017).

Prime Minister Malcolm Turnbull stated Abdel-Magied had made a 'very serious error of judgement' and explained 'she should very carefully reflect on that error of judge-ment' (Bickers 2017). Senator Abetz called for Bishop to sack Abdel-Magied from her position on the Council of Arab Australian Relations (CAAR) board. Bishop declared she was 'satisfied' with the ABC host's response. Abdel-Magied removed the post on the same day, apologised profusely, and 'did not seek to defend her words'. In terms of her position on the board of CAAR, she had 'communicated a positive image of Australia as an inclusive, tolerant and multicultural nation where civic participation of Arab-Australians, and particularly women, is valued'.

The responses from both the Prime Minister and the Foreign Minister convey two very clear and interrelated positions on the issues of 'speaking' as a Muslim woman in Australia. The patronizing response from the Prime Minister is a prime example of how Muslim women often find themselves publicly reprimanded for veering off-script. When viewed in light of a history of colonial discourse, the Prime Minister's words are both patronizing *and* threatening. They imply that the 'very serious error of judgment' could cost Abdel-Magied her moderate status. This is significant because the only voice within the Muslim community that is superficially considered as holding equal weight within the framework of Whiteness is the moderate voice. The response from Bishop reveals further the confines of the script for the moderate, stating Abdel-Magied 'did not seek to defend her words' and thus her position on the matter reveals the bindness, or as Morsi (2017, 4) calls it, 'the traps of Whiteness', within which moderates find themselves. At the centre of this condition in which the moderate is positioned is the imperative that a trade-off be made between being heard and being frank about the inequalities that implicate the Muslim community in Australia. In the next section, we turn to delineate this condition of the moderate.

The moderate voice and Islamophobia

The 'moderate Muslim' has long been referred to in public discussions around both Muslims and Islam. The accepted kind of Muslim a 'secular' society seeks to produce is 'a particular kind of religious subject who is compatible with the rationality and exercise of liberal political rule' (Mahmood 2006, 325). Kunandi (2016, 17), similarly, argues that Islamophobia deploys the categories of moderate and extremist by 'forcing' on

> [...] every Muslim the question of whether they are 'moderates' [...] But this question is not posed directly; it is always displaced onto the plane of culture: do they accept Western values? This framework imposes itself relentlessly on Muslim public expression, rendering suspicious anyone who refuses to engage in rituals of loyalty to Western culture.

For Kunandi (2016, 17), 'Muslim dissent against empire is never heard as dissent but only as extremism'. Thus, the 'moderate' Muslims are the Muslims who are emptied of their politics, their dissent, their resistance. The ideal moderate therefore is simply a cosmetic addition to a multicultural display with no overt political inclinations and certainly no agenda to unsettle or destabilize the centrality of Whiteness on which Australia exists as a nation. The 'moderate' Muslim is only allowed to perform 'safe criticisms', which 'must air only within the safe coordinates of society's democratic values' (Morsi 2017, 45). Any dissent or denunciation of state violence must be preceded by the Muslim's 'commitment to pursue white respectability' and hence dissent is only allowed 'within the scope of mainstream expectations of being the good Muslim' (2017, 45).

Modood and Ahmad (2007) argue that the moderate Muslim relies on a contrast with the non-moderate Muslim for validity. The effect of this contrast is a delineation between the legitimate and the illegitimate Muslim, wherein the moderate comes to be considered the legitimate voice (Spalek and Imtoual 2007, 196). Anna Mansson McGinty (2012) argues that in the United States, despite having entered a period of heightened Islamophobia, Muslim advocacy groups have maintained 'less confrontational' approaches to advocacy. This is partially attributed to the scrutiny these organizations have been subject to after 9/11 and the war on terror, and part of the pursuit 'for the "tolerable", "good", and "moderate" Muslim versus the supporter of Islamic terrorism' (2963). Moderate Muslims therefore become representative of the type of Muslim that might be encompassed by the state. They are governable, they are 'with us' not 'against us' – they are non-disruptors of the status quo. This is important in constructing a kind of normalcy around particular types of Islam, whilst demonizing those that differ. The moderate Muslims are easily contained in the rhetoric of belonging because they never seek to draw attention to the illegitimacy of White power. This is deeply problematic for Muslims who do not support 'terrorism' but who, equally, challenge or question the 'soft' approaches to advocacy, including engagement with mainstream media.

McGinty (2012) refers to the kind of Islam that maintains the status quo in the American context as 'American Islam'. This she argues has 'essentializing tendencies overlooking particular voices and geographies within the Muslim community in the USA'. The emphasis on American Islam as constituting part of the mainstream focuses on the 'sameness' of the moderate Muslim in the American context. Similarly, Sohrabi and Farquharson 2015, 638), in a study relating to Australian Muslim leaders and the discourse of normalization, note there is a strong desire from the perspective of the Muslim leaders interviewed to want to be 'invisible'. This invisibility is a marker of social and cultural acceptance and the normalization of Islamic practices. While patriarchy and fundamentalism are problems faced by numerous communities, for Sohrabi and Farquharson, Muslim communities are subject to an exceptionalism that depicts Islam as incompatible with the West (639). It is this invisibility we consider an inherent Whitening of Islam and Muslims in Australia. To be truly invisible, Muslims need to be the same. Difference cannot be encompassed in the governance of everyday Muslims. Inherent in the normalization discourse is therefore the notion of integration.

One of the effects of Islamophobia is its institutional and structural power to elevate and privilege the voices of some Muslims over others. In an environment where 'diversity' is managed by a White centre, only a narrow range of Muslim voices is allowed space in the mainstream public domain. The racialization of Muslims can bring about the homogenization of Muslims into a single, monolithic category. Yet, as we often see, the war on terror has split the racialized category of 'Muslims' into 'good' and 'bad' or 'moderate/mainstream' and 'radical'. Because Islamophobia and Whiteness encounter Muslims only via these two racialized categories, it cannot cope with a spectrum of viewpoints. Every intervention must be collapsed and folded into either of these two boxes. The 'moderate' personality is lauded and elevated to the status of a 'representative' of Australian Muslims. With social media now being used as content in media reports and stories, it is increasingly the case that when media is covering a story and a 'Muslim' response is included, a tweet from Mariam Veiszadeh, founder of Islamophobia Register, or more recently Abdel-Magied, will be used. If Waleed Aly, television personality and social commentator of Egyptian-Muslim descent, has spoken or written about the matter at hand, he will inevitably be quoted. In New South Wales, the likes of Jamal Rifi and Silma Ihram (community spokespeople) often stand in as the face of moderate Muslims. For the mainstream, left liberal media, these voices will be packaged as a representation of moderate Islam. For the conservative media, these figures are deviously using their 'moderate' persona as a masquerade for a more sinister, radical agenda. Community leaders such as Rifi and Ihram might, themselves, legitimize their discourse as *taqqiya* – a practice of avoiding persecution. This conservative discourse then comes to liken Hizb ut Tahrir, Keysar Trad or even in the past, Sheikh Al-Hilaly, to 'represent' 'radical' or 'bad' Islam. The fluidity of these categories is apparent when we consider the easy slippage between 'moderate' and 'radical'. Take, by way of example, Sheikh Shady Suleiman, president of the Australian National Imams Council. On the one hand, he is lauded as a 'moderate' sheikh who attended the Prime Minister's Ramadan iftar and signed a statement against domestic violence. On the other hand, he is presented as the 'radical' sheikh who is said to deliver misogynistic and homophobic sermons (Keany 2016). The sweeping and consistent effect of this slippage is that the 'radical' personality is demonized, marginalized and pitted against the 'moderate' and 'progressive' personality.

The voices of Australian Muslims are therefore compressed into two categories only. 'People who speak' are promoted to the status of *spokespeople*. Celebrated voices become celebrities. The extent to which Muslims are complicit in this dynamic and covet these public roles is another matter. We are not suggesting that the people we have mentioned in this article collectively share the same motives or agendas. The least we can say, however, is that as public figures who identify as Muslims and therefore bear the burden of being part of the most visible global 'Other', every intervention is politically loaded and further reproduces a problematic binary. This is a bind not of their making. There is no luxury of neutrality nor is there any credibility in any claim to speak 'as an individual not a representative'. No matter how sincerely the 'public Muslim' believes they represent themselves only, Islamophobia will sooner or later be there to remind them they have no such right. The right to speak as an individual is a privilege only the White mainstream can claim.

When Islamophobia permits a religious population to speak only via a select few voices, the spectrum of ideas and dissent is denied. One troubling consequence of this dynamic is the chilling effect it has on dissenting Muslim voices who seek to destabilize efforts to produce and reproduce Islamophobia's good/bad, moderate/radical dichotomies. For the privileging and valorization of 'moderate' voices results in the silencing and *self*-censorship of Muslims who disagree with the narratives espoused by these moderates. Such Muslims find themselves in a double bind. How does one oppose the 'moderate narrative' and its complicity in Islamophobia without contributing to a wider climate of Islamophobia? How does one reject the Islamophobic attacks a moderate is subjected to while claiming the right to critique the same person's politics? Such an exercise requires a level of nuance that is at odds with the way in which debates are allowed to play out. Any criticism is perceived as 'piling on' a person who is already being targeted and vilified and so the individual's politics are considered beyond reproach.

This brings us back to one of the enduring problems raised earlier, namely, how the White liberal logic's individualization of Islamophobia obscures its hegemonic power. The only Islamophobia Muslims are permitted to fight is the 'obvious' kind – harmful headlines, media witch hunts, social media trolling, individual threats to person or property. How does one speak back to the Islamophobia that demands a Muslim cannot be criticized because of their race-gendered marginalized identity? How can one fight the hegemonic social structures that squeeze Muslims into pre-fixed false categories without critiquing the politics of those who owe much of their profile and public standing to these same categories? The 'good' Muslim is treated as fragile and infallible, protected *from* Islamophobia *by* Islamophobia. Alternatively, how does one defend a 'radical' against Islamophobia without one's defence being equated with condoning the 'radical's' particular politics? By demanding solidarity at all costs, the diversity and complexity of Muslim identities are denied. The only axes of difference allowed pivots on the meaningless points of 'moderate/good' and 'radical/bad'. To critique or defend is always personalized and individualized. The politics of representation – you are either with us or against us – silences and censors.

Not all voices are defensible

What interests us about the Abdel-Magied controversy is not just what the backlash against her says about the elasticity of the 'moderate Muslim' double bind. What also interests us is how many of the voices in support of her operated under the dichotomous logic of moderate and radical. The impulse to defend Abdel-Magied derived more from her 'moderate credentials' than a principled stance against Islamophobia. Those whom liberals choose to defend, *and* those whom they ignore, reveals how Islamophobia organizes Muslims into defensible and indefensible categories, even among those who purport to be defending Muslims against Islamophobia. Among the liberal defenders of Abdel-Magied, there exists a robust defence of 'moderates', an appeal to trust that the moderate Muslim is 'one of us', accepting of liberal rule. The moderate Muslim is deserving of defence because he or she represents compatibility and reconciliation with Australian values, political and social life. One prominent journalist, writing in defence of Abdel-Magied, argued: 'Abdel-Magied's most vehement critics are those who say they oppose extreme Islam. Most experts will tell you their best shot of doing this is through empowering progressive Muslims.' (Baird 2017).

We certainly do not seek to engage in a discussion of how to 'oppose extreme Islam', but rather we simply wish to point out that a number of rather rational and highly nuanced voices are swept up in the category of 'extreme Islam' because they refuse to be co-opted through the category of moderate, not necessarily of their own choosing but because they are perceived as not being 'ordinary' enough. Take, for example, the incident with a group of young Muslim male high school students from Hurstville Boys in Sydney's south who were labelled 'disrespectful' for not shaking hands with women. The media was in a frenzy. Channel 9 TV news ran a story with the tagline: 'Handshake Policy: Muslim school boys at Hurstville Boys Campus of Georges River College are allowed to refuse to shake hands with women'. The story was even reported in the U.K.'s *Independent*. The likes of anti-Muslim One Nation leader, Pauline Hanson, and conservative Australian businessman and personality, Dick Smith, were called to comment on the issue, stating it was 'Un-Australian' and it taught the young men not to respect women (Seymour 2017). Misogyny, harassment, sexual assault and threats of rape by male students have all been reported in some of Sydney's most exclusive private boys' high schools. That a story about a few Muslim students declining to shake hands with women and instead placing their hands across their chest as a mark of respect attracted a media storm and accusations of misogyny, sexism and being 'unAustralian' demonstrates the capacity of the media to call upon an entrenched narrative of the 'extremist' Muslim in order to serve the ends of the Whiteness. And yet the narrative was unchallenged, and the disproportionate outcry over handshakes compared to rape threats and sexual assault among Sydney's elite male students was ignored. We argue this is an example of how Islamophobia works at its best when it is directing and shaping *anti-Islamophobia* such that the 'extremist' Muslim is constructed as indefensible. Islamophobia creates a discursive environment in which it becomes impossible to state, for example, that a true appreciation of difference would consider the fact that in Islam physical contact with the opposite gender is limited. Instead, the 'moderate' Muslim voice is hailed to discipline the 'extremist' Muslim voice. On behalf of the Muslim community, Keysar Trad and Kuranda Seyit were repeatedly quoted as saying it was up to each individual to choose their position on the issue of hand-shaking, and Trad was quoted on News.com (2017) as saying:

> I used to apologise profusely and pray they were not offended, I used to feel so guilty. I did some research and they explained the whole idea is to protect women from unwelcome touching, if it's an innocent handshake, it's OK. It's better not to offend a woman. I changed my approach.

Trad, who is usually a voice of extremism on matters of Islam (take for example his continued association with the legalization of polygamy in Australia), now becomes a voice of moderation. Trad is the Muslim here, who saw the light. Trad's realization that 'it is better not to offend a woman' becomes the position against which these young men are pitted. This positions these high school students as 'extraordinary', the kind of Muslim that cannot be tolerated, the kind of Muslim man in particular who will grow up to disrespect women and who once again conjures the image of the barbaric Muslim whose masculinity is not only deeply dangerous but who is being groomed in high schools in Australia. Many of the articles also cited a law that had recently been passed in Switzerland that stated Muslims, like all Swiss children, were required to shake hands with their teachers at the end of each lesson and any child who refused could be fined (BBC 2016). The allusion to a state governing or disciplining again becomes evident, and though media reports did not suggest that this should also occur in Australia, the association between the event and the law is enough to insinuate that here is an example of how other Western nations manage their waste.

The selectivity of defence was further notable in the silence among Abdel-Magied's defenders in response to the attacks on Sydney University law academics Ghena Krayem and Salim Farrar, just a month later. This particular moral panic started with a story by the *Daily Telegraph* (Haughton 2017) about two law courses being taught at no less than Australia's 'most prestigious law school', Sydney University. The courses, 'Muslim Minorities and the Law' and 'Introduction to Islamic Law', included – as part of the set reading materials – the book *Accommodating Muslims under Common Law: A Comparative Analysis*, written by Krayem and Farrar. 'Sydney University adopts law courses pushing for recognition of sharia law, polygamy and young marriage in Australian legal system', screamed the headline, accompanied by photographs of a niqabi Muslim woman and a bearded Muslim man who had refused to stand in court, a video of a 'sharia law punishment' in Indonesia and large profile photographs of Krayem and Farrar (Daily Telegraph 2017). The ensuing controversy was predictably sensationalist and hyperbolic. Muslim academics were apparently advocating for a dual legal system, seeking to introduce sharia law into Australia (where sharia law is constructed as barbarism, misogyny, child brides and violence). The 'scandal' of whether there is 'a place for sharia law in Australia' was discussed on a breakfast television programme (Sunrise 2017), in which one of the interviewees, Mark Latham, referred to the 'imbeciles doing that kind of thing in an Australian law school'. 'Australia's shariah university', screamed another headline, led by a large photograph of Krayem and the tagline 'Sharia fan and Sydney University course instructor' (Blair 2017). An article on Channel 10 News weighed in with an equally fear-mongering article about the courses potentially having 'massive ramifications on legal teachings across the country' (Channel 10 2017). Even the Federal Education Minister Simon Birmingham had something to say, suggesting the teaching of shari'ah law amounted to an effort to undermine the principle of equality under the law and subvert Australia's legal framework. Just as disconcerting was the minister's office responding to the *Daily Telegraph*'s report by issuing a cautionary tale to warn universities they must 'keep in touch with Australian community expectations and that includes respect for and adherence to Australian law', and issue a reminder that 'taxpayer "funding" to universities is "used" to deliver benefits to all Australians'. Here was another Muslim woman – this time a distinguished law academic who had never sought any public spotlight – whose career, commitment to 'Australian values' and trust-worthiness was being questioned. And yet the voices who rallied in support of Abdel-Magied were notably silent.

Thus, the discourse of moderate/extreme Islam is applied as a condition of defensibility. As we have suggested so far, essentializing Muslims into the politicized categories of 'good' and 'bad/'moderate' and 'extreme' has consequences on how the broader public and Muslims themselves respond to Islamophobia when 'extremists' are the target. In her research of public self-representations of Muslim American leaders, McGinty (2012) found the self-representation of 'mainstream Muslim' is 'a politicized category that stresses compatibility with American political and social life' and is 'closely related to issues of power and authority'. 'Mainstream Muslims', she argues, 'as a minority group negotiate and perform politics of belonging and inclusion in the United States through the appropriation of powerful notions of what represents 'the mainstream' (2957). In this section, we want to unpack how this negotiation and performance recently played out among Australian Muslims in response to a controversy involving the contentious Australian wing of the global organization Hizb ut-Tahrir. The incident reveals how Muslims are trapped in a double bind of challenging Islamophobia *and* addressing internal religious and social problems. It is our contention that to perform any speech acts in the context of this double bind inevitably reifies certain voices, discourses and identities within the Muslim community, thereby reinforcing the narrative of good/bad Muslim.

In April 2017, a video was posted on the Facebook page of the Women of Hizb ut-Tahrir Australia. The video is a 33-minute recording of a discussion between two women engaged in an exegesis of a particularly misunderstood and controversial verse of the Quran (verse 34 of chapter 4). In the video, the women discuss the mutual rights and responsibilities of husbands and wives and repeat normative interpretations and rulings of the verse, including that men 'are permitted, not obliged to, not encouraged, but permitted to hit' their wives, stressing this 'is symbolic in nature and it's not as what people have understood or what people would like to have understood'. The video was a private recording for a closed women's meeting and was mistakenly shared on the group's public page. When the media picked it up, the community, media and political backlash was swift and intense. Federal members of parliament spoke out against the 'abhorrent' video, talkback radio was in a frenzy and domestic violence and the rights of women were suddenly the concern of the same journalists and shock jocks who had participated in some of the most vitriolic campaigns against Muslim women (Burke 2016). Comments on social media were predictably outraged at the women's 'support for violence' whilst simultaneously abusing and vilifying the women. On Channel 10's *The Project*, Waleed Aly noted the views expressed in the video belonged to a 'radical group' and the Muslim community had a year earlier produced a video of prominent Muslim clerics categorically denouncing violence against women, which, he lamented, had not attracted anywhere near the same amount of publicity 'these jerks got'. This was a valid observation. A public video by Muslim scholars and faith leaders condemning domestic violence was largely ignored, while what was supposed to be a private video received widespread attention. And yet, to make this point, Aly fell into the trap of constructing a binary between 'good' and 'bad' Muslim. Media reports quoted tweets from Yassmin Abdel-Magied and Mariam Veiszadeh, in which they condemned the video and domestic violence, and prominent members of the Muslim community released a statement clarifying that Islam unequivocally rejects domestic violence. In fact, one of us, [author 1], signed the statement, only to regret her decision and post a retraction on Facebook the following day.

We recount this in order to demonstrate how fraught and complicated Muslim responses to Islamophobia can be, especially in circumstances involving media and political frenzies over contested aspects of Islam. That the video was not intended for public distribution was no longer relevant. It was in the public domain: two Muslim women discussing the 'symbolic' nature of being struck with a miswak and the permissibility of a husband hitting his wife. The qualifications and attempts at a nuanced reading of the verse did not undo the damage of Muslim women endorsing and reinforcing this interpretation. Complex questions of jurisprudence were now being openly discussed by non-Muslims and Muslims in the media. Compounding the issue was the fact that the interpretation offered by the two women in fact reflects a common and standard understanding of the verse's meaning. This meaning, however, sits uneasily with unequivocal denunciations of domestic violence by the same Muslim scholars who would repeat the miswak analogy. Navigating such contradictions and complexities is impossible in a media and political landscape that trades in sound-bites and short grabs and whose ideas of 'diverse' opinions involve pitting people from opposite ends of the spectrum against one another.

The response of Muslim scholars, religious and community leaders and prominent figures (described as an Australian Muslim collaborative) was to seek to reclaim the narrative by releasing a statement clarifying Islam's unequivocal rejection of domestic violence. The statement ended by 'reiterat[ing] that views that are not widely shared amongst the Australian Muslim community should not be sensationalized' (Australian Muslim Collaborative 2017).

There was a sense of urgency, particularly among Muslim women, that a public statement was needed to reinforce to the wider community, but especially the Muslim community, that domestic violence was unacceptable. The urgency was compounded by the fact that two women repeating this interpretation was seen to run the risk of legitimating and vindicating male voices within the community who either qualified denouncements of domestic violence or justified violence via the verse. According to Morsi (2017, 38), the War on Terror narrative 'sets the scene' for the Muslim to speak. The Muslim is interpellated into:

'speaking in its language impregnated by a meaning that is not "inside ourselves but outside." It sets the themes and expectations, gives us the vocabulary and from that moment we become'.

For Morsi (2017, 38), 'when a Muslim accepts this narrator's call [...] we accept the role of telling our story, telling it within the story of the war of terror; a story-within-a-story; when we accept its vocabulary, when we remain blind to its trap'. There were two 'traps' the statement fell into, which highlight how Islamophobia constrains the ability of Muslims to speak on their own terms, in their own vocabulary, because every speech act becomes a reflex and is absolutely and undeniably situated within the larger context of Islamophobia.

The first problem was that the statement was reactive. The attempt to define Islam's position on violence was done in relation to the wider society via an imbalance in power relations. As a reaction, the authors and signatories of the statement had no control or say over the initiating terms and frame of the discussion. The power relations inherent in the ritual of reaction, condemnation, clarification and response were clear given the statement was not issued on neutral territory, outside the realm of politics and power (Abdel-Fattah 2017). Instead, no matter the intentions of the authors and signatories, the Islamophobic media's siren call was answered.

The second problem was that the statement explicitly relied on a mainstream/fringe binary in an effort to distance the 'mainstream/moderate/majority/good' Muslim collective from the 'fringe/minority/extreme/bad' Muslim collective. Yet this binary reveals how essentializing certain views and positions as mainstream or fringe is a deliberate elision of a shared and dynamic jurisprudential tradition. It is difficult to justify the statement that the views expressed in the video 'are not widely shared' given they represent a fairly stock standard and oft-repeated interpretation of the verse. In seeking to construct a 'mainstream moderate' version of Islam pitted against a 'fringe' Islam, complex theological debates and Muslim community realities were completely ignored. When 'extreme' Muslims on social media sought to point out the interpretation expressed by the women was no different from that expressed by popular speakers and scholars, the impulse to rescue the image of 'mainstream' Muslim from the image of a miswak-wielding violent extremist was too seductive. Islamophobia does not offer Muslims the luxury of addressing these complexities in the public domain, not when the Muslim is an a priori category of misogyny and patriarchy – a stereotype Muslims rally against both outside and within their communities. And so, rather than call out the Islamophobia that creates false and politicized categories at the expense of conservative Muslims, the response was to attack conservative Muslims in order to privilege the voices and authority of moderate Muslims.

Here, we refer back to the quote with which we opened this article and the entitlement of never questioning the authority of a White person to speak and the difficulty attributed to listening. What becomes apparent is that being asked to listen without interruption requires a true internalization of difference as acceptable. The oppression Islamophobia seeks to conceal is not the openly violent act of accosting a Muslim woman in hijab, nor is it the death threat to the local mosque or Islamic community organization. The great oppression of Islamophobia is the erasure of nuance in the hope of making the Muslim palatable. It is the public humiliation that accompanies a divergence from the moderate-script. It is the patronizing tone with which young men who do not wish to shake hands with a woman are reprimanded and accused of being sexist, when in their world view they are in fact being respectful. It is the subtle insinuation that no matter how accustomed a Muslim is to the Australian way of life, there is always the potential for deceit.

Free speech as privilege

The arguments around free speech in Australia have manifested in a discussion of the repeal of Section 18C of the Racial Discrimination Act 1975, which prohibits others from insulting, offending, humiliating or intimidating others on the basis of their race. Conservative commentators have argued repeatedly that Section 18C is a limit to free speech and have campaigned for the repeal of this section of the act. It has been well established that such a repeal and the defence in the name of free speech actively benefit and protect those from privileged White communities, but leaves racial minorities vulnerable and unprotected. In this example, we see that the right to free speech is positioned as a right that should not be compromised for White Australia. Minorities, and others who oppose the repeal, are positioned as being too sensitive, or too politically correct (Shanahan 2016). Similar logic is evident in how the right to speak is considered a privilege that must be granted by the White mainstream in relation to Muslim communities.

Hage (1998) speaks of the tendency for the White nationalist and the White Multiculturalist to position themselves at the centre of the nation believing they are authorities on dictating who belongs and who does not. This similarity across both nationalist and multicultural approaches is pertinent because it highlights the positioning of White Australia irrespective of political leanings. Here, who speaks is not authorized by the minority community who is being spoken for, rather the position is filled by whomever ticks all the boxes. The moderate Muslim is required to apply for the position and is then endorsed based on their credentials, 'celebrated' so long as they do not draw attention to the Whiteness by which they are bound.

Dreher (2009) reminds us the 'material resources for speaking is inadequate unless there is also a shift in the hierarchies of value and esteem accorded different identities and cultural production'. As we see above, there is no real value in offering space to the Muslims to speak in the Australian context if they are bound by the expectations that they will reinforce the status quo; rather, in order to truly value this intercultural exchange, a power disparity must first be acknowledged and then remedied. As is demonstrated in the examples above, the moderate Muslims are not being asked for new ideas and innovations, rather they are asked to speak to the issues of concern of White Australia. Abdel-Magied in her appearance on *Q&A* was not giving an impassioned account of what her religion meant to her as a woman; she was responding to the discourse that Islam can only be oppressive to women, a discourse not generated within the community necessarily, but one that has proven to be a preoccupation of mainstream Australia (Ho 2007).

The examples explored above recognize that speaking is represented as a privilege only afforded to those who deserve it. Those who deserve it are only those who seek to leave the hegemony of the state, organized by and through Whiteness, firmly intact. Those who do so have permission to speak, but unfortunately, they are unlikely to be able to say whatever they like without consequence. Instead they are bound by the constraints of their status as outsiders trying to find a way in by virtue of proving their sameness and erasing their difference. To truly be heard outside of this position requires a re-ordering of the nation based on a true appreciation for difference, not simply based on the right to exist if you're different with the expectation that you will attempt to prove your sameness.

Note

1. ANZAC Day is a national day across Australia marking the first military action during World War 1 by Australia and New Zealand Army Corps.

Disclosure statement

No potential conflict of interest was reported by the authors.

References

Abdel-Fattah, R. 2017. "Islamophobia and Australian Muslim Political Consciousness in the War on Terror." *Journal of Intercultural Studies* 38 (4): 397–411. doi:10.1080/07256868.2017.1341392.

Australian Muslim Collaborative. 2017. *Media Statement: Australian Muslim Collaborative Denounces Domestic Violence.* April 13. Australia: Australian Muslim Collaborative.

Baird, J. 2017. "Yassmin Abdel-Magied: The Latest Woman to Be Roasted on the Spit of Public Life." *The Sydney Morning Herald*, July 14. http://www.smh.com.au/comment/yassmin-abdelmagied-the-latest-woman-to-be-roasted-on-the-spit-of-public-life-20170714-gxb6qh.html

BBC. 2016. "Switzerland: Muslim Students Must Shake Teacher's Hand." *BBC World News*, May 25. http://www.bbc.com/news/world-europe-36382596

Bickers, C. 2017. "Coalition MPs Call on Julie Bishop to Sack Yassmin Abdel-Magied from Australian-Arab Committee." *news.com.au*, April 28. http://www.news.com.au/national/politics/coalition-mps-call-on-julie-bishop-to-sack-yassmin-abdelmagied-from-australianarab-committee/news-story/a74c55865f1adce4f4339dd42c9a7634

Blair, T. 2017. "Australia's Sharia University." *Daily Telegraph*, July 14. http://www.dailytelegraph.com.au/blogs/tim-blair/australias-sharia-university/news-story/4247218fc501f6f97266a51205a7d4af

Burke, L., 2016. "'He's Permitted to Hit Her': Alarming Video Appears to Condone Domestic Violence." *news.com.au*, April 14. http://www.news.com.au/lifestyle/relationships/marriage/hes-permitted-to-hit-her-alarming-video-appears-to-condone-domestic-violence/news-story/f6f517cac59eccad98e0768d4604feb0

Daily Telegraph. 2017. *Sydney University Adopts Law Courses Pushing for Recognition of Sharia Law, Polygamy and Young Marriage in Australian Legal System.* July 13. Sydney: Daily Telegraph.

Dreher, T. 2009. "Listening across Difference: Media and Multiculturalism beyond the Politics of Voice." *Continuum* 23 (4): 445–458. doi:10.1080/10304310903015712.

Eddo-Lodge, R. 2017. *Why I'm No Longer Talking to White People about Race.* London: Bloomsbury.

Fairclough, N. 1995. *Media Discourse.* London: Bloomsbury Academic.

Frankenberg, R. 1993. *The Social Construction of Whiteness: White Women, Race Matters.* Minneapolis: University of Minnesota Press.

Hage, G. 1998. *White Nation: Fantasies of White Supremacy in a Multicultural Society.* London: Routledge.

Hage, G. 2002. "Citizenship and Honourability: Belonging to Australia Today." In *Arab-Australians Today: Citizenship and Belonging*, edited by G. Hage, 1–15. Melbourne: Melbourne University Press.

Haughton, J. 2017. "Sydney University Adopts Law Courses Pushing for Sharia Law, Polygamy and Young Marriage in Australian Legal System." *Daily Telegraph*, 14 July. http://www.dailytelegraph.com.au/news/nsw/sydney-uni-adopts-law-courses-pushing-for-sharia-law-in-australian-legal-system/news-story/2a7fc86e24920b10164945b50e5ed5ae

Ho, C. 2007. "Muslim Women's New Defenders: Women's Rights, Nationalism and Islamophobia in Contemporary Australia." *Women's Studies International Forum* 30 (4): 290–298. doi:10.1016/j.wsif.2007.05.002.

Keany, F. 2016. "Malcolm Turnbull Regrets Hosting Homophobic Islamic Cleric Sheikh Shady Alsuleiman at Kirribilli." *ABC News*, 16 June. http://www.abc.net.au/news/2016-06-17/pm-criticises-islamic-clerics-homophobic-comments/7520884

Kunandi, A. 2016. "Islamophobia: Lay Ideology of US-led Empire." *Draft paper.* http://www.kundnani.org/draft-paper-on-islamophobia-as-lay-ideology-of-us-led-empire/

Loussikian, K., and S. Rawthorne. 2017. "Yassmin Abdel-Magied: ABC Activist's Vile Anti-Diggers Remark Slammed as 'Deeply Reprehensible'." *Herald Sun*, April 25. http://www.heraldsun.com.au/news/yassmin-abdelmagied-abc-activists-vile-antidiggers-remark-slammed-as-deeply-reprehensible/news-story/f54327495066e049cabbb7cd36eb3a98

Mahmood, S. 2006. "Secularism, Hermeneutics, and Empire: The Politics of Islamic Reformation." *Public Culture* 18 (2): 323–347. doi:10.1215/08992363-2006-006.

McGinty, A. 2012. "The 'Mainstream Muslim' Opposing Islamophobia: Self-Representations of American Muslims." *Environment and Planning A* 44 (12): 2957–2973. doi:10.1068/a4556.

Modood, T and Ahmad, F. 2007. "British Muslim Perspectives on Multiculturalism." *Theory, Culture and Society* 24: 187–213.

Moreton-Robinson, A. 2004. *Whitening Race: Essays in Social and Cultural Criticism.* Canberra: Aboriginal Studies Press, Australian Institute of Aboriginal and Torres Strait Islander Studies.

Morsi, Y. 2017. *Radical Skin, Moderate Masks: De-Radicalising the Muslim and Racism in Post-Racial Societies*. London: Rowman and Littlefield.

News.com. 2017. "Muslim Schoolboys Allowed Refuse Women's Handshakes." *News.com*, 20 February. http://www.news.com.au/lifestyle/parenting/school-life/muslim-schoolboys-allowed-to-refuse-womens-handshakes/news-story/4d8384afed9ff684c971d872b735b38b

Seymour, B. 2017. "Muslim Students at NSW Public School Allowed to Refuse to Shake Hands with Women." *Yahoo7*, 20 February. https://au.news.yahoo.com/a/34456252/muslim-students-at-nsw-public-school-hurstville-boys-campus-can-refuse-to-shake-hands-with-women/

Shanahan, D. 2016. "Repeal 18C or Say Farewell to Free Speech: IPA." *The Australian*, December 13.

Sohrabi, H., and K. Farquharson. 2015. "Australian Muslim Leaders and Normalisation Discourses." *Ethnicities* 15 (5): 633–651. doi:10.1177/1468796814547371.

Spalek, B., and A. Imtoual. 2007. "Muslim Communities and Counter-Terror Responses: 'Hard' Approaches to Community Engagement in the UK and Australia." *Journal of Muslim Minority Affairs* 27 (2): 185–202. doi:10.1080/13602000701536117.

Stratton, J. 1998. *Race Daze: Australia in Identity Crisis*. Sydney: Pluto Press.

Sunrise. 2017. "Is There a Place for Sharia Law in Australia?" *Channel 7*, July 14. https://au.tv.yahoo.com/sunrise/video/watch/36374048/is-there-a-place-for-sharia-law-in-australia/#page1

Van Dijk, T. A. 2006. "Ideology and Discourse Analysis." *Journal of Political Ideologies* 11 (2): 115–140.

Inquiry mentality and occasional mourning in the settler colonial carceral

Micaela Sahhar and Michael R. Griffiths

ABSTRACT
The settler state is vested in the incarceration of non-white bodies. Yet, the coincidence of settler states and liberal polities also means a consistent concealment of this carceral system within forms of governmentality that represent it as a system of protection or rehabilitation. Forms of settler governmentality silence subjects of colour within and beyond the borders of the settler state even as they enclose, incarcerate and eliminate the very bodies that would enunciate an objection to the transnational networks of dispossession in which the settler state is imbricated. This article addresses how speech is managed and circumscribed within the operations of settler colonial liberalism, by focusing on such forms of speech as protest and government inquiries. It does so through an analysis of recent practices of incarceration – particularly of refugees in off-shore detention and of Aboriginal people in Australian prisons and youth detention centres – and of the modes of speech that resist them in Australia.

It is not only 'un-Australian' to be, through experience, a whistle-blower against nation-building mythology. Simply 'to be' one of those who have been abused by the Australian nation is to be 'un-Australian' (Birch, 2001, 21).

Introduction

The settler state is vested in the incarceration of non-white bodies. Yet, the coincidence of settler states and liberal polities also means a consistent concealment of this carceral system within forms of governmentality that represent it as a system of protection or rehabilitation. Forms of settler governmentality silence subjects of colour within and beyond the borders of the settler state even as they enclose, incarcerate and eliminate the very bodies that would enunciate an objection to the transnational networks of dispossession in which the settler state is imbricated. Within this nexus, the disciplinary application of power to bodies also manifests through a parallel governmentality, a strategy of appropriating the late liberal language of protection (Povinelli 2014). To claim to ameliorate the suffering of disciplined Aboriginal lives is one such form of governmentality even as the settler state protects its subjects from the incursion of refugee alterity on the other. To take seriously, a critique of the settler state involves an analysis of the management of difference that manifests both internally in relation to Indigenous bodies and externally in relation to migrants – and, in particular, irregular migrants (Giannacopoulis 2013; Moreton-Robinson 2007). The complexity of the settler colonial carceral means that analysis of its contours can hardly be captured even in an analysis crossing multiple authors with diverse backgrounds. Acknowledgement of such positionality is a key disclosure to the current article: the authors of this essay are quick to assert that they do not speak for all the positions of precarity engaged by this essay. The first author is both displaced and the beneficiary of a settler inheritance, a diasporic Palestinian and settler Australian, raised on Yorta Yorta Country. The second author is also a beneficiary of the privilege of being a settler Australian raised on Noongar Country and currently residing in Gadigal Country.

This essay asks how some bodies are disappeared in order to maintain the proper meaning of the liberal settler polity. Settler liberal states and subjects, we suggest, mourn this trauma as a means to manage the very violence that the settler state perpetrates. Those privileged with such conditions as whiteness and citizenship often maintain their privilege precisely through such forms of speech as mourning. As such, liberal discourse strips the political identity of refugee agents while it purports simultaneously to ameliorate the constitutive politics of the refugee. Liberal discourse simultaneously claims to address the conditions of Aboriginal bodies even as it reconstitutes constitutive settler violence against Aboriginal lives. In many cases, the forms of speech that have challenged this settler colonial liberal discourse rearticulate the terms of liberal debate in such a way as to maintain frameworks of governmentality. Where they refuse to be complicit in such governmentality, they are frequently met with silencing criminalization. This essay addresses the way modes and manifestations of speech are managed and, at times, circumscribed, within the operations of settler colonial liberalism by focusing on such forms of speech as protest and government inquiries. In so doing, we unravel the way forms of speech that critique or challenge settler colonial sovereignty are often restrained and circumscribed from breeching the liberal discursive form by which the settler state manages difference.

'[N]ot one boat': anxieties of sovereignty in settler-colonial australia

There is a language of crisis that now defines settler colonial liberal states. In the case of the refugee, this language of crisis obfuscates by referring to humanity as such and not the exceptional position of the most vulnerable. This obfuscation, in turn, covers over the plight of people forced into a crisis of geography (statelessness) and the claim of asylum which such stateless subjects could once, require of states. Alternative descriptions of the refugee demonstrate an entrenched linguistic regime of naming 'unwanted bodies' while the plain language meaning of the term itself has come to undermine the way the administration of asylum seeker policy now functions in Australia. Terminological power is at its base a violence that begins in language, transforming mentality, systems and approach. The hollowing out of the term, 'refugee', is a state crime, reproduced infinitely and under our watch.

Refugees have experienced increasingly limited possibilities for accessing asylum in Australia. Policy has progressed from limitation to outright prevention of access; a process (which is both a series of practical mechanisms but also a mentality) in which bodies have become a crude byproduct. Yet, an ill-defined but pervasive threat is attached to those subjects seen to unsettle the national body. Thus, the machineries of asylum seeker policy represent a protective mechanism to Australian, which it now posits as a constitutive element of national security. Indeed, the early twenty-first century Australian approach to refugees was to determine, as a matter of quotas rather than the compelling nature of a case, who would be regarded as a refugee in the eyes of the state (Burnside 2015). These linkages between security and border protection have, as Giannacopoulos, Marmo, and De Lint 2013, 560) argue, constructed the problem as one of numbers and people which, as De Lint and Giannacopoulos (2013) also argue elsewhere, circumscribes a humanitarian impulse with the ancillary assumptions of the sovereign right to exclusion, as determined by questions of security (Giannacopoulos, Marmo, and De Lint 2013, 626). In the 25-year history of the current regime of management to which refugees are subjected, Robert Manne (2016) writes that the conditions which have made possible a system devoid of humanity and yet so unremarkable and unremarked upon at moments of travesty/tragedy, is not a result of any one policy. Rather, he argues, it is the historic scaffolding to current policy, beginning with mandatory detention in 1992, that has diminished the capacity of the nation to apprehend the cumulative effects of refugee policy as deserving of serious structural repudiation and critique. Or, as Giannacopoulos, Marmo, and De Lint 2013, 561) argue, the Pacific Solution has reduced the possibility of scrutiny through questions of immediacy, thus reducing overall accountability. Manne invokes the most famous of Arendt's extrapolations from *Eichmann in Jerusalem*, 'the banality of evil', arguing that it is this incremental development of policy and attitude which has meant that

> [...] as a nation we gradually lost the capacity to see the horror of what it was that we were willing to do to innocent fellow human beings who had fled in fear and sought our help (Manne 2016).

Yet, while the incremental reform of process is, as Manne argues, what enabled Australian Immigration and Border Protection Minister Peter Dutton to assert after yet another tragic death in offshore detention: 'that people self-immolate so they can get to Australia' such that a remark as this goes unnoticed for its brutality. There is also a dimension of the current system which has been enabled by Australia's response to the so-called War on Terror (Manne 2016). In particular, it has enabled a host of political and social issues to be sequestered into the seeming neutrality of security issues. This, and much else, is indicative of the legal fictions on which Australia's white history stands, by which narratives of entitlement and in this instance, dis-entitlement, are supported through a reified legal lens.

The 2013 legislation, which excised the entire Australian mainland from the migration zone, is indicative of the structural brutality of the current system. The objective of the bill, which received bipartisan support, was to deter the arrival of asylum seekers to Australian shores, where previously, such arrivals were protected at law from the possibility of offshore processing. Effectively, this meant even refugees arriving to Australian shores were no longer legally recognized as arrivals; the new law purporting to sever the Australian continent from categorization as a migration zone. Yet, ridicule of this extraordinary policy, famously by the late satirist John Clarke and his comedic partner Bryan Dawe (*7:30 Report*, 2012), has to the contrary been subsumed by the bureaucratic mechanisms and language of border control such that neither outrage nor critique is sustained to enable the radical rethinking of a framework that obscures the positioning of refugees to Australia: essential elements if there is to be sufficient impetus to completely and systemically revise the current Australian regime on asylum.

Hage (2017, 37–41) observes that there is now a class/apartheid structure that regulates how kinds of people may access or cross borders. This observation intervenes in the nexus between late twentieth century work on transnational cosmopolitanism on the one hand and the neo-liberal 'use' value attributed to individuals which is increasingly prominent in the twenty-first century. He writes that, while the national border constitutes an obvious boundary, separating nation-states, what is less obvious is as follows: 'a racialized class border [...] where a "third-world-looking" transnational working-class and underclass citizens live, and are made to feel that national borders are exceptionally important and difficult to cross' (39). The particular problem of refugees, according to Hage, is that 'in becoming the maroons of the enslaving order of national borders, they are endangering more than the already collapsing national borders; they are also endangering its global apartheid structure' (40). No refugee is simply or only a refugee whom the Australian navy is preventing from transgressing Australian national borders. Rather in these physical encounters, what is represented symbolically, is the preservation of the class/apartheid borders (40–41). It is thus in managing boundaries and the bodies that threaten to besiege the nation that the refugee problem is instrumentalized as a system of governmentality rather than with reference to, for example, international laws and conventions which could provide alternate modes of regulating the passage of refugees on more compassionate grounds.

The existence of such international conventions indicates the possibility of other modalities for responding to refugees. Yet, even as the problem posed by humanitarian frameworks are significant, the solidification of humanitarian spaces as camps – or offshore centres – leaves refugees imprisoned such that while they are kept in a condition of mere life, they do not – as Weizman (2011, 58–62) argues – attain the status of properly political spaces. These exceptional spaces come to lack the conditions for the development of a politics outside of the agential practice of survival. The question in Australia, however, is positioned as a problem not at origin but at destination, indicative of the ancillary anxiety of the settler colonial state, whose settlers are differentiated from refugees only by the time and manner of their arrival, rather than by a distinctly different or unequivocal claim to 'belonging' (Benjamin 2002, 104). To the contrary, one might regard the problematic of the settler colonial state, faced with the claim of the refugee, to be in a sense reminded by its own incurably illegitimate claim to the nation, ethically speaking, irrespective of what settler-laws may purport to 'make good'.

The continuity between refugee policy and the selective and exclusionary practices of Australian immigration – characterized by the White Australia policy – indicates towards a continual process aimed at remedying settler-colonial anxieties about legitimacy and belonging, in this case by delimiting what in fact is characteristic of Australian identity, values or national character. This is necessarily a mythologizing of the nation, which purports both to erase the memory of those whom it has supplanted (Aboriginal people) and exclude those perceived to threaten the character of the nation (refugees). As Hage (2017, 100–101) notes, such a process of polarization, 'works through the valorization of a certain definition of "humanity" that the domesticator aims to "evacuate" from the domesticated'. However, he argues that the humanity of the domesticator 'is something that is never complete but needs to be continuously aspired for' (101). Indeed, there is a permanent difficulty for settler-colonial states in securing an identity that lays claims to 'naturalness'. Thus, the notion of granting refugees the formal equality of citizenship and the rights which flow from it, troubles the state's identity.[1] It is perhaps for this reason that at least one study sympathetic to the negative impact on refugees of current policy and discourse, nevertheless poses the question of whether refugees consider themselves as 'human beings' as one worth asking (Reid and Khalil 2013, 18).

Although Manne argues that the current system of refugee management does not share the obvious and foundational racism of the White Australia policy, he nevertheless considers that a significant feature of the current treatment of refugees, is immigration *absolutism* – that is, a culture of control – premised on the idea that the ideal situation is where 'not even one asylum seeker boat reaches our shores' (Manne 2016). While this accounts descriptively for current practice, as Hage argues, it is mistaken to consider the current system as only peripheral to questions of race. In fact, the system signals to Hage, racism in crisis. Furthermore, to refuse to acknowledge the continuity of disciplinary technologies of exclusion when they are not codified as applying to all migrants (for instance, economic migrants) is to ignore the more insidious operations of racialized governmentality.

Racism is, according to Hage (2017), one tool that enhances colonial practices, which, as a discriminatory method of organization and control, has offered great benefit to its colonial practitioners. Historically, it has functioned as an effective practice of management and has supported a network of justificatory arguments that work to cure fundamentally illegal forms of wealth and land accumulation on which capitalism relies. Thus racism is not in itself a crisis. Rather, Hage argues, the crisis is born when racism fails to do its job (29). Yet, if the current refugee problem is an index of racism in crisis, both the length of time in which current policies have operated and accretions of practice (where previously they may have seemed easier to dismantle), have made Australia's method of handling asylum seekers appear to its citizens, if it is not so regarded abroad – although Australia has provided a model elsewhere for more extreme forms of exclusion and refusal – a matter of normalcy (Lowenstein 2016).

It is in this milieu that one might consider the prevailing attitude in Australian politics and political discourse towards refugees. Since the 'Tampa' crisis in 2001, the federal position has been bipartisan, in which 'turn back the boats' and similar mantras have characterized policy pursued by all successive governments. However, something that does not inevitably follow from this bipartisan response to ever increasing numbers of displaced people, a figure which has vastly escalated since the 2003 Iraq war and the ongoing chaos of the Syrian conflict since 2011, is the attitude of Australians towards in the first instance, government policy, and in the second instance, refugees themselves.

In the first respect, the widespread campaign, 'bring them here', aims through a series of actions and protests throughout Australia to close all offshore processing centres and detention camps. There have also been instances in which individuals held in offshore camps have been brought to Australia for medical treatment and whose removal back into detention has been blocked by protesters holding 24-h vigils. One particularly well-publicized case of this nature was that of a baby burnt on Nauru and brought to a hospital in Brisbane in 2016 (Tapim 2016). Such activism has at least the effect of raising the profile of an issue and renewing, however briefly, public attention. However, notwithstanding the discreet value of such localized interventions in specific cases, no actions have produced any material effects on policy-makers and making in Canberra to date.

In terms of Australian attitudes to refugee treatment in offshore processing centres, the death of Reza Barati, an Iranian refugee held at Manus Island, in February 2014, harnessed a particular sense of public outrage against Australia's 'Regional Processing Centres', or more precisely, offshore detention on Manus Island (this centre now closed at the time of writing, amidst condemnation of Australia's decision to abandon inmates to life in PNG notwithstanding public outcry to bring the remaining refugees to Australia) and Nauru. In April 2016, two men were sentenced for Barati's murder: the trial uncovered a scene of utter chaos. Testimony indicates that there were multiple employees at the centre involved, while the cause of death – severe head trauma resulting from multiple blows to the head with a piece of wood with a nail in it, and finally a rock – demonstrates the brutality of the crime. In recognition of the widespread mismanagement by employees in subduing a riot, which a 2014 Senate inquiry found to be 'eminently foreseeable', the presiding judge acknowledged that 'in sentencing these two prisoners, I do not make them "guinea pigs" to bear the brunt of punishment for those who are not here and have not been prosecuted' (Tlozek 2016).

Yet, it ought to be noted that in the interim, the *Australian Border Force Act 2015* came into effect, provisions of which seek to 'gag' employees from disclosing, under threat of jail-time, anything they come across in off-shore processing centres while doing their jobs (Barnes and Newhouse 2015).[2] In short, the institutional approach to misconduct has been to suppress its wider publicity rather than to address the inhumane treatment in detention centres or, more radically, to abandon a policy that is systemically abusive.

In the public outrage at Reza Barati's murder, one sees a short-term capacity in the Australian public to horror at the treatment of refugees in offshore processing centres, but that in the absence of practical strategies or ideas aimed at significant structural reform, this outrage is easily dissipated and unable to produce meaningful change. In the wake of the death, well-attended candlelight vigils were held around Australia under the hashtag '#LightTheDark'. People carried banners and placards reading 'not in my name', 'ashamed to be Australian' and 'Justice for Reza Barati'. It would be disingenuous to say that the outrage was not real, that people did not cry at these protests, and that they did not mean it when they shouted for justice, compassion, or closing the centres. However, the idea that dominated in the series of protest speeches was one of atone-ment, of a clean slate, that creating a public 'resting space' for Reza Barati was the work of an evening.[3]

We contend that it is the responses of the vigils themselves that are demonstrative of the crisis in public discourse in the first instance, and in particular the failing of left politics, to reframe or determine a future direction for refugee policy. To the contrary, in the vigils inspired by Barati's murder, one witnessed a tendency in the protesting public to dissociate themselves from the policies that have led to this state of affairs and thus absolve themselves of responsibility for the continuing perpetration of these crimes. Thus, the mode of public dissent, rather than being capable of harnessing a collective force, is personalized and individualized. This is captured in particular by the refrain 'not in my name', which expresses this sense of individual horror and refusal, but lacks the transformative impact required for the structural re-framing of discourse.

It is similarly this individualized discourse, reflected in the media, which deflects attention from structural problems by focussing on individual cases. A recent 'good new story' in the *Sydney Morning Herald* related to an Iraqi doctor, 50 years of age, taking his HSC in New South Wales (Sinhai 2017). Although the article did note that a system to recognize international qualifications existed, it had not in this case been able to recognize the qualifications of Hekmat Alqus Hanna, since proof of the qualification could not be obtained. The positive framing of the piece was rather directed towards the optimistic spirit displayed by Mr Hanna whose chief desire is to requalify as a medical doctor in Australia, demonstrating his 'use' value to the Australian host society.

In a discussion at the University of Melbourne in 2011 entitled 'An Indigenous Welcome for Asylum Seekers', Hage described the issue in Australia as a pathological inability to deal with people other than through a mode of instrumentality (Birch et al. 2011). He notes that this is specific to a kind of sovereignty associated with private property, rather than a sovereignty which engages in the upkeep of the dignity of the other. As Hage (131) has recently argued, the detention centres serve Australia's purpose, 'the opposition to them [...] is largely moral'. At the same discussion, the strategy offered by two Aboriginal speakers, the late Ray Jackson and Tony Birch, was to address the fundamental anxiety of settler-colonial governmentality in Australia and offer an alternative register for thinking about refugees. Birch (2001, 20–21), in an earlier piece, urges that Aboriginal people

> [...] must also assert more moral authority and *ownership* of this country. Our legitimacy does not lie within the legal system and is not dependent on state recognition [...] And we need to claim and legitimate our authority by speaking out for and protecting the rights of others, who live in, or visit *our* country. (Birch et. al. 2011)

In bringing together the anxiety of settler-colonialism and the positioning of refugees, Jackson insists on Australia's foundational illegality as crucial in explaining government approaches to refugees but also the power of Aboriginal communities (however symbolically) in definitively rejecting that position. Indeed, he argues that the incurable illegality of white Australia is constitutive of the brutality towards both Aboriginals and refugees. Thus, he urges the power of alliance between these two embattled groups with respect to the Australian state, an identification that circumvents its claims to sovereignty and refuses the importance of state recognition at all:

> I object very strongly to the governments of this country saying that refugees and asylum seekers are not welcome. [...] I have been approached by Palestinians, Iranians, by others, could I arrange a welcome to country? They wanted to feel a part of this country. They didn't go to the government to seek that. They came to the real owners of this land. They came to us, the Aboriginal people. So I say welcome, WELCOME to the refugees. And I'm damned sure that none of these governments speak in my name. (Birch et. al. 2011)

This welcome is, in a profound sense, a gesture that can only be given by Indigenous Australians, and as we have previously noted, neither of us are Indigenous to the land on which we write. Nonetheless, it is absolutely essential that the carceral operations of settler colonialism not only touch on its excised spaces of exception from properly political space (Weizman 2011). As such, we turn to the internally colonial carceral within Australia's borders.

Inquiry-mentality and the criminalization of aboriginal resistance

Indigenous bodies in the late liberal archipelago of dispossession are now killed, removed, disappeared and incarcerated at incredible rates. In Canada, there is the pervasive question of missing and murdered women – predominantly of First Nations and Aboriginal filiation and affiliation. In Australia, the question of death and torture in custody has been recently found once again to overlap with the removal of children as more and more Aboriginal teens, subject to removal have been subjected to and subjectivized as incarcerable subjects – the case of Dylan Voller is a key example. As Michael Griffiths (2013) has elsewhere argued, building on Hage's foundational claims about the field of whiteness in settler nation-states such as Australia: 'while the gaze of governmental belonging does not question whether indigenous persons *belong within* the nation [an assertion of Hage's], this gaze clearly claims the desire to evaluate *how such subjects belong* (both together and within wider imaginaries)'. Similarly, the target-ing of refugee bodies might function through the production of exceptional zones of off-shore detention, but *as bodies* Aboriginal subjects are also subjected through the lens of racism to exceptional (and exceptionally cruel) treatment within the territoriality of the settler nation-state. As such, the settler state subordinates the Aboriginal subject through disciplinary measures comparable to those targeted at the refugee, even as – in the case of Aboriginal subjects – they produce a governmental logic of protection as the alibi of this carceral project. The settler state manifests an officially liberal self-presentation, concealing its own disciplinary measures within a putatively affirmative biopolitics (Esposito 2008).

In this year's Interim Report of the Royal Commission into the Protection and Detention of Children in the Northern Territory (RCPDCNT), Commissioner Mick Gooda presents the following caveat to Australian policy:

> There have been up to 50 earlier reports and inquiries on the issues covered by the Commission's Terms of Reference. Despite these efforts, the situation of children and young people in the child protection and youth detention systems in the Northern Territory appear to have deteriorated.

Noting this rate of reporting, the RCPDCNT continues, drawing on the 2016 words of Senior Counsel Assisting Commission Peter Callaghan SC: 'There is a need to confront some sort of "Inquiry Mentality", in which investigation is allowed as a substitution for action and reporting is accepted as a replacement for results'. This is hardly surprising since few of the recommendations of either the 1992 report of the Royal Commission into Deaths in Custody or the 1997 *Bringing Them Home* Report into the removal of Aboriginal and Torres Strait Islander children from their families have been implemented (Commonwealth of Australia 1997). While *Bringing Them Home* recommended compen-sation for survivors of the Stolen Generations and while several individual cases have ended in such compensation, no commission of compensation has been established.

Similarly, extensive measures had been recommended by *Bringing Them Home* to prevent the repetition of racialized child removal – for instance that Aboriginal and Torres Strait Islander children be removed from family only in the most extreme of instances and, where possible to Indigenous extended family. There are now around 15,000 Indigenous children in out of home 'care' nationally, where there were less than 3000 in 1993.[4]

This section critiques this 'Inquiry Mentality' by making the claim that the governmental subordination of Indigenous bodies to surveillance and violence deploys a swathe of technologies of power that shelter within late liberal policies of abandonment (Povinelli 2014). Building on Audra Simpson's work, one can observe that settler states require the death and disappearance of Indigenous people to establish and maintain their patriarchal white sovereignty (Simpson 2016; Moreton-Robinson 2007). Incarceration plays a central role in this structure of dispossession since settler society's 'multicultural, liberal, democratic structure and performance of governance seek[] an ongoing settling of this land' (Simpson 2016, 1). As such, such forms of speech as political performances of liberal settler shame are themselves annexed to the structure of dispossession that they claim to ameliorate. Inquiry-mentality is a late liberal technique of government designed precisely to precipitate the disciplinary and necropolitical power over non-white subjects who, as in the case of Aboriginal people, are designated as belonging to the settler nation (however tenuously or tokenistically) and, in the case of migrant subjects such as the refugee – are refused belonging *tout court*. Inquiry-mentality produces a din of discourse about the 'tragic' violence to which Aboriginal subjects are subordinated without implementing the measures which might not only ameliorate such conditions but dismantle the settler colonial carceral as such.

The language of governmentality centres its mourning on the nation that was always the subject of dispossession. In clarifying his official statement, Australia's Attorney General, George Brandis, stated as follows:

> I have decided to make a new reference to the Australian Law Reform Commission, to ask them to examine the incarceration of Indigenous Australians, and to consider what law reform measures can be put in place to help ameliorate this *national tragedy* (quoted in Conifer et al. 2016, italics ours).

The Indigenous body has always been made manifestly disposable by patriarchal white sovereignty – yet the trope of tragedy has been the rhetorical alibi for this violent disposal's occultation (Moreton-Robinson 2007).[5] Yet, the discourse of *national tragedy* retains rhetorical occlusion of dispossession that abandons Aboriginal bodies to incarceration – a settler logic of dispossession engendered by Brandis's own *hubris*. Attorney generals are not the tragic heroes in a story that has seen Dylan Voller held in the interventionist conditions of violence that manifest through Don Dale Detention Centre's or Mulrunji Doomadgee's death in custody on Palm Island – both instances of the ongoing reduction of bodies to 'bare life' (Agamben 1998). Dylan Voller's body was subjected to torture – the spectacle of settler sovereignty in all its eliminationist violence. Mulrunji Doomadgee's death led to resistance riots, which were criminalized by the Queensland Police (Anthony 2013, 165–191). Inquiry transforms sovereign power and the spectacle of violence against the Indigenous body into biopolitical indices: facts about detention and incarceration to be recorded, tabled and mourned – all in order to reify the settler nation.

Often, articulations of settler-colonial discourse (such as *national tragedy* – informed as it is by an amnesia about Indigenous Country) are met with a commiseration, even when they are staged by such voices (such as Brandis) within late liberalism who have a vested interest in the grounded fruits (land) of slow and fast violence and the extractions it entails (Nixon 2013; Berlant 2007; Nichols 2017). Povinelli (2014, 22) argues that neoliberalism is 'neither a social formation in which the state allows the market to proceed on the basis of one set of principles and the market allows the state to proceed on another set of principles'. Instead, she argues, 'we need to start asking what are the measures of failure, the arts of failure, such that people believe and experience cultural recognition and social welfare as failures' (23). The disposability of Aboriginal bodies within the settler colonial carceral is not, then, simply a tragic failure of a system vested in a Benthamite doctrine such as rehabilitation. It is not simply that the suffering of Aboriginal young people under incarceration was a failure of state care or protection. Rather the alibi of protection and rehabilitation is deployed to undergird a system designed to remove Aboriginal bodies from their traditional Country. Such a statement is not legible in the language of free speech or in racist cartoons such as that produced by Bill Leak (discussed in detail in Evelyn Araluen's article in this issue of *Continuum*). The failure of the Northern Territory youth rehabilitation system is a cunning one designed to absent Aboriginal presence – precipitating the creation of a silo effect in which the sovereign power to take life (as was done to Mulrunji) or subject bodies to torture (to which Dylan Voller was subjected) is made possible residually even within a framework presented as protection and designed to inhabit late liberalism as such a form of governmentality. Colonial governmentality, thus remains the normative framework of the settler-liberal logic of power even as it permits and precipitates residual disciplinary violence and sovereign putting to death.

Resistance to this wing of the settler colonial carceral is often marked by a suppression and criminalization of Aboriginal voices. As Thalia Anthony (2013) has argued, attempts by Indigenous people to challenge this logic through assembly, resistance and riot are criminalized while exonerating the sovereign killing of agents of the settler state (165–191). For Anthony, the riot is 'a contest over territory', wherein the criminalized are articulating their resistance to the ongoing colonization of their land and the incarceration of the bodies of kin (169). Institutionalized operations of policing assert themselves as agencies of care and protection over Indigenous bodies and particularly those of Indigenous children, but all too often this late liberal governmentality covers over an ongoing apparatus of carceral violence and killing. Where these agents and their carceral killing are not punished by the late liberal apparatus, Anthony's work suggests that the riot is a political response – a form of speech from an 'alternative social world' (in Povinelli's sense) that is resisting ongoing colonization. This political speech act is, however, consistently coded as criminal. On Palm Island, community leaders such as Lex Wotton were criminalized and penalized for taking a leading role in the political resistance of the riot that had seen police point 'rifles on the crowd and were prepared to fire'. (R v Wotton 2007: [6]–[7] cited in Anthony 2013, 186, 187). As Povinelli (2014, 165) argues, the ethical substance of such alternative social worlds is put aside in settler colonies wherein: 'complex rhetorical crossings provide a dense knot where late liberal figurations of tense, eventfulness, and ethical substance aggregate harm and suffering in such a way that every ethical and political claim of an alternative social world [...] can be deferred'. The riot is a political act of resistance over land – a form of speech that is always criminalized and threatened by further violence on the part of agents of the settler state. The rioter in articulating resistance is nonetheless subject to criminalization by the late liberal apparatus of settler governmentality. Governmentality covers over settler state discipline in a contradictory double logic. Where the death tolls and incarceration rates of this double logic are addressed it is only through the reporting of aggregates – an inquiry-mentality that refuses to dismantle its carceral structures, instead multiplying late liberal governmental speech.

Where the social form of protest that becomes recognized as a 'riot' is a political response to this double logic of settler colonial carceral and its alibi in late liberal governmentality, the riot becomes pathologized in relation to Indigenous culture. As Neale (2013, 181) has argued, claims of cultural pathology work through misrecognizing Indigenous culture and misrepresenting it through anecdotal ethnography. For Neale, a recent tradition of ethnographic glosses on: '"traditions" and "culture" allows the knotted intricacies of inherited practices, negotiated responses and the modern forma-tion of Indigenous subjects in remote Australia to appear as malignant nostalgia: unavailable to most and pernicious to the remainder'. Practices of political assembly and resistant speech and action respond to the double disciplinary-governmental logic of settler colonialism, but become subject to a representation of cultural pathology of the kind Neale identifies in such ethnographic and, indeed, mass-media gloss. However, where Neale is addressing the attempt by the settler state to ascribe pathology to traditional practice, the double logic of settler colonial incarceration and inquiry men-tality seeks to suppress forms of Indigenous culture that are a direct response to discrimination's history and persistence in settler institutions.

Writing of African-American culture, Spillers (2006, 25) notes that 'black culture [...] is born in the penumbra of the official cultures that are historically emergent at a particular moment that we could quite rightly call modernity'. For Spillers, the relation between black culture and modernity is one of dialectical relation and invention. She argues that 'black cultures arose in the world of normative violence, coercive labor, and the virtually absolute crush of the everyday struggle for existence, its subjects could imagine, could dare to imagine, a world beyond the coercive technologies of their daily bread, but meditating the historical possibilities steadily marks [an] immense labor of emancipa-tion' (25–6). The culture of the colonized is not only traditional and continuous or (in the case of diasporic cultures) a utopian emergence of exchange and creolization (though it is often emergent from both of these lines of filiation). Just as African-Americans elaborated black culture in relation to such normative violence and coercive labour, similarly, Aboriginal people have had to produce culture through a labour of emancipa-tion. As Spillers elaborates: '[b]ecause it was set aside, black culture could, by virtue of the very act of discrimination, become culture, insofar as, historically speaking, it was forced to turn its resources of spirit toward negation and critique' (26). The riot is just one such continuous practice of negation and critique. It asserts the need for justice in a space wherein the state agencies of late liberal governmentality are also the perpetra-tors of incarceration and killing. The riot is a form of assembly – an articulation that aims to reframe the terms of debate even as its *praxis* is consistently subject to both liberal rhetorics insisting on its irrational violence and also state practices that criminalize and target resistant Aboriginal subjects. Where the management of justice remains subject to an inquiry-mentality – an agglomeration of discourse without action – the riot substitutes a political speech act of outrage and direct action, even, as we have noted as the former is labelled legitimate and the latter delegitimized as violent and irrational.

Conclusion

The framework of racialized class apartheid we saw in the forerunning discussion of the settler state repression of refugees is, then, present on the Australian mainland in a modified form. Its internal colonization functions as a method to acquire and shore up land and resources, with inquiry-mentality operating, in turn, as a performative governmental strategy that conceals knowledge of the ongoing disciplinary intervention into Aboriginal lives. Inquiry-mentality is, precisely, the state production of critical discourse against state practice that stands in place of more radical systemic transformation. It is a form of speech designed to take the place of action. Protests, in this space, are a form of speech. Yet, this speech is, as we have seen, variously constrained and redefined within settler discourse. In one instance, the vigils for Reza Berati were constrained in time – seeking to mourn as the work of an evening at the risk of addressing ongoing structures of refugee incarceration. This occasional mourning operates as a mode of enunciation that fails to address such settler structures. In the other instance, the political enunciation of the riot against death in custody was everywhere constrained, whether by physical force on the part of the police, or via discursive force by representing the rioters as irrational violent subjects and not as the active political agents they were and are.

As we have consistently affirmed, settler colonialism and its self-sanitization as late liberal multiculture is structured by the disposability of bodies. In articulating the relation between settler colonialism and the elimination of (crucially, but not only) Indigenous bodies as well as (crucially, also) as those of irregular migrants of colour, we join with such scholars as Giannacopoulis (2013) and Aileen Moreton-Robinson (2007) as seeing the undergirding racist co-constitution of settler states such as Australia. This double logic of offshore and onshore incarceration should lead to a consideration of agency, both with regards to the people positioned as outside and even inimical to the interests of the settler state and those positioned within the state who are moved to protest its brutality. One has the late-liberal spectre of the revivified Indigenous identity whose success in merely surviving, let alone a capacity to resist, poses a threat to the Australian nation. The coherence of an indigenous identity is not shared by other marginalized groupings, such as refugees, in so far as that identity is not held together by an ancillary geontological claim to the Australian nation (Povinelli 2016). Rather, the refugee identity is vertiginous and externally imposed. What links refugees together in the Australian context is not the histories that lead them into exile but rather the imposition of Australian state policy on obstructing their arrival. Refugees come to have a common identity less because of the varying violences they have fled and more for the uniform way this settler colony manages them.

In the face of this violence, certain forms of speech are privileged and others forms are silenced. One sees in moments of collective 'resistance' such as the riots that led to

Barati's murder, the (morally incompetent) struggle of state mechanisms to manage an accumulated collective identification, yet nevertheless the refugee identity vis-a-vis the Australian state is not fixed. Aboriginal riots, the so-called 'History Wars' and increased awareness in how white-solidarity should function creates a particular body of resistance such that the date for Australia Day (however tokenistically) has become the subject of national debate. On the other hand, the incarceration of refugees in off-shore detention has the effect, whether primary or residual, of disabling collective resistance amongst refugees themselves or the capacity to develop appropriate partnering strategies and campaigns between the subjects of violence and their supporters. Rather, since protests for refugees are, as we saw, constituted by Australian citizens, it is unclear what interests the very subjects of protests they (or, indeed, the broader voting public) might have in maintaining the systems of repression that they nonetheless object to.

The problem we should now consider is not whether indigenous communities can accept their dispossession, or whether the international community will continue to tolerate Australian approaches to refugees, since in the former case it seems they must and in the latter case that they will. However, rather we must ask the question of how we might arrest the appalling violence that settler-colonial states perpetuate in the ongoing effort to conceal the founding violence from which the settler state derives (however precariously) and from which the continuing violence must be seen as a futile strategy in maintaining but never completing that project of domination.

For those of us with the privileges secured by Australian citizenship, it seems incumbent that we use that privilege in ways that others cannot. One may be wary of the value of reactive activism, or left-liberal talk, and with good reason. Practical outcomes towards radical transformation are urgently needed. However, not talking, not criticizing, not acting – in obnoxious volumes and with the vigour of the faithful – or in short, falling silent on these atrocities, is surely the worst response that there might be.

Notes

1. Lorenzo Veracini makes this argument in the context of exogenous groups and the Law of Return in the case of Israel: 'Settler colonial studies and the politics of interpretation: reframing Israel-Palestine' (Veracini, conference paper supplied by the author, September 2016).
2. It should be noted that in 2016, the law was reformed to the extent that it exempted doctors and nurses from commenting on abuses (Hall 2016).
3. '#Light the Night' (2014).
4. Report on Government Services: Chapter 15, Vol. F. (Commonwealth of Australia 2016); *Bringing Them Home*. Chapter 21 (Commonwealth of Australia 1997).
5. Griffiths (2011) engages and critiques the trope of Aboriginal death as tragedy.

Acknowledgements

As well as benefiting from the feedback of two anonymous referees, this article was improved by some feedback from Juan Marcellus Tauri. Any oversights remain our own.

Disclosure statement

No potential conflict of interest was reported by the authors.

References

"#Light the Night Melbourne 500+ People Candlelight Vigil for Murdered Refugee Reza Barati." *youtube*, posted February 23, 2014. https://www.youtube.com/watch?v=GUIJ17oVyf8.

Agamben, G. 1998. *Homo Sacer: Sovereign Power and Bare Life*. Trans. Kevin Attell. Stanford: Stanford University Press.

Anthony, T. 2013. *Indigenous People, Crime and Punishment*. Abingdon: Routledge.

Barnes, G., and G. Newhouse. 2015. "Border Force Act: Detention Secrecy Just Got Worse." *ABC News*, May 28. http://www.abc.net.au/news/2015-05-28/barns-newhouse-detention-centre-secrecy-just-got-even-worse/6501086.

Benjamin, A. 2002. "Refugees, Cosmopolitanism and the Place of Citizenship." *Architectural Theory Review* 7 (2): 104. doi:10.1080/13264820209478460.

Berlant, L. 2007. "Slow Death (Sovereignty, Obesity, Lateral Agency)." *Critical Inquiry* 33 (4): 754–780. doi:10.1086/521568.

Birch, T. 2001. "The Last Refuge of the 'Un-Australian'." *UTS Review* 7 (1): 17–22, 20–21.

Birch, T., G. Hage, R. Jackson, T. Kohn, J. Pugliese, and J. Rogers. 2011. "An Indigenous Welcome for Asylum Seekers." *Crucial Conversation Lecture Series*, October 26, The University of Melbourne. http://arts.unimelb.edu.au/ssps/resources/videos/crucial-conversations-lecture-series-an-indigenous-welcome-for-asylum-seekers

Burnside, J. 2015. "Getting the Facts Straight on Refugee Resettlement." *Huffington Post*, September 7. Accessed July 2017. http://www.huffingtonpost.com.au/julian-burnside/getting-the-facts-straigh_1_b_8097326.html

Commonwealth of Australia. 1997. *Bringing Them Home: Report of the National Inquiry into the Separation of Aboriginal and Torres Strait Islander Children from their Families*. Canberra: Government Printer.

Commonwealth of Australia. 2016. *Report on Government Services*. Canberra: Government Printer.

Conifer, D., A. Henderson, H. Belot, and S. Anderson. 2016. "Indigenous Incarceration a 'National Tragedy': George Brandis Announces Inquiry." *ABC News*, October 27. http://www.abc.net.au/news/2016-10-27/indigenous-incarceration-inquiry-announced/7970186

De Lint, W., and M. Giannacopoulos. 2013. "Framing Migration: A Handbook for Policy Makers." *Griffith Law Review* 22 (3): 619–647. doi:10.1080/10383441.2013.10877015.

Esposito, R. 2008. *Bios: Biopolitics and Philosophy*. Trans. Timothy C. Campbell. Minneapolis: University of Minnesota Press.

Giannacopoulis, M. 2013. "Offshore Hospitality: Law, Asylum and Colonisation." *Law, Text, Culture* 17: 163–183.

Giannacopoulos, M., M. Marmo, and W. De Lint. 2013. "Irregular Migration: Emerging Regimes of Power and the Disappearing Human." *Griffith Law Review* 22 (3): 559–570. doi:10.1080/10383441.2013.10877012.

Griffiths, M. R. 2011. "Biopolitical Correspondences: Settler Nationalism, *Thanatopolitics*, and the Perils of Hybridity." *Australian Literary Studies* 26 (2): 20–42.

Griffiths, M. R. 2013. "The White Gaze and Its Artifacts: Governmental Belonging and Non-Indigenous Evaluation in a (Post)-Settler Colony." *Postcolonial Studies* 15 (4): 415–435. doi:10.1080/13688790.2013.777993.

Hage, G. 2017. *Is Racism an Environmental Threat?* Cambridge: Polity.

Hall, B. 2016. "A Huge Win for Doctors." *Sydney Morning Herald*, October 20. http://www.smh.com.au/federal-politics/political-news/a-huge-win-for-doctors-turnbull-government-backs-down-on-gag-laws-for-doctors-on-nauru-and-manus-20161019-gs6ecs.html

Lowenstein, A. 2016. "Australia's Refugee Policies: A Global Inspiration for All the Wrong Reasons." *The Guardian*, January 18. https://www.theguardian.com/commentisfree/2016/jan/18/australias-refugee-policies-a-global-inspiration-for-all-the-wrong-reasons.

Manne, R. 2016. "A History of Cruelty." *ABC Religion and Ethics*, 28 October. http://www.abc.net.au/religion/articles/2016/10/28/4565087.htm.

"Minister Explores Migration Semantics with Clarke and Dawe," 2012. *7.30 Report, video, Australian Broadcasting Corporation*, November 1. http://www.abc.net.au/7.30/content/2012/s3623692.htm.

Moreton-Robinson, A., ed. 2007. "Writing off Indigenous Sovereignty: The Discourse of Security and Patriarchal White Sovereignty." In *Sovereign Subjects: Indigenous Sovereignty Matters*, 86–102. Crows Nest: Allen and Unwin.

Neale, T. D. 2013. "Staircases, Pyramids and Poisons: The Immunitary Paradigm in the Works of Noel Pearson and Peter Sutton." *Continuum* 27 (2): 177–192. doi:10.1080/10304312.2013.766317.

Nichols, R. 2017. "As the U. S. Oligarchy Expands Its War, Middle Class White People Must Take a Side." *Abolition: A Journal of Insurgent Politics*. January 31.

Nixon, R. 2013. *Slow Violence and the Environmentalism of the Poor*. Cambridge, MA: Harvard University Press.

Povinelli, E. A. 2014. *Economies of Abandonment: Social Belonging and Endurance in Late Liberalism*. Durham: Duke University Press.

Povinelli, E. A. 2016. *Geontologies: A Requiem to Late Liberalism*. Durham: Duke University Press.

R v Wotton. 2007. QDC 181 (07/2087) Nase DCJ. 25 May.

Reid, C., and A. A. Khalil. 2013. "Refugee Cosmopolitans: Disrupting Narratives of Dependency." *Social Alternative* 32 (3): 14–19.

Simpson, A. 2016. "The State Is a Man: Theresa Spence, Loretta Saunders and the Gender of Settler Sovereignty." *Theory and Event* 19 (4).

Sinhai, P. 2017. "Oldest HSC Student in 2017 Is a 50-Year-Old Iraq Refugee and Medical Doctor." *Sydney Morning Herald*, June 19. http://www.smh.com.au/national/education/oldest-hsc-student-in-2017-is-a-50yearold-iraq-refugee-and-medical-doctor-20170616-gwsp7o.html

Spillers, H. J. 2006. "The Idea of Black Culture." *CR: The Centennial Review* 6 (3): 7–20. doi:10.1353/ncr.2007.0022.

Tapim, F. 2016. "Brisbane's Lady Cilento Children's Hospital Refuses to Release Badly Burnt Nauru Baby." *ABC News*, February 13. http://www.abc.net.au/news/2016-02-12/brisbane-hospital-refuses-to-release-nauru-baby/7165470

Tlozek, E. 2016. "Reza Barati Death: Two Men Jailed over 2014 Murder of Asylum Seeker at Manus Island Detention Centre." *ABC News*, April 19. http://www.abc.net.au/news/2016-04-19/reza-barati-death-two-men-sentenced-to-10-years-over-murder/7338928

Veracini, L. 2016. "Settler Colonial Studies and the Politics of Interpretation: Reframing Israel-Palestine." Conference paper supplied by the author.

Weizman, E. 2011. *The Least of All Possible Evils: Humanitarian Violence from Arendt to Gaza*. London: Verso.

What does racial (in)justice sound like? On listening, acoustic violence and the booing of Adam Goodes

Poppy de Souza (ID)

ABSTRACT

At the height of public debate surrounding the sustained booing of Indigenous AFL footballer Adam Goodes between 2013 and 2015, several media commentators routinely misheard the roar of the crowd as nothing other than acceptable social behaviour. To ears invested in the established order, the distinction between a 'boo' and a 'boo' is non-existent; to racialized others, like Adam Goodes, hearing the difference – and calling it out – is an act of resistance, sovereignty, and survival. Taking the booing of Adam Goodes as its starting point, this paper argues for a notion of political listening that attends to the sonic and sonorous histories of racial violence without displacing, or indeed replicating, its wounding effects. I consider the entangled relationship between sound, power and violence, moving beyond the sporting field to examine other acoustic territories where struggles for sovereignty, power and racial justice are playing out. By attending to the ways sound is unevenly deployed to target, silence, assimilate or oppress others along racial lines, this paper hopes to unsettle the listening logic and privileged position of the white, settler-colonial ear, to expose the norms of attention that condition and solidify their appearance.

The roar of the crowd

At the height of public debate in August 2015 around the sustained booing of Adnyamathanha man Adam Goodes – one of the country's most successful Australian Football League (AFL) players, two-time Brownlow Medal winner and 2014 Australian of the Year – there were competing voices and polarized views in the media about whether the crowd's behaviour was, or was not, a display of racism. Goodes had been the target of repeated booing and simmering racial abuse since mid 2013.[1] By 2015, opposition crowds booed Goodes at all grounds he played at, and were 'particularly unsporting and vehement in Perth' (Judd and Butcher 2016, 76). Somewhat ironically, the booing intensified in the wake of the AFL's annual Indigenous Round, a round in the AFL calendar that celebrates and recognizes Indigenous players and Indigenous culture and which is regularly attended by a crowd of over 80,000 at the MCG (Melbourne Cricket Ground), the largest sporting venue in the country. In that weekend's game, Goodes performed an Aboriginal war cry dance on the field to celebrate a goal. The dance was taught to him by members of the under-16 Flying Boomerangs, the Indigenous AFL youth squad (Goodes cited in Curley 2015) and incorporated moves to reflect the words 'strong', 'fast', 'hunting' as well as the action of throwing a boomerang (Booth and Ahmat 2015). As Goodes described in a press conference the following day, the Indigenous Round was the first opportunity he had to perform the war cry and 'show that passion and that pride about being a Warrior and representing my people and where I come from' (Goodes cited in Curley 2015).

Yet, his expression of cultural pride, leadership and Indigenous sovereignty (Phillips and Klugman 2016, 193) was a predictable lightning rod for criticism in sporting commentary and popular opinion. Larissa Behrendt (2015) expressed bafflement than an expression of Aboriginal culture is seen as 'un-Australian', but as Judd and Butcher (2016, 70) have argued, the resultant booing of Goodes and its justification as 'socially acceptable crowd behaviour' occurred *precisely* because he had 'dared to insert Aboriginal cultural meanings, including Aboriginal understandings of history, into the national game'. Not surprisingly, both high profile media commentator and Collingwood Football Club president Eddie McGuire, and former Victorian Premier and former Hawthorn Football Club president Jeff Kennett, publicly criticized Goodes' act as deliberately provocative, defending the crowd's behaviour as acceptable. Kennett was unambiguous in his position: 'this isn't an act of racism; this is an act where many in the community feel as if they've been provoked, and they are responding to that provocation' (ABC Radio National 2015). But as Maxine Beneba Clarke (2016) insists, 'denial is crucial in maintaining the status quo. When you are accustomed to privilege, equality feels like oppression'. By late July, the booing had intensified further and Goodes made the decision to sit out of the following weekend's fixture.

Kennett's public comments denied racism by focusing attention back on Goodes, depoliticizing the booing by likening the sporting field to a modern-day Colosseum (ABC Radio National 2015). His analogy of football-field-as-sporting-Colosseum plays on an established tradition of sledging and verbal abuse in sport, where booing players on the opposing team is understood as an everyday, acceptable part of the game; a part of the theatricality of the sport. Following Kennett's performative logic, provocation of the crowd – intentional or otherwise – both solicits and deserves a hostile response. Setting aside the problem with this logic for the moment, Kennett's Colosseum analogy touches on a deeper, troubling, truth. In the popular imagination at least, the roar of the crowd is the sonic barometer that measures who is accepted and who is rejected; who belongs and who is banished; who is loved and who is hated. In other words, the Colosseum is an acoustic territory of unevenly distributed power and populism, with the sound of violence at its very heart.

How, then, do we make sense of the refusal to hear racism in the crowd's booing of Adam Goodes, as epitomized in the comments of Kennett and others? I propose that the failure to register anything other than acceptable crowd behaviour is not so much an *inability to hear* than a *wilful mishearing* conditioned through, and which naturalizes, the privileged position of 'white ears'. These white ears wilfully mishear the long history of racial abuse directed against Aboriginal players in the history of the AFL; they also erase previous acts of aboriginal resistance, sovereignty and leadership in the face of such abuse.[2] This leads me to a second, related, contention – namely that the discourse of 'hurt feelings' is increasingly hollowed out and redeployed to dismiss claims of racism. For example, former non-Indigenous AFL player

Jason Akermanis publicly accused Goodes of being a 'sook' and 'playing the victim' (AAP/ABC 2015) in response to his temporary withdrawal from the game. This accusation simultaneously dismisses the serious wounding caused by racial violence at the same time as reproducing and perpetuating its logic. Through the narrow focus on individual fragility, hurt feelings are untethered from the broader category of moral injury to which they belong. Shifting the focus from individual fragility onto the ways in which the denial of dignity, respect and justice occur is crucial to understanding how structures of racism are articulated in everyday life.

As a category of moral injury, hurt feelings are a relational, inter-subjective harm: it is hard to envisage how one could hurt one's own feelings, for instance. The concept of moral injury connects to notions in critical theory and moral philosophy around mis-recognition, disrespect and injustice (Bernstein 2005; see also Fraser and Honneth 2003). The wilful mishearing of hurt feelings as individual fragility (rather than as moral injury) both *displaces* the harm from one conditioned through unequal social relations to one that arises from the individual experience alone, and at the same time, *diminishes* its scale and depth. By insisting that hurt feelings as a form of moral injury, we can see how they may arise through differences in power and privilege, including acts that press those differences onto others.

From these initial provocations, the following questions arise: how do established hierarchies of attention (Dreher 2009) and dominant listening practices mishear the serious moral injuries of racial abuse? How do they reinforce systems of oppression and the privilege of whiteness? And how can claims of racial injustice be heard and taken seriously without reducing the discussion to an issue of free speech, or in this case, 'the freedom to boo'?

This article takes up some of these questions by arguing for an expanded notion of 'political listening' (Bickford 1996) that attends to the sonic histories of racism as a way of unsettling the listening logic and privileged position of the white ear. For Bickford (1996, 129), oppression works, in part, through 'not hearing certain kinds of expressions from certain kinds of people'. Her notion of political listening both challenges the valorization of speech and asserts a charge of ethical responsibility to others: 'just as speakers must reflect on how to speak (and what to say), listeners must be self-conscious about how they listen (and what they hear) (129)'. Similarly, Tanja Dreher (2009) argues that political listening is crucial in shifting focus onto the conventions, hierarchies and discourses which shape not only *what* is and is not heard and valued but also *who* is and is not heard.

I suggest that by further extending the notion of political listening to include attention to sound and the sonic register of racial injustice, it becomes possible to push beyond predictable rights-based arguments that privilege freedom of speech as well as liberal discourses of tolerance or diversity. Making this move opens up space for me to register these very particular and distinct kinds of moral injury without displacing, or replicating, their wounding effects. It allows me to pose the critical question: what does racial (in)justice sound like?

In the next section, I briefly turn to the public debate and media commentary around issues of free speech and racial vilification legislation to place the booing of Adam Goodes in the broader context of contemporary race politics in Australia. I then introduce the notions of acoustic violence and the listening ear as analytical tools for political listening. In the second half of the paper, I follow the sounds of racialized violence beyond the football field to other acoustic territories to map overlapping struggles where questions of race, sovereignty and power play out. I examine the use of sonic warfare in the occupied West Bank, before moving in later sections the sounds of racial injustice in the United States. I return in the final section to Goodes and the football field, and conclude by reflecting on the decision by Yorta Yorta woman, soprano Deborah Cheetham not to sing the national anthem at the 2015 AFL grand final.

Listening, speech and the ear of the law

Proposed changes to Section 18C of the Commonwealth of Australia (1975) (the Act) in 2011, and renewed pressure to amend the Act by conservative Senators David Leyonhjelm and Cory Bernardi in early 2017, have oriented public discussion towards the appropriate limits (if any) on the rights of individuals and freedom of speech. Such discussions underplay the serious and disproportionate negative impacts particular speech acts have on racial and ethnic minorities while claiming they limit the rights of others to free expression.

Contrary to the popular prevailing view that the Act makes it unlawful to offend someone on the basis of their race, ethnicity or religion, Section 18D of the Act provides a number of exemptions which makes some forms of speech legally permissible – including racial vilification – within certain limits: speech uttered 'in good faith', of 'genuine belief', 'reasonably' and in a 'fair' manner is protected (Commonwealth of Australia 1975, Section 18D). What is interesting here is that the 18D exemption opens a sonorous space attuned to both *tone* and *mode of address* in determining whether a particular speech act falls within the boundaries of lawful speech. It connects speech to ethical behaviour and injurious speech to the exercise of power; it also pays close attention not only to what is said, but *how* it is said and to what effect. In other words, 18D constitutes a space of attention between the intention (of speech) and intensity (of affect) in determining what speech *means* and what speech *does*.

In 2011, prompted in part by the Federal Court's upholding of a high-profile case successfully brought against conservative commentator Andrew Bolt under by nine Aboriginal applicants under Section 18C of the RDA, the then Abbott-led federal government proposed a series of amendments to Sections 18C and 18D of the Act. The subsequent exposure draft sought to remove the words 'offend', 'insult' and 'humiliate' from section 18C, along with the words 'reasonably' and 'in good faith' from Section 18D.[3] These two amendments in particular expose the hierarchies of attention that structure the ear of the law in determining what counts as unlawful speech under the Act. At the time, the Attorney-General Senator George Brandis – the highest ear of the law in parliament – argued the words offend, insult and humiliate 'describe what has sometimes been called *hurt feelings*' (ABC Radio National 2015; italics mine). This listening logic is the same logic behind Akermanis' comments about Goodes being a 'sook' and 'playing the victim' described earlier. Framing the impacts of racial abuse in terms of hurt feelings alone is a wilful mishearing of moral injury that reinforces white privilege. When then Senator Nova Peris, the first female Indigenous federal member of Parliament, asked about the government's plans to amend the Act, Attorney General Brandis' responded that 'people have a right to be bigots' (Commonwealth of Australia 2014).

In a second attempt to change the legislation in March 2017, the Turnbull government proposed to remove the words 'offend,' 'insult' and 'humiliate', this time replacing them with the words 'harass' and 'intimidate'. The bill was ultimately defeated in the Senate. Despite these unsuccessful attempts to change the legislation, what becomes clear is that it is precisely those sections of the Act that require attention to the affective qualities of a speech act or utterance that are the most problematic for conservative critics. The concerted push to remove the word 'humiliate' from Section 18C (in both the 2011 exposure draft and the 2017 proposed amendments) also seems particularly significant, despite the claim that many see it as merely 'an operatic outbreak of gesture politics' (Murphy 2017) on the part of the Government. Wiradjuri man, journalist Stan Grant (2016) has described Indigenous people's shared recognition of the 'howl of humiliation' at work in the boos targeted at Adam Goodes, a settler-colonial form of violence that works through the deployment of sound. It is clear that humiliation has a sound that carried through history, borne by those who bear the wounds of that history. The claim that Aboriginal people are 'too sensitive' does not account for ongoing colonialisms, oppression and dispossession that produce such howls of humiliation in the first place.

Another challenge when thinking about the booing aimed at Goodes is that while booing is a speech act, it is an utterance that denies a reduction to words. This is part of the reason why it can neither be defended nor fully understood through recourse to ideas of freedom of speech (on the one hand) or cultural diversity and tolerance (on the other) alone. It is worth noting also that booing is a particular kind of utterance that has a series of perlocutionary effects. A boo is a transitive utterance; it is directed *at* an object. In other words, it is an utterance with direction – it moves. However, the injury it can perform is not a simple case of cause and effect. As Butler (1996, 204) asks:

> [...] is it the utterance or the utterer who is the cause of the injury, or does the utterance perform its injury through a transitivity that cannot be reduced to a causal or intentional process originating in a single subject?

What Butler makes clear is that intentionality and causation are not always necessary for wounding to occur, and their relationship is far from straightforward. It carries both direction and movement *towards* its target, asserting a charge that is not always clear or unambiguous but which generally communicates disapproval or displeasure. Focussing on the intention of the crowd or a single 'booer' alone fails to account for the ways that booing gains both its force and power to inflict moral injury as a collective, yet dispersed, utterance that is amplified and intensified as it circulates through the crowd, increasing the acoustic violence. Sounds come from somewhere; they have a history. Individuals who are 'swept up' with the crowd are also entangled in this larger history (recall the 13-year-old girl who was unaware that calling Adam Goodes an 'ape' was racist or was historically used as a racial epithet). However, the utterance also has a sound. The force of the word is always also a sonic force: the sheer sound of it as it echoes through the body politic.

The listening ear

There was one passing mention in print about the fact that Goodes had played over 300 football games and had enough experience to gauge the mood – *or tone* – of the crowd and therefore able to distinguish between standard rowdy behaviour and racially motivated verbal abuse. Yet, this aspect of racism – its particular sonorous and sonic quality, and the wounding that it causes – was noticeably absent from public debate and remains critically under-examined. One notable exception was academic and broadcaster Waleed Aly (2015) whose comments provide a sonic entry point into the analysis of racial injustice and violence:

> Anyone listening to those boos who is familiar with the dynamics of racism can *hear it in the boos*. There's a certain quality to them. There's something about it that sounds markedly different from the other boos that players get (italics my own).

What Aly identifies is what I am calling the acoustic violence of racism. Federico Miyara (1999) has described acoustic violence as 'violence exercised by means of sound', where violence involves either force or threat of force causing damage, unrest, hurt or harm. Significantly, he adds that it can also cause 'unease, discomfort and helplessness', under certain conditions, regardless of intention. As an expression of power, acoustic violence carries with it the possibility for both moral and political injury. Thinking about the booing of Adam Goodes in terms of acoustic violence brings into view the ways in which racism creates a hostile sensory terrain that certain populations and individuals must navigate on a daily basis. These sounds, then, embody far more than what is at first apparent to the untrained ear.

In the above quote, Aly stops short of unpacking the precise quality and dynamics that make some boos distinct from others. Yet his insistence on the distinction – and their uneven distribution along racial lines – warrants serious consideration. At the heart of his critique lies an important observation, perhaps drawn from his embodied experience: those who are the targets of racialized violence become *attuned* to sonic qualities that are indistinct to untrained ears. In this, there are two points. First, to distinguish between a 'boo' and a 'boo', a particular structure of intelligibility is required (following Butler 2009). In Aly's formulation, a precondition for hearing racism is an already present familiarity (a pre-disposition perhaps?) with the dynamics of racism. The distinction between a 'boo' and a 'boo' may be altogether absent to the untrained ear, but to those exposed to its injurious effects, parsing this distinction can be a challenge against ongoing injustice and, in some cases a necessary act of survival, as I discuss further on. Second, the repeated exposure to racialized violence produces *expert listeners* attuned to the sounds of that violence. In other words, it is their very exposure that marks out as expert listeners; they are ears trained to *hear* racism.

In her illuminating examination of sound, race and the cultural politics of listening in the United States, Jennifer Stoever (2016) exposes the systems that produce and regulate cultural ideas about sound to theorize what she calls the 'sonic color line' (13). Focused on the history of African American music and literature in particular, she explores listening as 'a form of agency, a technique of survival, ethics of community building, practice of self-care, guide through racialized space, site of racialisation and mode of decolonising' (17). Central to her analysis are the contrasting figures of the 'listening ear' and the 'embodied ear', concepts useful to my own acoustic analysis. For Stoever, the listening ear is

> [...] a figure for how dominant listening practices accrue – and change – over time, as well as a description for how dominant culture exerts pressure on individual listening practices to conform the sonic color line's norms (7).

In contrast, the embodied ear represents how

> [...] individual listening practices are shaped by the totality of their experiences, their historical context, and physicality, as well as intersecting subject positions and particular interactions with power (the listening ear) (15).

This tension and interplay between the listening ear and the embodied ear reveals how established hierarchies of attention are produced and maintained through a continued investment in the values, norms, practices – and sounds – of the dominant culture. Listening practices attuned to racialized histories of sound and, relatedly, attention to the way sound can be deployed as a weapon of force, can unsettle the structures of power that condition and normalize their appearance.

Sound and violence

The relationship between sound and violence has a long and complicated history. Sound has been used as a weapon of force in the exercise of power, dominance and control over individuals and populations, including as a tactic to disarm political dissent. For example, in 2014, Jordanian-British artist and researcher Lawrence Abu Hamdan was approached by Palestinian human rights organization Defense for Children International (DCI) to conduct an acoustic analysis of the sounds of gunfire deployed by members of the Israeli police on a group of unarmed Palestinians in the occupied West Bank that resulted in the death of two Palestinian teenagers, Nadeem Nawara and Mohammad Abu Daher (Defense for Children International 2014). As Abu Hamdan described, the case hinged upon an audio-ballistics analysis of the recorded gunshots to determine whether the soldiers had used rubber bullets, as they claimed, or had 'broken the law by firing live ammunition at the two unarmed teenagers' (Abu Hamdan 2016). Abu Hamdan analysed the sound recordings of the incident, examining both lethal and non-lethal shots fired that day into the crowd. To the untrained ear, the lethal and non-lethal shots sound identical. However, spectrogram analysis – a form of analysis which visualizes and strands out different frequencies of a noise – revealed a distinct difference between the sound signature of live ammunition as compared to ammunition fired through a rubber bullet extension.[4]

When Abu Hamdan synced up the CNN news footage of the incident to the audio recording of the gunfire, it was evident the Palestinian crowd reacted in dramatically different ways to the rounds of live ammunition than they did to shots fired through a (non-lethal) rubber bullet extension, rapidly dispersing to seek shelter only when live shots were fired. From this, Abu Hamdan concluded that for this group of Palestinian civilians, constant exposure to this kind of 'sonic warfare' (Goodman 2010) marked them out as expert listeners able to distinguish between the sonic characteristics of live gunfire and gunfire masked with a rubber bullet extension, something that sounds identical to the untrained ear but could be visualized through spectrogram analysis. In his video installation *Rubber Coated Steel* (2016), which built on the work Abu Hamdan did for DCI, the sonic signature of the killings stands as another form of public testimony: they 'do not preside over the voices of the victims', but rather seek to 'amplify their silence' (Abu Hamdan 2016). He insists:

It is the sound that needs to enter our acoustic consciousness, because in all cases across the world it is the sound where the tools of institutional violence cross the threshold into acts of wanton bloodshed.

How might the example of sonic warfare in the Middle East help us think through the ways that sound and violence can work to dominate and regulate the lives of racialized others more broadly? What can it tell us about the ways individuals and communities routinely targeted become finely attuned to the practices and tactics used to achieve this? In the above case of sonic warfare, the stakes are a matter of life and death. This may seem far removed from the sonic sites of racial injustice and expressions of everyday racism I'm thinking through in this paper. However, I suggest their difference is a matter of degree, not of kind.

Hearing racism

In his 2016 *Quarterly Essay*, 'The Australian Dream: Blood, history and becoming', Stan Grant makes an unequivocal connection between the racist booing targeted at Adam Goodes on the football ground and the legacy of settler-colonial violence and Indigenous dispossession:

> I can't speak for what lay in the hearts of the people who booed Adam Goodes. But I can tell you what we heard when we heard those boos. We heard a sound that was very familiar to us. We heard a howl. We heard a howl of humiliation that echoes across two centuries of dispossession, injustice, suffering and survival. We heard the howl of the Australian Dream, and it said to us again: you're not welcome.

Grant's account pushes further than Aly's distinction between a 'boo' and a 'boo'. The 'howl of humiliation' is at once a political metaphor and an embodied response to a particular register of settler-colonial violence directed at First Nations peoples, one that re-appears, circulates and is expressed in different forms. Indigenous people navigate racialized sonic space where the white ear marks out the sonic boundary between belonging and non-belonging (or un-belonging), inclusion and exclusion; where words and sounds perform another kind of dispossession and displacement. At the same time, the boos directed at Goodes are but one articulation of the howl of humiliation, intimately entangled with a larger history of racial injustice that condition their appearance.

Ahmed (2017, 61) reminds us that, for many people of colour who experience and are the target of racism and humiliation, 'to remember violence is to bring the *sound of violence* into the present' (my italics). Ahmed illustrates this point by citing Audre Lorde, whose activist writings and poetry critique the workings of power and privilege in the construction of race, sex, and gender. Lorde recounts a particular sound she was repeatedly exposed to as a child:

> As a very little girl, I remember shrinking from a particular sound, a hoarsely sharp, guttural rasp, because it often meant a nasty glob of grey spittle on my coat or shoes an instant later. My mother wiped it off with little pieces of newspaper she always carried in her purse. Sometimes she fussed about low-class people who had no better sense or manners than to spit into the wind no matter where they went, impressing upon me that this humiliation was totally random [...] But it was so typical of my mother when I was young that if she couldn't stop white people spitting on her children because they were Black, she would insist it was something else (Lorde, cited in Ahmed 2017).

I quote from this passage at length because it powerfully highlights the intimate entanglement between acts of racism and their visceral, embodied and sonorous qualities. The sound of being spat on as a child – that 'hoarsely sharp, guttural rasp' – carries with it the memory of humiliation. The sound of the rasp is the sonic cue for the child Audre to shrink away in bodily anticipation of what comes next. It is not the spit alone, but *the very sound of the utterance*, that sharpens her humiliation. The spit travels onto the body of the child Audre, but the sound of the spit collapses both space and time, wrenching up a larger history where the sounds of hate carry meanings and power connected to white supremacy and racial dominance. If we return to Grant's words reflected through Lorde's account above, it becomes clear that the 'howls of humilia-tion' – whether the boo of the crowd or the sound of spit – cannot be disentangled from the violent histories that condition their very appearance.

Critically attending to these sites of acoustic violence – following the sounds – opens up a route to examine other racialized sonic spaces, not with the aim of comparison, but rather to bring into view how the force of sound is used to humiliate, exclude and to put racialized others in their 'place'.

When American tennis player Serena Williams described her experience of being booed and taunted by the crowd at the 2001 Indian Wells tennis tournament in California, she spoke of the undercurrent of racism and the pain it caused her (Williams 2015b). Both Serena and her sister Venus have been subject to hostile crowds and racial taunts for years, most dramatically at the 2001 Indian Wells[5] final, after Venus had defaulted to Serena in the semi-final to the great displeasure of the largely white crowd in a predominantly white sport. Both sisters subsequently boycotted the tourna-ment for over a decade, with Serena only returning to the tournament in 2014. In 2015, Serena Williams wrote a piece in *Time* magazine about her experience at the 2001 final:

> As I walked out onto the court, the crowd immediately started jeering and booing [...] The undercurrent of racism was painful, confusing and unfair. In a game I loved with all my heart, at one of my most cherished tournaments, I suddenly felt unwelcome, alone and afraid. [...] When I was booed at Indian Wells – by what seemed like the whole world – my voice of doubt became real. I didn't understand what was going on in that moment. But worse, I had no desire to even win. It happened very quickly. This haunted me for a long time.

Williams' account of simultaneous non-belonging, isolation and fear must be taken seriously to fully register the dynamics of racism beyond racial epithets and speech acts alone. In the above excerpt, it is clear that the booing and racial abuse had multiple and complicated effects for Williams. First, the sounds of jeering and booing were 'confusing' and disorientating: she did not understand what was going on. Second, and echoing the quote from Grant (2016) cited earlier, the booing made her feel 'unwelcome', rupturing her sense of belonging by sonically marking out a space of difference; they were a threatening form of exclusion, making her feel 'alone' and 'afraid'. Third, they were a haunting.

Attempts to justify or defend the crowd's behaviour by citing the Williams' sisters' bad sportsmanship – a justification also used by some to defend the booing of Goodes – does not account for the repeated and disproportionate booing Williams has been subject to throughout her career, and the expectation that she conform to the stereo-type of the 'exceptional black athlete' by suffering racial abuse graciously and without complaint. While Williams is not immune to the injurious and exclusionary effects of this repeated sonic violence, like Goodes, she too refuses to let them go unchallenged.

Poet and cultural critic Claudia Rankine (2015) argues that while Williams has discarded the white racist gaze, it 'doesn't mean she won't be emotional or hurt by challenges to her humanity'. It is precisely in her refusal that her grace and excellence is demonstrated:

> Serena's grace comes because she won't be forced into stillness; she won't accept those racist projections onto her body without speaking back; she won't go gently into the white light of victory. Her excellence doesn't mask the struggle it takes to achieve each win. For black people, there is an unspoken script that demands the humble absorption of racist assaults, no matter the scale, because whites need to believe that it's no big deal. But Serena refuses to keep to that script. Somehow, along the way, she made a decision to be excellent while still being Serena.

Challenging racism for athletes like Williams and Goodes involves putting their bodies on the line, refusing to absorb racist insults by challenging their very legitimacy and disrupting the norms of whiteness that make such assaults acceptable. They dismantle the 'unspoken script'. They *hear racism* and call it out; unsettling and challenging otherwise socially acceptable or normalized behaviours (in some cases, celebrated behaviours like the booing of one's opponent) by insisting such behaviour cannot be separated from histories and practices of racism. The sporting field, the tennis court, and so forth, are not spaces quarantined from history, culture and politics. To *not* hear racism in booing of Goodes and Williams is a refusal to hear the testimony of racialized others, and a denial of voice. It is made possible through what Cate Thill (2009) calls 'selective listening' which functions to 'preserve, rather than transform, established hierarchies of attention'.

Goodes' temporary withdrawal from the game in August 2015, his decision not to speak, was significant. Taking time to spend with his family, to be on Country,[6] Goodes also removed himself from the media storm that was swirling around him. His dignified public silence in the face of intense media scrutiny brings to mind the words of Butler 2009, 12) who argues the 'refusal to narrate' can 'call into question the legitimacy of authority' by attempting to circumscribe a 'domain of autonomy' for the subject. In this sense, silence becomes a defiant act of self-relation that asserts itself through a withdrawal from established terms and frames of recognition and legitimacy, in this case, from the competing and conflicting demands of the public and the media pressing down on him for a response. More broadly, this 'politics of refusal' (Bond 2016) shifts the very terms and frames of the debate. Goode's silence – his absent-presence – invites us to reflect on other silences that deny Indigenous sovereignty and consolidate settler-colonial power: 'the Great Australian Silence' (Stanner 1969); and, more recently, 'the silence at the heart of the Constitution' (Williams 2015a, 121).

Voice, silence and resistance

> What forms of resistance and healing does silence make possible? What nuances, strategic forms of engagement and ways of navigating or resisting power are made possible through silence? What alliances might be enabled as we learn to read [or hear] silences? Under what conditions is it productive to move between voice and silence? Rowe and Malhotra 2013, 7).

In this final section, I turn to another acoustic territory where the struggle against racial injustice takes centre stage, and is staged, in several ways. In the months following the booing of Goodes, Deborah Cheetham, an internationally renowned soprano, was invited by the AFL to sing the Australian national anthem at the 2015 Grand Final. In response to this invitation, Cheetham proposed she sing the anthem with amended lyrics, replacing the line 'for we are young and free' with 'in peace and harmony'.[7] After some consideration, AFL management found they could not support her proposal and she graciously declined to perform. In a subsequent article written for *The Conversation*, Cheetham (2015) explained her reasons:

> As an Indigenous leader I simply can no longer sing the words 'we are young and free'. For that matter, as an Australian with a strong desire to deepen our nation's understanding of identity and our place in the world, I believe we can and must do better.

To be asked to sing in front of a live audience of tens of thousands of people and sing the national anthem is, in Cheetham's (2015) words, 'every performer's dream'. By declining to sing, Cheetham performs a political act of leadership and resistance that unsettles the nation's complacency about ongoing injustice. Her decision not to sing questions the legitimacy of the anthem and its role in perpetuating a settler-colonial narrative of the nation. Cheetham is a highly respected Indigenous public figure and soprano. As an Indigenous leader, Cheetham spoke to the ways in which the anthem is both hurtful to and excludes Indigenous people. As a soprano – whose very instrument of expression is her voice – to choose silence over sound is a powerful act of both resistance and hope. Cheetham enacts leadership by challenging the white ear that naturalizes the national anthem as benign and patriotic. In hearing the logic of white possession (Moreton-Robinson 2004) in the anthem's lyrics, Cheetham's enacts Indigenous sovereignty through performative silence.

As an expert listener – both in a musical sense and in the sense of racialized attunement I have been describing – Cheetham draws attention to how the national anthem operates as a form of sonic dominance that perpetuates a settler-colonial narrative of *terra nullius* and legitimates the founding myth of the nation state. If singing the anthem performs a kind of acoustic violence, the lyrics recite a narrative violence that both denies Indigenous sovereignty and fails to recognize Australian history prior to 1788. Predictably, there was anger in some sections of mainstream and social media in response to Cheetham's decision not to sing the anthem.[8] However, in an interview ABC radio, she spoke about how singing the anthem with the current lyrics also deeply affects many Indigenous people: 'how hurtful it is to Indigenous Australians to really be excluded, because when we sing that "we are young" in that anthem, that really does set up a false premise'. To yield to Cheetham's authority as an expert listener attuned to the sonic traces of racial injustice opens a space of both democratic and sonic dissonance – the lyrics don't *ring true*. Cheetham's performative silence insists we ask a broader question: how might we register Indigenous claims to sovereignty, beyond legal or constitutional forms of recognition alone?[9]

Conclusion: what would justice sound like?

By attending to the ways sound is unevenly deployed to target, silence, assimilate or oppress others along racial lines, this paper has ultimately aimed to unsettle the listening logic and privileged position of the white, settler-colonial ear, in Australia and beyond. If political listening asserts a charge of responsibility towards others in the pursuit of more just and equitable futures, it must also refuse listening positions that solidify forms of settler-colonial power or reproduce ongoing colonialisms. In taking up sound as frame of analysis, I have argued for an expanded notion of political listening that attends to the sonic histories of racialized violence, but which also registers acts of sovereignty, resistance and hope in the face of ongoing injustice. Not only is this move analytically useful, opening fresh lines of 'sonic' inquiry which bring into conversation the struggles of those whose lands and life-worlds continued to be structured by colonial and imperial logics; it is also politically necessary to 're-sound' the public sphere (Lacey 2011, 9) and, in turn, pose the critical question: what would justice sound like?

Notes

1. In May 2013, Goodes was called an 'ape' by a 13-year-old girl in the crowd at a game between the Sydney Swans and Collingwood.
2. For example, Nicky Winmar and Michael Long in the 1990s and early 2000s, respectively.
3. Bolt was found to have breached the Act for a series of articles he wrote which claimed certain Aboriginal people sought professional advantage from being 'fair-skinned' (see Federal Court of Australia 2011). The Court ruled Bolt was in breach of the Act and not exempt under section 18(D), which pertains to fair comment in the matter of public interest, because of his failure to act 'in good faith', along with errors of fact in his claims.
4. Abu Hamdan's video analysis of the shooting, including the audio-ballistics and spectrogram analysis, can be accessed here: http://lawrenceabuhamdan.com/blog/2014/11/21/pre view-to-my-audio-balistics-investigation-into-the-murder-of-nadeem-nawara .
5. It is worth noting the land on which this tournament is played, Indian Wells in California, US, is a site of First Nations dispossession and colonization brought about by the arrival settler explorers and gold prospectors to the area in the nineteenth century that devastated the Indigenous population.
6. In Australia, the term Country has a specific meaning for Indigenous people and is incommensurable to non-Indigenous or geo-political definitions of country/land/territory (see Moreton-Robinson 2004). Indigenous people's ontological connection to Country describes their spiritual, physical, social and cultural attachment and sense of belonging to their ancestral lands.
7. Cheetham later pointed to alternative lyrics to the Anthem – penned by Judith Durham in consultation with Muti Muti singer-songwriter Kutcha Edwards – that include and celebrate the history and culture of First Nations Australians, as a starting point for a broader public conversation around settler-Indigenous relations.
8. A similar level of anger was directed at boxer Anthony Mundine when he declared he would not come out when the national anthem was played at the start of his fight, saying 'we are not young and free … my people are still being oppressed' (Herald 2017). A similar point has been made by Stan Grant (2016). In 2016, African American football player Colin Kaepernick sat down or knelt, rather than stood, when the US national anthem was played, to draw attention to police brutality and racial injustice in that country.
9. It is interesting that mainstream media receptions of the 'Uluru Statement from the Heart' – arising from the First Nations National Constitutional Convention – were negatively framed as a 'refusal' of recognition, rather than the need for a First Nations Voice and a desire to 'be heard'. This invitation to listen insists Indigenous sovereignty be placed at the heart of healing injustice.

Acknowledgements

The author would like to thank Marnie Badham, Tanja Dreher, Michelle Evans and two anonymous reviewers for their constructive feedback. This paper also benefited from roundtable discussions during a workshop on Acoustic Justice at Melbourne Law School in July 2017.

Disclosure statement

No potential conflict of interest was reported by the author.

ORCID

Poppy de Souza ⓘD http://orcid.org/0000-0003-4958-9146

References

AAP/ABC. 2015. "Adam Goodes Playing the Victim over Booing, Says Former AFL Star Jason Akermanis." *ABC News Online*, July 31. Accessed 10 October 2016. http://www.abc.net.au/news/2015-07-30/jason-akermanis-says-adam-goodes-is-a-sook/6659344

ABC Radio National. 2015. "Jeff Kennett on Bishop and Goodes." *RN Drive*, July 30. Accessed 29 March 2017. http://www.abc.net.au/radionational/programs/drive/kennett-on-bishop-and-goodes/6661120

Abu Hamdan, L. 2016. *Earshot*. Exhibition notes. http://lawrenceabuhamdan.com/new-page-1/

Ahmed, S. 2017. *Living a Feminist Life*. Durham and London: Duke University Press.

Aly, W. 2015. "Racism and Adam Goodes." *The Minefield*. ABC Radio National, July 30. Accessed 6 August 2015. http://www.abc.net.au/radionational/programs/theminefield/racism/6656974.

Behrendt, L. 2015. "The Backlash against Adam Goodes Is the Reason His War Dance Is Important." *The Guardian*, June 1. Accessed 29 March 2017. http://www.theguardian.com/commentisfree/2015/jun/01/the-backlash-against-adam-goodes-is-the-reason-his-war-dance-is-important.

Bernstein, J. 2005. "Suffering Injustice: Misrecognition as Moral Injury in Critical Theory." *International Journal of Philosophical Studies* 13 (3): 303–324. doi:10.1080/09672550500169117.

Bickford, S. 1996. *The Dissonance of Democracy: Listening, Conflict, and Citizenship*. Ithaca and London: Cornell University Press.

Bond, C. 2016. "Refusing to Play the Race Game." *The Conversation*, 29 September. Accessed 6 April 2017. https://theconversation.com/refusing-to-play-the-race-game-66043

Booth, A., and N. Ahmat. 2015. "That Adam Goodes War Cry Used a Boomerang Not a Spear: Choreographer." *NITV News*. SBS. Accessed 18 September 2017. http://www.sbs.com.au/nitv/article/2015/08/03/adam-goodes-war-cry-used-boomerang-not-spear-choreographer.

Butler, J. 1996. "Burning Acts: Injurious Speech." *The University of Chicago Law School Roundtable* 3 (1): 199.

Butler, J. 2009. *Frames of War: When Is Life Grievable?* London: Verso Books.

Cheetham, D. 2015. "Young and Free? Why I Declined to Sing the National Anthem at the 2015 AFL Grand Final." *The Conversation*, October 20. https://theconversation.com/young-and-free-why-i-declined-to-sing-the-national-anthem-at-the-2015-afl-grand-final-49234

Clarke, M. B. 2016. "Our Unnamed Racism Holds Us Back." *The Monthly*, August 13. https://www.thesaturdaypaper.com.au/opinion/topic/2016/08/13/our-unnamed-racism-holds-us-back/14710104003607

Commonwealth of Australia. 1975. *Racial Discrimination Act* (RDA). Consolidated, Accessed January 2014. https://www.legislation.gov.au/Details/C2014C00014

Commonwealth of Australia. Parliamentary Debates. 2014. "The Senate. Questions without Notice: Racial Disrimination Act." (Hansard) March 24: 1797–1798. doi: 10.1101/gr.176784.114

Curley, A. 2015. "Proud Goodes Stands by War Cry Celebration." *AFL News*, May 30. Accessed 6 May 2017. http://www.afl.com.au/news/2015-05-30/proud-goodes-stands-by-war-cry-celebration

Defense for Children International. 2014. "Israeli Forces Shoot and Kill Two Palestinian Teens near Ramallah." May 17. http://www.dci-palestine.org/israeli_forces_shoot_and_kill_two_palestinian_teens_near_ramallah.

Dreher, T. 2009. "Listening across Difference: Media and Multiculturalism beyond the Politics of Voice." *Continuum* 23 (4): 445–458. doi:10.1080/10304310903015712.

Federal Court of Australia. 2011. *Eatock V Bolt [2011] FCA 1103. File Number VID 770 of 2010.* September 28. Federal Court of Australia.

Fraser, N., and A. Honneth. 2003. *Redistribution or Recognition? A Political-Philosophical Exchange.* London: Verso.

Goodman, S. 2010. *Sonic Warfare: Sound, Affect and the Ecology of Fear.* Cambridge, MA: Massachusetts Institute of Technology Press.

Grant, S. 2016. "The Australian Dream: Blood, History and Becoming." *Quarterly Essay* 64 (1): 1–80.

Herald, S. M. 2017. Anthony Mundine Refuses to Acknowledge National Anthem before Danny Green Fight', 30 January. http://www.smh.com.au/sport/boxing/anthony-mundine-refuses-to-acknowledge-national-anthem-before-danny-green-fight-20170129-gu131n.html

Judd, B., and T. Butcher. 2016. "Beyond Equality: The Place of Aboriginal Culture in the Australian Game of Football." *Australian Aboriginal Studies* 1: 68–84.

Lacey, K. 2011. "Listening Overlooked: An Audit of Listening as a Category in the Public Sphere." *Javnost-The Public* 18 (4): 5–20. doi:10.1080/13183222.2011.11009064.

Miyara, F. 1999. "Acoustic Violence: A New Name for an Old Social Pain." *Hearing Rehabilitation Quarterly* 24 (1): 18–21.

Moreton-Robinson, A. 2004. "The Possessive Logic of Patriarchal White Sovereignty: The High Court and the Yorta Yorta Decision." *Borderlands E-Journal* 3 (2). http://www.borderlands.net.au/vol3no2_2004/moreton_possessive.htm.

Murphy, K. 2017. "Coalition's 18C Overhaul a Hollow and Operatic Outbreak of Gesture Politics." *The Guardian*, March 21. Accessed 28 March 2017. http://www.theguardian.com/australia-news/2017/mar/21/coalitions-18c-overhaul-a-hollow-and-operatic-outbreak-of-gesture-politics.

Phillips, G., and M. Klugman. 2016. "The Land We Play On: Equality Doesn't Mean Justice." *Griffith REVIEW* 53: 185.

Rankine, C. 2015. "The Meaning of Serena Williams. On Tennis and Black Excellence." *The New York Times*, August 25. Accessed 28 March 2017. https://www.nytimes.com/2015/08/30/magazine/the-meaning-of-serena-williams.html

Rowe, A. C., and S. Malhotra. 2013. "Still the Silence: Feminist Reflections at the Edges of Sound." In *Silence, Feminism, Power: Reflections at the Edges of Sound*, edited by S. Malhotra and A. C. Rowe, 1–16. London: Palgrave MacMillan.

Stanner, W. E. 1969. *After the Dreaming. Black and White Australians: An Anthropologist's View.* Boyer Lectures, 1968. Sydney: Australian Broadcasting Corporation.

Stoever, J. L. 2016. "'The Sonic Color Line and the Listening Ear.' Introduction." In *The Sonic Color Line: Race and the Cultural Politics of Listening*, edited by J. L. Stoever, 1–28. New York: New York University Press.

Thill, C. 2009. "Courageous Listening, Responsibility for the Other and the Northern Territory Intervention." *Continuum: Journal of Media & Cultural Studies* 23 (4): 537–548. doi:10.1080/10304310903012651.

Williams, G. 2015a. "Recognising Aboriginal and Torres Strait Islander Peoples in the Constitution." *University of Tasmania Law Review* 34 (2): 114.

Williams, S. 2015b. "I'm Going Back to Indian Wells." *Time Magazine*, February 4, sec. Tennis. Accessed 6 April 2017. http://time.com/3694659/serena-williams-indian-wells/.

The 'free speech' of the (un)free

Yassir Morsi

ABSTRACT

This auto-ethnography explores the ways in which storytelling can illuminate the ways in which an 'Islamist' can(not) engage in 'free speech'. It argues the double bind that Muslims find themselves (condemn OR be condemned) in the War on Terror exposes the 'liberal swindle' that is free speech. Through storytelling and a ring composition, the author analyses his own engagement in academia and how as a Muslim he is compelled to code his dissent through toying with academic *form* rather than *content*.

Erasing which we must repress

Patricia Williams asks a provocative question. *Are we accommodating different audiences or erasing that which we must repress?* The question came in her fifth lecture in *The Genealogy of Race* (1997) where she mentions Ford motors. The company had photographed 'ethnic looking minorities' from among their workforce. They wanted to use them for a commercial that showed their workforce's diversity. But, an odd (perhaps predictable) twist shortly followed. For their Polish audience, Ford prepared an 'ethnically cleansed' version of the commercial. Incredibly, they Photoshopped white faces onto their worker's black and brown bodies. Ford employee Douglas Sinclair described the following. 'His body was there, but not his face. ⋯ dressed in my overalls, the rings on my fingers were still there, but I had glasses on and a white face' (ibid).

Williams brilliant final words point out the Thing so many people of colour must repress. She describes herself at her desk writing the very lecture she delivers. We read how she 'reaches for a little bottle of White-Out'. She brushes the 'correctional fluid' over her fingers. In seconds, they melt to the knuckle. Watching herself disappear, the author assures us she feels no pain. It is the 'subtlest of sensations' (ibid). She erases what she must repress, her blackness, her otherness.

I have never forgotten this story. As I read it the imagery became so clear in my mind's eye. I saw knuckles disappear, saw how the author was at her desk. In that auto-ethnographic tradition, she wrote about writing, showed rather than told. And so, both her style and story compelled me to listen and to remember. The question she asked is both powerful in its content and form, its delivery and message and ever since the words have circled in my mind whenever I think about my other otherness: 'accommodate', 'erasure', 'white-out', 'correctional', etc. I have not thus stopped wondering how much I must repress? How much correctional fluid, how much whiteness? How much should I erase as a writer to accommodate my academic audiences?

Since I speak of erasure, I ought to pause and be cognitive and careful. Yes, I am a person of colour and a Muslim who writes against the racial logic of – but also because of – the War on Terror. Heading William's warnings about erasure, I wish to acknowledge a significant difference however. Unlike Williams, I am not black, am not a black woman. As an Arab man, I cannot speak of her experience as if I share a non-white commonality. I cannot speak of the lasting acts of racial violence that target black women. Although I am indebted to black scholarship, both its form and content have taught me about the world and of the questions we should ask it. Grateful, especially to Fanon. He made me aware of the arsenal of complexities that I have inherited as a non-white subject. A subject formed by its pursuit of the white gaze (Fanon 1967). But, I am also indebted in another way, indebted by where my body lives.

Williams' analogy works to explain my aim. My paper wishes to highlight the place of the erased body in our discussions of free speech. A body we must repress to accommodate liberalism's swindle and its white audience. And so on this note, and against the liberal logic, I want to acknowledge that I too sat at my desk when I wrote these words. I sat in a building on the land of the Wurundjeri people of the Kulin nation.

Would it be amiss for me to ask if Europe gave us the intellectual style of modern academia? I ought to begin with stating my 'research' question, or that which pretends to be a question. Too often the research article follows a neutral 'Westernese' form. In the main it is also written with an academic sound, an accompanying and an assuming 'objective' tone and professionalism. This I assume is so because the imperial accredited style of science designed what we have come to know as knowledge (Hesse and Sayyid 2002, 150; Sayyid 2003). The Enlightenment and its positivist elements provided certain conventions and expectations. I am obliged to adhere to them to win a PhD, or so I was taught. Thus, general 'academic' rules (and what that name evokes) come to decide in my mind what is 'discipline' and what is 'scholarship'. Following this, I have often come to suspect that the research article itself has a rigid (read:cultural) form. So, Suresh Canagarajah in *A Geopolitics of Academic Writing* (2002, 41) asks, does a Eurocentricism shape its structure? Is there is less than visible geopolitics that guides our writing and its standards? For instance, the dominant Introduction-Method-Results-Discussion now comes without saying because it goes without saying (83,109). It has for me always plagued me with a (research) question, does this structure effect only how but *what* I can say.

In response, my paper's lack of 'proper' academic *form* is then its *content*. It is its research question. It stutters with stories rather than stack premises and builds conclusions. I want to stumble and repeat myself and to be circular in my argument for a reason. For this research paper's nonlinear logic and its absence of sequence embodies my struggles as an 'Islamist' and as a scholar to speak freely within set institutional and racialized norms.

But to give further context to this, I should be more honest about what motivates me. I find within me a strong will to identify an institutional demand for me to write in a particular way, and in turn a will to resist this. I have long harboured a strong wish to be unscientific. For the word science is always tied to power and race for me. Echoing Linda Tuhiwai Smith (1999) in her wonderful *Decolonizing Methodologies*, science like the term research is a 'dirty' word to me (xi). In my experience (on studying Muslims), it represents the articulation of white supremacy more than a path to truth. I want to disrupt what I see as the standards of institutions, then. I know why too. Yes, I am Muslim, but that is not enough. I am political, am an 'Islamist' (in scare quotes) and even as I write this, I recognize that in an instant I become a constructed Other of the West when I say it out loud. For a perverse desire comes from being their 'Oriental'. Thus, I internalize within myself a voice of a subject awry and a desire grows to disrupt the way 'they' expect me to speak through the brushes of a white-out bottle. I cannot help but feel any adherence to rules erases parts of me.

I actually recognize that my will to say 'no' to institutional norms arrives without proper direction and this in itself is of curiosity. But also, why does this resistance so often latch on to the word 'Islamist'? Why am I not brave enough to use this label without scare quotes? For now, all I know is that these half thoughts come to me through writing like this. Unhindered, in circles, and through stories I write to figure out my free speech as a Muslim, as an academic, as an 'Islamist', and all the limits that come with this. It is as I say a curious feeling that drives this article's question. And, I do know that necessary academic convention exists to protect and build research. I agree with these, to an extent. And to be fair I have rushed through my above points, for a reason. This paper is not written to make generalizations and a sustained argument against academic standards. Instead, I want to trace through an auto-ethnography on why I feel there exists a need to erase the Islamic side to me.

My gratitude goes to Tanja Dreher and Michael Griffiths. The editor's invitation to contribute to this special edition flatters me but it also gives me (and my reader) greater clarity in describing my article's objective. Their special edition asks a key question, how can we shift the debate on free speech? It was then with some delight I read their abstract and its line of questions. How can we speak beyond the limitations of the liberal free speech paradigm? Can decolonization or the ethics and politics of listening offer alternatives? How can we shift the terms of the debate? All these resonated and told of my ambition to reorient my voice and my method. A dutiful echoing call to 'speak from (or listen to) below' rang throughout their abstract as it does through me. It also offered me the bravery to try and tamper with both form and content.

With all this said, there was one moment in the abstract that had me pause and reflect further on how I could contribute and to what exactly my aim might be. The editors spoke of 'their promise to open up new ways to defend difference···' I hesitated when reading this sentence without fully understanding why. Perhaps because my political ambitions have lived, died and survived by the word 'promise' and its many meanings. I see the word as commitment, hope and potential.

I read their sentence in such a way, in all ways and again as a crucial way to speak of my own paper. First, a promise is as Tanja and Michael describe theirs. It is a pledge that speaks to their/our commitment to imagine freedom and equality in new ways. Also, it gives hope. A wish, at least for me and for the Islamicate, to go beyond the liberal (white) 'I' and thus liberate the Muslim's Islamic eye. To speak and not be spoken for, to look at, and not only be looked at. To speak within the coordinates of our fantasies and beyond the lines colonialism drew. Such a hope leads us to the final echo of the word: promise. It speaks of the potential of Islam's rich and old scholarly works. I have long sought a pathway for (in)sight into the other discourse. This is opposed to us speaking after I accept myself as the Other of discourse.

Above all then, the word promise evokes another meaning. It recalls its opposite and recalls a place from where many of my anxieties about erasing my own sense of self stem. It tells of a promise as a swindle, the swindle of liberalism (Khiabany and Williamson 2015, 583).

My auto-ethnography shows little interest in answering whether I can or ought to have free speech. But it speaks more of the promise of free speech in all of that word's various meanings. My auto-ethnography thus works through examples of a Muslim's life, works through my internalized fantasies as an Other and other stories of when I have tried to fulfil this promise, when I have believed in it and when I have seen it for the swindle it is. I will thus try to think through free speech's promise and what lays between and beyond the scare quotes to my own claim to an 'Islamist' speech.

The liberal fantasy

The TV shows a van with bullet holes. An image of a wounded survivor follows. She sits on the curb surrounded by concerned paramedics. And then, a few frames later, comes the portrait of the van's owner. We see the face of the 'alleged' terrorist. I hear myself give a selfish whisper of 'not again'. I know by his name he is Muslim. I divert my eyes and say a prayer for the families of lost ones. Then a second bout of guilt arrives and another prayer follows. May God bring justice to all.

A minute later on the same screen comes a Muslim spokesperson. An imam, a 'leader', a lawyer, or whoever. Someone always arrives on set to speak about Islam and Muslims. We have all played that role, played it from the beginning. A black or brown face brought to condemn another black or brown man's act, as an act done against his religion and our collective decency. For white anxieties about the threat of terror need someone who looks like me to say, 'not all of us'.

What would I say if I were that spokesperson? What could I say?

I have unfortunate recurring fantasy where I sit opposite an 'expert on counter-terrorism'. I mumble and shake my head: what a hopeless task. And so, in the days after, to deal with my silence, to deal with feeling hopeless, I do something. I often daydream about this exact scenario. I take up the task.

We are on some television panel. Real anxieties come when I imagine this. I even feel them as I write it now, feel the pressure, and can even smell that cologne I wear for big occasions. The red flashing dot above the live camera is there. I can see the silhouettes of an audience, in the dark, who stares back at me.

My mind makes my opponent in the image of how I see power. A clean shaved white conservative male with spectacles and a red tie who wears a black suit. He is a counter-terrorism expert, and his job is to trace (my) Islamic excesses. And, I can hear his voice, hear it well, like I've heard it before: on the news, from my principal, from my lecturer. He uses well-rehearsed liberal lies in a restrained tone. It is so well done, and nothing seems to disrupt its balance. But then, there is that moment. A moment that comes when he enjoys curving his lips around a provocative and racist point. A moment where I can feel the audience move closer. A post-racial moment where a pent-up racism against Muslims feels justified to be said. In this fantasy, I give the expert the uppity prose of a Hitchens (2007). There is something about the British accent that feels authoritative to me. It gives his intellectual content an imperial echo. It sounds truer. And, so inserting the accent helps me explain the colonial relationship. Imagining this helps position me against what I see as a privileged opponent. It is not him or his ideas I combat, it's also that he sounds right. Who speaks truth and who does not come with acoustics. Maybe that's why I find Hutchins brilliantly cutting in his contempt for Islam. As, he says, it:

> [···]insists that some turgid and contradictory and sometimes evil and mad texts, obviously written by fairly unexceptional humans, are in fact the word of god. I think that the indispensable condition of any intellectual liberty is the realisation that there is no such thing. For, faith is the surrender of the mind. (ibid)

It is then that I ask again: what would I say if I were that spokesperson? I also imagine my frustration as I listen, as I keep trying to interrupt for even in my fantasy I am silent. The camera feels focused on my lack of a reaction, on my face. It compounds the problem, makes it more immediate, irreversible. The focus on my face frames me as someone who has in faith 'surrendered his mind' and who has as a ···

> [···] Muslim spent decades defending what is both unknowable and unfalsifiable in their silly books, rather than show an ounce of career for their kind. It is beyond the cognitive capacity of any person to claim without embarrassment that the lord of creation spoke his ultimate words to an unlettered merchant in seventh-century Arabia. [···] Yet, Muslims use this as license for murder and rape. And I do not care if ten billion people intone the contrary to what I say. Nor should I have to. But the plain fact is that the believable threat of violence undergirds the Muslim demand for 'respect'. (pause) And why should we? (ibid)

In my mind I see the audience nod. While the expert plays up to what I assume is their overt secular sensibilities. He toys with his words, enjoys the habit of pausing as if he waits for them to recognize the potency of his point. Relishing the elegant prose, they like his question.

Why should we respect them? And, after he has framed the debate, the host turns to ask: 'your reply?'

How should I respond when my body is an object of phobia and the site of my own fears? The inner troubles, the spiritual ones, the blinking red dot, all come from within. They silence me more than his words. How do you seek respect when you think any such claim violence 'undergirds' your demand?

While researching to write this paper I wanted to read up on new works about Muslims and free speech. This took me to Khiabany and Williamson (2015). I enjoyed their concrete historical examples of highlighting the liberal state's double standards that filled their pages. Free speech is not for all. Consider how in recent times, the UK alone investigated over 20,000 people for online comments. Most of them were Muslims (ibid). In 2012, police charged a British Muslim teenager for an offensive tweet. He wrote 'all British soldiers should die' for the deaths of innocent Afghanis (Greenwald 2015). In contrast, the authors noted how we find no prosecution of those who celebrated deaths in Gaza (ibid).

Further cases against Muslims supported the point about double standards. In 2006 France charged the rapper Richard Makela with 'offending public decency'. He had called France a 'slut' (583). And in 2014, the French Interior Minister moved to ban comedian Dieudonne M'Bala for hate speech (ibid). Two notable instances show how the state criminalized anti-establishment speech. This took place in a context in which France banned the veil in public spaces. France had also become the first country to ban pro-Palestinian demonstrations. And it is not only the French state who have double standards. Charlie Hebdo defended its right to publish Islamophobic cartoons. It sacked its cartoonist Maurice Sine. He had refuse to apologize for antisemitic comments about President Sarkozy's son (ibid).

It is worth asking where do Manning, Assange and Snowdon fit in debates about free speech? For I caught myself nodding as the authors took up Hal Draper's review on Marx's argument of the 'democratic swindle' (573–5). The charming use of the phrase, my desire to believe it, and its relevance to my own aim for this paper buoyed me. In its spirit, their argument explains how those in power use freedom. Governments, for example, see threats against them as infringements on 'liberty'. Freedom is thus a rhetoric, is a way to advance the state, to advance powerful elite interest (ibid). I could not help but racialize this, bring it back home. A long tradition of suppressing exists in liberalism's name. The liberal state has long asserted who the free 'man' is and who is not. A history where African slaves who built America and peoples of the ex-colonies were all excluded from this category 'man'. I realized how many who champion 'free speech' are using it to police the current and assumed threat but also to erase a history from which freedom was helping define "white".

My friend Mohamad dropped me off to the studios to conduct a pre-interview on the television show *The Project*. I was a special guest in a piece titled 'Muslim-Australians Traveling to Syria/Iraq'. The panellists would ask me on my thoughts on why young Muslims joined the Islamic State. Earlier that month, Islamic State of Iraq and Syria (ISIS) had announced they had set up a 'caliphate'.

We drove through the upscale area of Melbourne's South Yara, around the bends of the river. And, I rehearsed. I could guess what they would ask me. I could also predict what my obligation as a Muslim should be. While thinking about my answers, I over-focused on disproving the jihadist. But, I had promised myself to sidestep this trap and made a personal pledge not to denounce ISIS. I concluded this not because I support or have sympathies for their cause. I wished to disrupt what I saw as a liberal society's insistent call for Muslims to condemn. I wanted to avoid playing what Salman Sayyid (2014) calls the role of 'therapist'. I hoped to free myself as Muslim from the always having to ease white anxieties.

The reality is many Muslims feel the pressure to speak the liberal language. As Sayyid (2014) argues, the racist kernel at the centre of Islamophobia is a dark wish to erase Muslims. In its extreme form, it shows itself through bombs, through calls for genocide. But, the logic has many measures. It also works as a way for Muslim's to perform their own self-erasure. It acts through the community's self-policing of dissenting and angry voice. It works through self-policing complex and ambiguous positions. It distrusts (and silences) those who refuse to play good or bad Muslim. Why should I choose sides? There is more to this than whether ISIS is Islamic or not.

But, I knew something else. And the closer we came to the studio the more it became a must. The reality is many Muslims feel the pressure to speak the liberal language and erase ourselves as threats, erase how freedom has a particular racial meaning. We feel the need to say the right things. We must repeat our belief in society's democratic 'promises'. I thus knew it would be easier to denounce the violence of the western state only after I show I am a 'good Muslim' who believes in the liberal swindle. So, I thought about performing the tactic of giving a little, taking a little. I would condemn ISIS and then talk about the Iraq War and colonialism. I would point the finger back and say 'racism' is always at play. I would then hope audiences would defend my 'free speech' if I was attacked for having provocative views. Upon reflection, this has always been the negotiation in my mind, before the camera or in the experience of everyday. This performance of saying criticisms within the paradigm of the liberal promise equates to an initiation act. It equates to a democratic playing up of one's critical agency and shows I have 'self-reflection', which I disagree only after I fundamentally agree.

At the *centre* of the war on terror

A double bind exists within the War on Terror for Muslims. The anger and the revulsion in the West towards Islamist violence foregrounds Muslims only to erase us. It frames the debate. We as Muslims are seen to be unseen. We speak not to speak because there is always a compulsion for us to conceal that which reveal us: terrorism. And I am left with a 'choice' (one within scare quotes). Either speak to confirm or deny what I am not, I can only contemplate the indeterminacy of my 'throwness' into this War. Its methods, battles, delusions, intimidations, and fabrications shape my subjectivity within its quotes. For, I can only speak freely after its paradigm decides me to be of unfree. That is to say, the content of who I am and what I wish to say is always dictated by the existing form of the conversation.

The liberal fantasy

I rehearsed my performance with Mohamad rather than my answers; I could see The Project's panellists frowns even then. I could see the worried look on my father's face, who came to me out of nowhere, perhaps as a reminder of who I might disappoint. Drenched in apprehension, pressing on my beard, I caught myself in the rear-view mirror. Severe doubts entered my head about using ISIS to enter a discussion on racism. I tried to talk myself out of it. For I knew, had been socialized into recognizing a basic rule. This is about survival, not about telling a truth. The Muslim community does not want you to be heroic here, they just want to mitigated the backlash. This is about making sure that the following day a sister does not get her hijab ripped of her head.

Just condemn ISIS I told myself. But, I also knew condemnation does not abate Islamophobia. It only defers the abject object of disgust onto another Other. Some brown person had to pay for ISIS, them, their supporters, or me. Condemnation would happen, without or without me. If I did not condemn openly, I would be that object. I eventually found myself sitting in the studios, leading up to my segment with the standard clichés rushing to mind, I felt trapped, still uncertain of what to say. I adjusted my falling earpiece. I could not hear the voice-over but I watched the panellists introduce my segment as they showed stock footage of ISIS, militants holding guns and their fingers to the sky. There was something soothing in seeing this image without sound. It felt like an analogy of sorts. Indeed, Muslim voices do not drive our analysis. The media interprets Muslims against 'frozen' stock silent images (Sardar and Davies 2010, 15). The War on Terror has framed Muslims. Anyone who speaks like a Muslim must adopt and internalize their impossibility, we are one stock image or another. Whatever mask I wear I can only ever appear to the West as terrorist or not. As Fanon put it, and as explained to me by my contemporary Arun Kundnani, 'turn white or disappear'. And, at that moment, within my apprehension, I felt a strength. I had long committed myself to a different politics. It was now about finding the courage to not disappear.

Khiabany and Williamson (2015, 576) also reminded me of Domenico Losurdo's work. They cite the author's engaging accounts of liberal history. He flushes out the contradictions in this tale of liberalism. Losurdo's first chapter answers what he calls 'a series of embarrassing questions'. He testifies to what united the great liberal thinkers. They shared a contempt for the indigenous people of the colonies and the working class. They participated in the systematic expropriation and the practical genocide of such peoples. And a willingness was there too, a willingness to use the most repressive of measures. These measures included genocide, slavery and child labour (see Khiabany and Williamson's summary, 576).

In his book, *Liberalism: A Counter-History*, Losurdo (2014) reminds us that Locke, Smith and Franklin shared a common enthusiasm. They all called to use violence in denying the rights of the Irish, and then of the Indians. They continued this dedication to 'black enslavement and the black slave trade' (20). Losurdo stresses that slavery was not something that preceded liberalism. It rather engendered its development (35).

Khiabany and Williamson highlight one passage that captures the point best. What they call 'the tangle of emancipation and de-emancipation' makes the argument. And, it comes with rebel colonists shouting out a slogan during the war of independence. They shouted 'We won't be their Negroes' (576). A confession lays within their call for the British to recognize their rights. In the very moment of it saying it they also endorse inequality for blacks.

From the start, Losurdo points out liberalism expressed the self-consciousness of slave owners. This consciousness formed as the capitalist system emerged and established itself. Thanks also in part to the ruthless practices of expropriation and oppression. Practices implemented at home and in the colonies. Practices that worked to exclude the Other experience from politics and speech (Losurdo 309). And, the power of capital in the land of 'barbarians' came not through 'peaceful competition'. It came through the barrel of a gun. Indeed, the Declaration of the Rights of Man said nothing about the rights of slaves, natives or women. (See Khiabany and Williamson's summary, 577.) The self-congratulatory account of liberalism fails to mention this 'exclusion clause' (Khiabany and Williamson 2015, 576). Instead, liberalism presents itself in the most favourable light.

Similarly, in their book, *The Crises of Multiculturalism*, Lentin and Titley (2011, 139) make a similar point. Following Peter Hervik, they argue the Danish cartoons controversy do not prove hypocrisy as some critics of free speech suggest. Yes, Western society dictates whose criticisms we value and whose we reject. But the author argues we must understand the history of the fascist and conservative past of Jyllands Posten. Their views show an inherent and consistent racism beyond the obvious point about hypocrisy. A civilizational hierarchy exists in their imagination, a hierarchy where Europe sits on the top. It is this imagination that drives the editor's excuses to print the cartoons. It is not just then because Muslims are simply a minority or the Other and we can easily discard their concerns. But, also their bodily presence as European citizens problematizes their sense of order and this imaginative hierarchy. As Stuart Hall puts it, cite Lentin and Titley, Muslims are 'in but not of Europe' and thus affront to Europeanness (25). And,

I have come to understand while writing this article that my own confusion about what voice I ought to have as a Muslim scholar in the West is historically formed by this formula. Yes, I am of in the West as a citizen, but that line from Hall 'in but not of' captures so well my relationship with academia.

In my fantasy as a Muslim spokesperson on TV, I want to respond, to speak from below, to reorganize the current status quo of how Muslims are posited within a framework of images that show death and terror. I want to explain how I am asked to speak after a van ploughs into innocent people, after the expert has dictated the language, the terms, the conditions of who I want to say the emotional settings dictate the content of my speech. And what can one say, really?

And so very often, even in my fantasy, I feel compelled to wear the mask of the moderate. I feel compelled to hide the traces of the 'Islamist' Other. Well before I drove to the studio with my friend Mohamad I have felt the persistent compulsion to speak in a 'human' language to ultimately soothe away the privileged fears about the threat of a radical Islam. Long before it became part of my fantasy to break the cycle, it became my landscape, for I have not stopped thinking about how to shape the Muslim voice to echo liberalism's abstraction, its lie, its swindle, to speak in a voice that works to erase the world of the body and its historical realities that shaped liberalism's imaginative hierarchy.

And so, even in the fantasy, I do, I very often respond to the Hitchen like expert as a way to practise how to survive real life. I practise how to say not all Muslims are alike, that we must not generalize. But I also teach myself to get used to the 'subtlest of sensations', get used to *that* feeling. For, as I speak in this fantasy I can feel part of myself being erased by myself. Sixteen years' worth of pressure to correct the ugly image of a violent Islam therefore informs my fantasy. It informs the blurring of my hope with painful self-reflections of the double bind that as a Muslim I face: condemn or be condemned. In this insidious context, within the parameters of this swindle, our own words are our White-Out. What erases our ability to tell our story is that we must tell the content of our stories within the ideological *form* set by theirs.

Erasing which we must repress

My auto-ethnography takes a fundamental point about storytelling that I learned from Walter Benjamin. His essay *The Storyteller* (1969) tells of the decline in the ways we share each other's experiences. For Benjamin, modernity's swift changes undermine the ways we reflect and understand ourselves in the world. The old art of forming narrative vanishes from of our academic speech. But in vanishing, it makes it possible for us to see more clearly the beauty of what is dying out (87).

I wondered about this lost beauty as I read Richard White's (2017) wonderful summary. And what I write here is in part informed by that summary. It would be wrong for me not to mention it. For as I read White I remembered when I first read Benjamin's essay. I picked up a sense of mourning something lost echo throughout his essay. But I ought to be careful, this sense of loss might be mine. Benjamin is a swifter thinker and a keener scholar of history than me. For him, the decline is a manifestation of secular and productive forces. As I understood it, he claims that this new age means the development of a modern form of communication. Spreading information becomes the principal way we engage with one another. No event any longer comes to us without the scientific tone of explaining things, or so I read him (89).

Here we have the key to what Benjamin describes in the first section of his essay and another way to explain my point about the importance of how academic *form* shapes academic content. We, argues Benjamin, are losing our ability to integrate or exchange personal experience. We no longer understand anything as truth except through its direct appeals to information and the explanation of facts. But, given the priority of information, how are we to grasp our most in-depth experiences? How can we communicate the most intimate and emotive aspects of our truths for others?

But it is here Benjamin got me, and White's (2017, 1–15) description helped. He goes on to describe the attitude of the listener. He speaks of the rhythm of the work. When it has seized the listener, they listen to the tales more intently. It comes in such a way that the gift of retelling them comes all by itself. This, then, is the nature of the web in which the gift of storytelling is cradled (Benjamin 1969, 91). In the end, there is no final separation between the storyteller and the listener. The listener is also a potential storyteller who hands down his version of the story to others. And, through storytelling, the collective experience of people is passed on. It moves from one generation to the next. Storytelling is something that involves the collective depth of cultural life. It is more than the individual's own experience.

Let me begin to conclude then by saying out perhaps I appealed to my fight for 'free speech' as an 'Islamist' because the word has its own rhythm and drama and brings certain emotions with it. It has its own story. I ought to point out that I put 'Islamist' then in scare quotes because it was the narrator of my story for struggle. I am not sure what being one means to be honest, or even if I am such a thing. I admit I tend to romanticize political Islam, yes. But the word comes to mean, for me, that which lays beyond the Westernese of liberal academia. It comes to mean a promise, unfulfilled and broken.

As Benjamin (1969, 91) puts it, 'Storytelling does not aim to convey the pure essence of the thing, like information or a report. It sinks the thing into the life of the storyteller, to bring it out of him again. Thus traces of the storyteller cling to the story the way the handprints of the potter cling to the clay vessel.' And perhaps, I used the word 'Islamist' as a way to cling to a story about the promise (in all its meanings) to remain potentially, radically, Other.

It has not escaped me while writing that perhaps I spoke as an 'Islamist' as a way to hide a problematic politics that I possess, to hide it from myself. I have often thought a hidden and unwarranted apology exists within me for those who resist the West through unethical use of violence. I hope not, but it may well lay dormant in me. But part of the problem is that it is hard to tell what my relationship is with this thing called the 'West' is, for I have to often had to wear masks. The hidden epistemic racism of powerful white institutions that demand sterile information about Islam requires a 'fugitive communication' (Conquergood 2000, 133, 2002, 146). As I have tried to show, my Islamic voice must learn how to lubricate its criticisms. The content of my dissent thus comes through the careful (mis)use of my embodied form as their Other. Or, an Other who is in but not of. Or, an Other who realizes he must make his intellectual content its form. For instances at many conferences I converse through intonation, not words. Arched eyebrows and smiles or confused stares work as ways to express my dissent. I change the pronouns and turn my statements into open-ended questions, 'have *we* thought about why Muslims⋯'.

Minorities in radical politics do not have the privilege of explicitness. We do not have the luxury of transparency and or of a free speech free from the punishments. Some penalties come as the subtlest of sensations. You get ignored. But even as I write these words, I hear doubts. I can hear the institutional voices whisper. Their suspicion about the validity of my argument is my doubt. Academia is a big place, many voices exist, and maybe I look for this argument to be true, to find solace. But academia is big with small circles. And I also wish to challenge the opposite of me, challenge those with power. But in their company, I can only speak of 'free speech' as an 'Islamist' from positions of awry that take me awry when I speak. I must assume the role of a fugitive who codes his stereotype. For the never-ending debate about Islam versus free speech works as a circular debate that demands the same thing from me. The intellectual content of the debate is about passing on information about who I am as Muslim that becomes irrelevant to the circular form that this debate makes. A form that typically follows the line of a Mobius strip. It assumes two sides: the free against the unfree, us and them. But it is one line that takes us in the same discursive circle.

So, if my purpose in writing like this is to point at anything let me point at one thing only. It is difficult to be a critic of liberalism and a Muslim scholar and not evoke stereotypes when you have been socialized into playing a prop in someone else's fantasy about the promise of freedom. The form of who I am as Muslim is far more powerful a Thing than the content of which I speak of. And it has occurred to me, we as Muslims of the West seem to walk in circles along the tracks of this fantasy in an attempt to grasp the object of our own identities.

Is not Said's (1979) underlining point that an oriental subject is a form without content. We are a thing whose discursive being is 'whited out' by the brushes of Orientalists. For, is this not the most basic truth of Orientalism's information about Islam? Muslims are what they see and not what we are. How many of you know of the Arabesque eyes peering through a niqab as an image of the world 'out there'? Images of dunes and camel caravans replace the content of Islamicate history.

Islam is thus a European 'Thing' from 'out there'. Those of you who have read *Orientalism* (1979) know this well. Images in Europe of Muslim's otherness have a long bibliography. We find Islam cited throughout European essays and imagination. It often serves as a blank canvas for many an Orientalist to name and to debate, to dispute and to circle. Of most note, it reaffirms Europe's rational and cultural borders. A Thing 'out there' to point at, but to also repress. Islam came to be an internal sublimated dialogue about what is foreign. But also, it becomes a way to teach Europe, an imperial way, to speak of and 'know' the foreign. Thus throughout, as Said argues, practising her creativity, Europe made the East. It created a distant and aesthetic thing to look at and oppose (7). It trained the European eye to look outward to see itself. In doing so, Europe set up its sense of superiority. The almost mythical traits of Islam helped make the West home to the West. Islam's otherness centred Europe as the cultural and rational core of the world. And, it helped legitimate a claim to Europe's universality because it was not this thing, Islam.

While for us designated 'Orientals' who live in but are not of the West, who grew up here, we live with some consequence. We live in what Said (1979, 29) calls a dehumanizing 'web of racism'. A web 'very strong indeed', it is a network of language and imagery that holds in the Orient. A nexus of knowledge and power that creates 'the Oriental' and yet obliterates us. It is the subtlest of sensations. So, I sit at my desk to write eight thousand words about this web, in the language of this web, to speak about not speaking. And, I had hoped to show the circularity of it all. That at the heart of these debates is an abstract liberalism for all 'people' and a concrete freedom for only some 'men', and for this, I hoped to mimic Williams' act. I write about the act of writing, to speak about the double bind at the heart of the War on Terror, at the centre of my paper.

My aim was to mirror Williams' symbolic act of reaching for a little bottle of White-Out. For me to speak as if I am free is to erase my body, the land I am on, to brush the 'correctional fluid' over, to melt away. It is to assume I am separate from the Orientalist web that gives 'Muslim' its informative meaning. And if I were to write like this I would arrive at where I began, and confront the same question. Am I accommodating different audiences or erasing that which I must repress?

Disclosure statement

No potential conflict of interest was reported by the author.

References

Benjamin, W. 1969. "The Storyteller." In *Illuminations*, translated by H. Zohn. New York: Random House.
Canagarjah, S. A. 2002. *A Geopolitics of Academic Writing*. Pittsburgh: University of Pittsburgh Press.
Conquergood, D. 2000. "Rethinking Elocution: The Trope of the Talking Book and Other Figures of Speech." *Text and Performance Quarterly* 20 (4): 325–341. doi:10.1080/10462930009366308.
Conquergood, D. 2002. "Performance Studies: Interventions and Radical Research." *The Drama Review* 46 (2): 1–12. doi:10.1162/105420402320980550.
Fanon, F. 1967. *Black Skin, White Masks*. Translated by C. L. Markmann, 2008 (reprint of the 1986 Edition) ed. London: Pluto Press.
Greenwald, G. 2015. "With Power of Social Media Growing, Police Now Monitoring and Criminalizing Online Speech." *The Intercept*, January 6. https://theintercept.com/2015/01/06/police-increasingly-monitoring-criminalizing-online-speech/
Hesse, B., and S. Sayyid. 2002. "The 'War' Against Terrorism/The 'War' for Cynical Reason." *Ethnicities* 2 (2): 12–17.
Hitchens, C. 2007. "God-Fearing People: Why Are We So Scared of Offending Muslims?" *Slate* 30 (June). http://www.slate.com/articles/news_and_politics/fighting_words/2007/07/godfearing_people.html.
Khiabany, G., and M. Williamson. 2015. "Free Speech and the Market State: Race, Media and Democracy in New Liberal Times." *European Journal of Communication* 30 (6): 571–586. doi:10.1177/0267323115597855.
Lentin, A., and G. Titley. 2011. *The Crises of Multiculturalism: Racism in a Neoliberal Age*. New York: Zed Books.
Losurdo, D. 2014. *Liberalism: A Counter-History*. New York: Verso.
Said, E. 1979. *Orientalism*. New York: Vintage.

Sardar, Z., and M. W. Davies. 2010. "Freeze Framing Muslims: Hollywood and the Slideshow of Western Imagination." *Interventions* 12 (2): 239–250. doi:10.1080/1369801X.2010.489698.

Sayyid, S. 2003. *A Fundamental Fear: Eurocentrism and the Emergence of Islamism*. London: Zed Books.

Sayyid, S. 2014. "A Measure of Islamophobia." *Islamophobia Studies Journal* 2 (1): 10–25. doi:10.13169/islastudj.2.1.0010.

Smith, L. T. 1999. *Decolonizing Methodologies: Research and Indigenous Peoples*. New York: Zed Books.

White, R. 2017. "Walter Benjamin: 'The Storyteller' and the Possibility of Wisdom." *The Journal of Aesthetic Education* 51 (1): 1–15. doi:10.5406/jaesteduc.51.1.0001.

Williams, P. 1997. "An Ordinary Brilliance: Parting the Waters, Closing the Wounds." In *The Genealogy of Race, Lecture 5*. BBC Radio 4: The Reith Lectures.

Silence and resistance: Aboriginal women working within and against the archive

Evelyn Araluen Corr

ABSTRACT
Representation of Aboriginal women in colonial archives has long been linked to strategies of silencing and erasure. These representations still bear considerable weight over the ways in which Aboriginal womanhood is perceived and permitted in Australian society. This essay explores a history of Aboriginal women self-presenting both within and in direct response to colonial archives, and the modes of cultural translation which function to hold archival representations accountable to the realities of Aboriginal womanhood.

Introduction

For Aboriginal women, 'the archive' is a material and symbolic space of imperial violence. The visual and discursive colonization of Aboriginal women's bodies, lands, and histories through the construction and circulation of tropes, stereotypes, caricatures, and catalogs since first contact with Europeans, denies Aboriginal women the right to experience and articulate their contemporary and ancestral heterogeneities without resistance. For many Aboriginal women today, the archive is to at least some extent a repository of family history, and thus has also become a site of recovery through community and government services. As French philosopher Jacques Derrida's *Archive Fever: A Freudian Impression* (1995) suggests, the archive (*Arkhe*) still bears within itself its nomological reference to the domicile of superior magistrates, those who command and represent the law, the *archons*. It is in their homes that those with authority guard, interpret, and enact the official documents of their society (9–10). Archives occur and take place under house arrest, a topo-nomological principle of archontic power which is driven also by consignation, by the gathering together and unification of signs. The archive is both institutive and conservative, revolutionary and traditional, it is capital and power, it is political, and it is violent: 'There is no political power without control of the archive, if not of memory. Effective democratisation can always be measured by this essential criterion: the participation in and the access to the archive, its constitution, and its interpretation' (11). Living within the temporal and spatial dispossessions of colonialism, Aboriginal realities are shadowed and concealed by projections of settler colonial archives onto unceded lands and bodies.

The power of the archive to administer and control perceptions of Aboriginal people was saliently demonstrated in the wake of ABC's *Four Corners* report into abuse in the juvenile justice system in July 2016, after significant controversy arose in response to Bill Leak's cartoon for *The Australian*, which depicts a male Aboriginal police officer holding a young Aboriginal boy by the neck of his shirt, telling an Aboriginal man 'You'll have to sit down and talk to your son about personal responsibility.' The Aboriginal man, who is slouched and holding a beer can, replies, 'Yeah righto what's his name then?' (*The Australian*, 4 August 2016). The ensuing criticism from both Aboriginal and non-Aboriginal commentators drew attention to other instances of Leak's work, which enter into the archival iconography of Indigenous savagery to explicitly configure the abuse of Aboriginal women as an inherent feature of Aboriginal culture. Responses to the cartoon from Aboriginal journalists and academics such as Celeste Liddle, Luke Pearson, and Chelsea Bond highlighted not only Leak's history of demonizing and ridiculing Aboriginal men and women, but also spoke to the broader structure of colonial vilification of Aboriginal bodies in which Leak's images operate. Leak's submission into the 18C parliamentary inquiry which was announced after Aboriginal woman Melissa Dinnison lodged a complaint with the Human Rights Commission against Leak and *The Australian*, pertaining to section 18C of Australia's Racial Discrimination Act, argued that his cartoon sought 'to expose the truth about the appalling levels of violence endured by Aboriginal women and children', and situated himself as an advocate of free speech in a culture of silence and political correctness. Later in the year, Bundjalung former ALP president Ngunggai Warren Mundine performed a similar critique of this supposed culture of silence around neglect and abuse in Aboriginal communities, claiming those communities protect and conceal violence against women and children. Many Aboriginal women, such as Darumbul and South Sea Islander journalist Amy McQuire, responded with outrage at these accusations, citing the efforts of Aboriginal women such as Jackie Huggins, Kylie Cripps, Megan Davis, Louise Taylor, Judy Atkinson, and Janet Hammill to work against community violence:

> [I]f you think Aboriginal women have been silent, it's only because you haven't heard us, our voices now hoarse after decades of screaming into the abyss of Australia's apathy (*The Guardian*, 5 October 2016).

Silence and erasure of Aboriginal women's voices have long been employed as a strategy of disempowerment by the settler colonial state and its imperial affiliations. Yiman and Bidjera academic Marcia Langton's (1993, 24) much quoted aphorism 'The easiest and most "natural" form of racism in representation is the act of making the other invisible' can be understood in reference to both the denial of Aboriginal presence, a process central to the colonial project, and the silencing of Aboriginal perspectives in favor of settler inscriptions thereof. The erasive and reconstitutive impact of settler colonialism on Indigenous women's ways of being and doing has been a central concern in the feminist writings of Indigenous scholars such as Lisa Kahaleole Hall (Kanaka Maoli) and Jackie Huggins (Bidjara and Birri Gubba Juru) over the last 30 years. Colonialism does not just physically threaten Indigenous bodies, Kahaleole Hall (2009) argues, but also threatens the Indigenous languages and practices capable of conceptualizing and celebrating the cultural specificities of Indigenous womanhood—a process inextricable from the expropriation of land and natural resources in which these beings and doings operate. The anthropological edifice of Aboriginality, Huggins states in *Always Was, Always Will Be* (1993), reveals more of the nature of Western ethnocentrism than it does the actual lives and knowledges of Aboriginal people. In rejecting Australian historian Bain Attwood's assertion that the 'new Aboriginal writing phenomenon' is an instance of Aboriginal people proclaiming Aboriginal identity, she configures emergent forms of textuality for Aboriginal people as acts of reclaiming place and history in Australian society (1993, 460).

This article builds on work engaging with the interstices of colonization and the evolving forms in which colonial representations of Aboriginal women are circulated, and further explores how Aboriginal women's resistance has challenged these modes. Resistance to silence can be located both within and against the colonial archive. In addressing some of the silencing strategies employed against Aboriginal women across the last 200 years, and by exploring trajectories of Aboriginal women speaking back to colonial representations with their own self-presentations of identity, culture, and agency, this article asks how making the archive visible can also be making the archive responsible.

Historicism and accountability

This interrogation has been initiated by recent critiques of the settler imaginary and its archival organization from Australian feminist historian Liz Conor, Eualeyai/Kamillaroi lawyer and academic Larissa Behrendt, and Narungga poet and researcher Natalie Harkin.

In *Skin Deep: Settler Impressions of Aboriginal Women* (2016), Conor confronts a series of racialized inscriptions invoked by settler Australians in the dispossession and misappropriation of Aboriginal people, which have been recirculated and reconstituted as dualisms to stabilize modern settler subjectivity. This source-based study of print media reveals a network of caricatures involved in the creation and curation of tropes of Aboriginal womanhood, many of which have been mobilized by state and protectorate powers for policies of discrimination and assimilation. Tracing the function of stereotype in colonial practice has been a feature of Aboriginal history writing since J.J. Fletcher's *Clean, Clad, and Courteous: A History of Aboriginal Education in New South Wales* (1989), which explores implications from the Aborigines Protection Board's drawing of explicit links between blackness and both physical and moral filth throughout the nineteenth and twentieth century. In this form Conor (2016, 238) cites former federal Minister for Aboriginal Affairs Peter Howson's claims that decades of child removal had rescued thousands of children from infanticide. Tropes of the 'cannibal mother' were recirculated by Queensland Senator Pauline Hanson in 1997 with unsubstantiated claims of widespread infanticide and cannibalism, presented to challenge prevailing guilt over white settlement, and further entrench the paradigms of savagery in which Aboriginal women have been implicated since initial invasion. *Skin Deep* is deeply concerned with the material consequences of what Benedict Anderson defines as 'print-capitalism', extending Patrick Wolfe's settler-colonial 'logic of elimination' into the relationship between imperialism and repetition, which Conor (2016, 33) calls the 'imperial copy'. It is through this imperial copy, as Langton has previously argued, that most Australians continue to 'know' Aboriginal people today.

Behrendt's *Finding Eliza: Power and Colonial Storytelling* (2016) executes a similar study of the consequences of imagined representations for real communities. In her research, Behrendt enters into critical and personal engagement with the Butchulla people who were bound to the colonial pornography of Eliza Fraser's 1836 shipwreck on the Southern-Queensland island of K'gari. Behrendt explores the symbolic rendering of Aboriginal women as the antitheses of idealized white womanhood, and the role of those renderings in justifying the religious and colonial suppression of the Butchulla people (54). Like *Skin Deep, Finding Eliza* argues that the construction and perpetuation of colonial and imperial epistemologies is the primary function of settler representations of Aboriginal people, and that these persisting representations are mobilized by colonial powers for the disempowerment of Aboriginal people today. Both Conor and Behrendt have publicly stated their belief that Leak's cartoons rely on, and recycle, colonial notions of primitivism and cultural violence. Despite extensive records of white convicts, settlers, and colonial agents performing violence against Aboriginal women; Conor documents that in the imperial iconography of the subjugated native woman, it is almost always the native man who subjugates. This narrative frontier of the settler-colonial project relies extensively on tropes of feminine subjugation, so as to justify the assimilation or, if necessary, the eradication of Aboriginal men. In this discourse of 'settler gallantry', it is the white man who lifts the Aboriginal woman from her primitive and violent environment, into the sanctity of the imperial nation. (Conor 2016, 136)

Historical studies of this nature can be mobilized to intervene and resist settler narratives of Aboriginal identity by revealing the various patterns of demonization, usurpation, and erasure which link these representations to the settler colonial project. Much work has been done to interrogate the deployment of such essentialisms in state policy in Australia, New Zealand, and Canada. However, personal and familial encounters with the archive has also become a source of critical and creative interrogation in the work of contemporary artists and writers. Harkin, who is researching archival poetics at the Yunggorendi First Nations Centre for Higher Education and Research, explores the textures of simultaneous archival recovery and loss in her essay *The Poetics of (Re) Mapping Archives: Memory in the Blood* (2014). For Harkin (2014), archive fever is a burning for what is beyond the official record, a desire to destabilize the archons guarding her grandmother's textual presence and erasure with her own 'critical Aboriginal-sovereign-woman's voice'. This remapping attends to the 'spectres of the archive' with a spectropoetics of resistance and transcendence; making both creative and critical claims on literary theory and psychology in her delineation of 'memory in the blood'. In her use of this trope, which has been widely interrogated across international networks of Indigenous scholars and writers to articulate individual and collective ancestral relations between land, body, and memory; Harkin (2014, 4–5) marks the archive as a site of bloodshed but also genealogy, and emphasizes blood memory as a site of mourning:

> This narrative, represented as truth in public discourse and informing the foundations of public policy, was inscribed and articulated as *the Aboriginal problem*. But these reports revealed something else that was both visceral-reality and created-imagined fantasy; something that anchored and centred and pulsed to and from the heart of it all. And that was *blood*. The revered and repulsed colonial obsession, written into the record. *Flowing. Stirring. Spilling. Dripping. Mixing. Blood.* Aboriginal blood and white blood. Full-blood and mixed-

blood. Half-caste and quarter-caste. Quadroon and octoroon. Sub-human and fully- human. The racialised assumptions underpinning a so-called real and true Aboriginality became absolute on the colonial blood-dilution-scale, and reinforced the actions of government. *Blood everywhere ... everywhere blood on the record.*

In 2014, for an exhibition titled *Bound and Unbouch: Sovereign Acts – Act 1*, a part of the TARNANTHI Festival of Contemporary Aboriginal and Torres Strait Islander Art, Harkin (2014) translated the archive back into cultural form through poetry and weaving. The radical historicism of investigating, remapping, and reforming the archive, as Harkin shows, 'allows us to consider ways to live more justly with the past, oppose the ongoing violence of neo-colonialisms, and theorise future responsibilities to history'. In a similar encounter with archival records of her Aboriginal great-grandmother, historian Lynette Russell explores the hidden histories which emerge from archives of Aboriginal history— reading contrapuntally to reveal underestimated agency, but also to confront the consequences of cultural ignorance. Russell's (2013) research into her great-grandmother's psychiatric records reveals accounts of 'auditory hallucinations', for which she was institutionalized. Emily told the doctors they were the voices of her spirits and ancestors. By remapping, reconstituting, or rearchiving this history in *A Little Bird Told Me* (2002), Russell, like Harkin, encourages a critical revision of the power of the archive to ascribe and control historic representations of Aboriginal women.

Notes on representation, aboriginality, and resistance

As colonial ways of perceiving Aboriginal women are so regularly performed as acts of violence against our bodies, children, and lands, representation of and by Aboriginal women must also be understood in embodied ways. Quandamooka academic Aileen Moreton-Robinson defines this concept through Bengali feminist and literary scholar Gayatri Chakravorty Spivak's two dimensions of representation to explore the ways in which Aboriginal women perform and embody Aboriginal women's realities. Representation, in Spivak's formation, can be understood as either 'speaking for', or as 're-presentation'; being that which involves interpretation. Moreton-Robinson (2000, xxii) establishes her own conception of 'self-presentation' to 'distinguish how one represents one-self through interpretations as opposed to how one is represented by another', in positions generated by proximity and privilege. For Moreton-Robinson, the study of narrative, expression, and testimony is also the study of the historical circumstances in which subordinately-positioned subjects live experiences inscribed and deployed by those occupying dominant subject-positions. The discourses of anthropology and eth-nography which so often characterize colonial archives, she argues, do not function to reveal or know Aboriginal women, but rather to inscribe difference and thereby define the settler subject (xxiii-iv).

As Langton highlights, both Aboriginal and non-Aboriginal people create Aboriginalities in different spaces and measures of proximity (Langton 1994, in Grossman 2003, 119). The right and responsibility to represent Aboriginality, and the parameters of 'Aboriginality' itself, have been central interrogations in the critical and creative work of many Aboriginal women since invasion. Although a term historically rooted in European Latinate notions of occupation and possession, for almost 200 years the language of Aboriginality has been reclaimed and reconstituted by its referents in an assertion of collective and eternal identities. The earliest known instance of a person identifying as 'Aboriginal' in Australia dates to the fourteenth of March, 1831. Dharug woman Maria Lock, daughter of Yellomundee, who she names as 'Chief of the Richmond Tribes', was a student of the Native Institution from 1814. After marrying convict carpenter Robert Lock in 1824 in the first officially sanctioned union between an Aboriginal woman and a white man, she petitioned Governor Darling in 1831 for her deceased brother Colebee's land grant opposite the Native Institute, which had been given to Colebee by Governor Macquarie for his services as guide. In signing this memorial, Maria identifies herself as an 'Aboriginal native of New South Wales' (Lock 1831, in B Corr 2016, 7). The letter is highly significant for its reversal of the language of ethnographic classification wielded against Aboriginal people during the first decades of settlement: remembered within the Hawkesbury community as 'a political statement about a collective and inclusive identity that resonates today' (Corr 2016, 61).

In 1846, Palawa woman Mary Ann Arthur concluded her letter protesting the mis-treatment of Tasmanian Aboriginal people on Flinders Island to the colonial secretary of Van Dieman's Land with the phrase, 'Your humble Aborigine Child, Mary Ann Arthur'. Similarly, her husband, Walter George Arthur, signed himself as 'Your humble Aborigine Servant, Walter G. Arthur Chief of Ben Lomond Tribes' (Heiss and Minter 2008, 12–14). These assertions, attached to subordinate positions of child and servant, directly appeal to the structure of patronage and protectionism in which those Aboriginal people of the nineteenth century who had escaped massacre and disease were ostensibly implicated, such as Bennelong's letter to Lord Sydney's steward articulated in 1796. Maria's demand for her late brother's land grant speaks to her rights within the logics of European property law and inheritance, a claim supposedly incompatible with the Aboriginality she asserts. Nonetheless, she proclaims her identity and entitlements within both spheres. A reading of the adoption and articulation of the language of these terms by Aboriginal people in the nineteenth century demonstrates the performativity of 'Aboriginal' status and its signifiers in the context of ethnographic inscription. Engaging directly with Aboriginal expression in this period does not reveal a reconciled endorsement of Aboriginality as a relational primitivism of colonial authority, but rather a pluralism of the modes in which Aboriginal people resisted the material implications of their racial status.

Popular discourse surrounding the recognition of Frontier Wars and Aboriginal resis-tance to invasion was most conspicuously sparked by Australian anthropologist W.E.H. Stanner's 1968 Boyer Lecture, and continued as a central site of contestation throughout the History Wars of the 1990s and 2000s. Stanner's notion of the 'Great Australian Silence' and Wolfe's 'logic of elimination' provide a structural language with which to understand and revise the erasures which shape historical narratives of settlement, many of which have been retrospectively applied by historians and politicians seeking to consolidate the legal implications of dispossession, such as is evident in D.G. Bowd's widely influential *Macquarie Country: A History of the Hawkesbury* (1979); 'The music and laughter of the Hawkesbury tribes have been silenced, their customs forgotten, and their traditions lost. Relics of a bygone age remind us that they used simple equipment to fulfil their daily needs' (37). The logic of the 'doomed race' implied by this imagery can be traced most notably to Charles Darwin's observations of Aboriginal people on his

1836 visit to New South Wales, in which extensive decreases in Aboriginal populations were attributed to ill health, alcohol abuse, and high rates of infant mortality resulting from 'the wandering life of these people'. As a visitor, Darwin was possibly unaware of the catastrophic effects of frontier warfare upon Aboriginal people, in celebrating the newfound civilization within the Australian wilderness, won by 'the white man, who seems predestined to inherit the country of the thoughtless aboriginal' (B Corr 2016, 19–20).

In such a context, the very survival of Aboriginal people can be viewed as resistance to the structure of genocide built on colonial assumptions, frontier warfare, and assimilation policy. However, there are inherent issues in the configuration of all Aboriginal expressions as politically resistant. Such an approach implicitly endorses the notion that Aboriginality exists only in dialect with colonialism, and contributes to gendered and racialized tropes of the angry black man or woman, as explored in the North American African American context by critical race theorists bell hooks and Audre Lorde. Nevertheless, as Australian literary historian Penny van Toorn (2006, 14–5) observes, the relationship between literacy and colonialism means that writing is not a politically neutral force in the lives of Aboriginal people:

> Writing was carried into their world by individuals whose skin colour was the same as that of the people who shot them, sexually abused them, poisoned their water, ruined their hunting grounds, took away their children, and dispossessed them from their lands. Literacy and alphabetic script entered Indigenous life-worlds as part of a foreign invasion [···] But writing also proved to be a most valuable political weapon when Aboriginal people wished to level complaints against mission and reserve staff, or halt government plans to sell off their adopted homes. The government and church bodies that funded and administered reserves and missions were highly bureaucratic. If Aboriginal people had complaints, they were required to put them in writing.

As such, a historical study of Aboriginal writing and expression also inevitably reveals histories of Aboriginal resistance. Given the multiplicity of Aboriginal narratives and forms, it is necessary, then, to understand resistance as a fluid and multifaceted phenomenon. As Moreton-Robinson (2000, 29) acknowledges, resistance to oppression in one form—say, that of resisting or disavowing the linguistic signifiers of state determined Aboriginality—does not necessarily disrupt socio-cultural practices and performances in other spaces. An increased focus on narratives of resistance in historical work, she contends, makes visible the relationship between resistance, recovery and revitalization, and reveals the multitude of ways in which the past acts upon present identities and interests. 'Resistance by the oppressed is the influence they have on their relationship with the oppressors', Moreton-Robinson argued in 2003: 'As a form of agency resistance manifests itself as the capacity to be oppositional' (in Grossman 2003, 128–9).

It is the 'tragedy of resistance', described by Palestinian literary theorist Edward Said (1993, 210), that this oppositionality must invent, recover, or reclaim forms and representations marked and infiltrated by 'the culture of empire.'. Said proposes a language of reinscription when he writes that for the colonial subject:

> [t]o achieve recognition is to rechart and then occupy the place in imperial cultural forms reserved for subordination, to occupy it self-consciously, fighting for it on the very same territory once ruled by a consciousness that assumed the subordination of a designated inferior Other (1993, 210).

Arrente artist and writer Jennifer Kemarre Martiniello (2002, 94–5) also employs a language of inscription to conceptualize the cultural dimensions of textuality for Aboriginal histories and bodies when she writes; 'I am bark, engraved by the continuous cartography of my peoples, their histories – I am Dream. The unsilenced. The ink that runs from the tongues of languages to their inscriptions in print, paper, minds'. By invoking these at times explicitly spiritual notions of haunting or spetropoetics, inscription and reinscription, as a form of radical historicism in our engagement with Aboriginal women's resistance to colonial representations, we are better situated to place Aboriginal women in active and embodied roles both in the consequences of these images and ideologies, and in the self-presentation of Aboriginal womanhood.

Reading in and against the archive

There are inherent issues in the reading of Aboriginal literature and expression through the frames of Western or even postcolonial theoretical praxis. In approaches to Aboriginal texts which explicitly reinscribe or enter into dialog with Western and colonial forms, or narratives which have been supressed by the archive and its archons, the task becomes that which van Toorn performs *Writing Never Arrives Naked: Early Aboriginal cultures of writing in Australia* (2006); the understanding of these texts in the historical, political, and cultural contexts of both Aboriginal and colonial worlds. Throughout *Writing Never Arrives Naked*, van Toorn contrapuntally reads a range of Aboriginal forms of textuality to reveal the hybridity with which Aboriginal people's written expressions in English speak against the conditions of their lives under colonial oppression, and explores historically the role that literacy played in the perception and treatment of Aboriginal women in the nineteenth century through the lives of Annie McDonald at Lake Condah Mission and Bessie Flower at Ramahyuck. This comparison of two literate and educated Aboriginal women whose epistolary records reveal distinct histories of resistance to their characterizations by the mission system, demonstrates the contradictory ways in which Aboriginal women's achievements could be mobilized for their continued subjugation (2006, 183–94). Conor's method in *Skin Deep* involves the exhaustive compiling of like representations of Aboriginal women to document patterns of repetition and recirculation throughout print media, and in many instances to trace these representations back to single, unsubstantiated sources, often invented for purposes of land acquisition. Behrendt's approach in *Finding Eliza* explores historical and legal sources surrounding Eliza Fraser's narrative of shipwreck and capture in dialog with a range of potential literary influences, as well as the Butchulla community, to reveal a number of inconsistencies and outright fictions, which nonetheless were used to justify violent putative expeditions on K'Gari in the 1850s. The work of these three historians approach narratives of inscription or resistance by situating each text in the historical, political, and cultural contexts from which they have been generated.

American Marxist literary theorist Frederic Jameson's focus on the historical relationship between textual form and economic and political realities has application in these dynamics. In *The Political Unconscious* (1981, 80), Jameson contends that for the West, literary or cultural texts—and indeed, the archive—function to aesthetically or symbolically resolve dissonance of cultural structure and identity, and thus the legitimate the dominant social order. Since the mid-sixteenth century conquest of the Americas, constructions of the *indigene* have been inextricably bound to imperialism and other forms of racial ideology which have worked to symbolically resolve or occlude the ethical contradictions of colonial capitalism. In this tradition, Aboriginal women have been implicated in Western constructions of the dualism of nature and civilization in both gendered and racialized forms. Jameson proposes a series of interpretive frames to expose these cultural and national contradictions, wherein the act of reading is itself the act of reconstructing—a formation in which we can approach the tragedy of resistance instead as an agential mode of rewriting and remapping the narratives and images used to silence, supress, and exploit Aboriginal women.

By challenging the text (or archive), as a site of consignation and investigating what the text (or archive) pushes against or seeks to conceal; the act or reading and rewriting becomes here a mode of historicism in which archival texts claiming to represent Aboriginality are encountered as embodied, agential forces which exist within a reality which they also bear and construct, we are better situated to emphasize the social and political consequences of textual acts on the lives of Aboriginal women, such as the writing of Governor Phillip's settlement orders, or the construction of assimilation policy; but also to highlight the agency of textual resistances deployed against such acts.

However, Jameson's (1981, 80–1) cautions against both the underestimation of the symbolic, and the overemphasis of the agency of a text to reorganize and reconstruct reality, rests upon the assumption that history can only be grasped through the text. The issue with his assumption arises in that the radical other of Aboriginal perpetuity is—and should be—inaccessible to most forms of critical, logocentric, and historical discourse. Aboriginal epistemology, in contrast to these forms, shows that history has its own agency in its embodiment and presence in land and through ancestors. Time and history act upon place and person without being textually read: we may not always be aware of history, but history is always aware of us —a haunting which Harkin's spectropoetics seek to reveal. This understanding of the world is explicitly demonstrated in Wright's (2013) novel *The Swan Book*, a text which resists Western hermeneutic relationships in its depiction of political and environmental dystopia as its protagonist Oblivia Ethalyne struggles to achieve sovereignty over her own mind. The novel does not consolidate political, environmental, or cultural futures, rather, it presents a world in which mytho-poetic and socio-political representations coexist, just as they coexist as realities for Aboriginal people. Throughout the novel, terms of cultural reference and geographical signifiers shift with the changing climate: the desert becomes the swamp, as desert people become swamp people, and what might within a traditional Western dystopia be perceived as the collapse of nature is in fact an articulation of nature's agency to transform and reinscribe. In an earlier essay on the politics of writing, Wright (2002, 3) states that for Aboriginal people:

> All times are important to us. No time has ended and all worlds are possible [⋯] The world I try to inhabit in my writing is like looking at the ancestral tracks spanning our traditional country which, if I look at the land, combines all stories, all realities, from the ancient to the new, and it makes ones – like all the strands in a long rope. Our stories are like the music which feeds the soul and the heart, which sometimes flies above the bitterness of pure logic and rational thought [⋯]

Such articulations demonstrate that in the reading of Aboriginal literatures and expressions, it is not possible to draw distinctions between texts which instruct and offer interpretive strategies to engage with Aboriginal resistance, and the texts to which those strategies are to be applied. In Harkin's performance, her voice is triangulated through literary theory, archival poetics, and traditional weaving. It is implicit in the interrogations of this article that truth and fiction are relative concepts deeply embedded within structures of power and discourse, and it is in the act of reading and revealing that these structures are put to question.

As this article has already indicated, many of the textual forms in which these acts of resistance operate either bear the material and ideological legacies of colonial inscription, or are themselves colonial forms of text and textuality. Formal distinctions can be arbitrary for textual landscapes which largely have not acceded to the naturalization of Western modes, but are a useful collective device when considering those forms against which they are responding, and historical teleologies of hegemony and resistance. This section will consider early colonial letter writing and testimony against the mission and reserve system; the liminality of Aboriginal women's life writing in the twentieth century; and examples of contemporary film and visual art which incorporate and recontextualize the colonial archive.

In the nineteenth century, the written word was mobilized by Aboriginal men and women within a broader struggle to survive and resist colonization. Although education for Aboriginal women across the mission and reserve system was limited, there are still extensive records of forms of personal and political writing, such as personal correspondence and petitions to colonial authorities. In the *Maquarie Pen Anthology of Aboriginal Literature* (2008), Aboriginal literary scholar Peter Minter and Wiradjuri novelist Anita Heiss chart the development Aboriginal authorship of this first century, particularly observing texts concerned with the conditions of life for Aboriginal people under the Aborigines Protection Board and Aboriginal Welfare policies (2008, 2–3). I have discussed earlier the articulation of identity and entitlement in Maria Lock's letter to Governor Darling, and made reference to Annie Rich and Bessie Flower's respective negotiations of authority in their letter writing. Women also played key roles in the writing and transcription of petitions, and it was for this reason that Mary Ann Arthur wrote her complaint to the Colonial Secretary of Van Diemen's Land in 1846, which appears in the anthology. After writing a petition to the Queen of England to represent the interests of the Flinders Island Aboriginal community with her husband, Walter George Arthur, the couple received threats from the superintendent Henry Jeanneret. Mary's letter seeks leniency but does not ask for forgiveness, and rearticulates her complaint that 'we do not like to be his [Jeanneret] slaves nor wish our poor Country to be treated badly or made slaves of' (Arthur 1846, in Heiss and Minter 2008, 12). Over 50 years later, Keerrupjmara woman Maggie Mobourne wrote and circulated a petition to the Vice-Chairman of the Victorian Board for the Protection of Aborigines, protesting the treatment of Aboriginal people by Reverend Johann Stähle on the Lake Condah Mission (Mobourne 1900, in Heiss and Minter 2008, 18). Both these texts demonstrate Aboriginal women's awareness of the way in which they were misrepresented and misused by local authorities, and take narrative control over their rightful protests and complaints, often by bringing their concerns to the highest available powers.

Letters and correspondence also held a significant social and cultural function for Aboriginal women for their capacity to maintain kinship connections despite extensive displacement and community disruption suffered throughout the nineteenth century. van Toorn demonstrates this in her reading of Koorie woman Kitty Brangy's letter to her sister Edith at Coranderrk in 1881, and Diyari woman Rebecca Maltilina's correspondence with her friend Dorothea Ruediger in the early 1900s, written in both English and the Diyari language. Both examples use writing as a tool of social attachment, reaffirming relationships to individuals but also to country. From the deeply affectionate affirmations of kinship in Kitty's letter, van Toorn reconstructs the context of devastating frontier expansion throughout Victoria in the nineteenth century. Kitty's letter, which is signed with eight-three kisses and informs her sister of the births, deaths, and lost connections of the family; moves against the divisive and disconnecting function of this process. The capacity for writing to maintain connection to country and community is performed in Rebecca's letters to her white friend Dorothea, who remained living in Rebecca's homeland of Killalpannina after she was removed at the age of 17. These exchanges perform what van Toorn refers to as the act of sending something of oneself home to their traditional country (2006, 196–8).

Affirming exchanges are rare in the colonial archive of this period. While writing was certainly a way of maintaining relationships between Aboriginal women across the country, it was also the form in which Aboriginal women, such as Lena Austin and Margaret Green, could resist the bureaucratic dispersal of family groups, and provide their testimony to plead for the return of their children. In a time in which Aboriginal children are being removed from their families at rates between nine and fifteen times more likely than non-Aboriginal children, these records are crucial interventions into the narratives of neglect and abuse which have been attached to Aboriginal mothers.

The political function of Aboriginal writing was in no way diminished by its movement into more explicitly literary forms, such as poetry and fiction, in the latter half of the twentieth century. After decades of influence from Minjerriba poet and activist Oodgeroo Noonuccal, who used her poetry to advocate for the rights of Aboriginal people and culture and resist programs of cultural imperialism, two key texts of Aboriginal women's life-narratives were published in 1987 and 1988; Sally Morgan's *My Place*, which narrates the author's research into her family's Aboriginal history, and Glenyse Ward's *Wandering Girl*, which tells the story of Ward's removal from her family and life on Wandering Mission and as a domestic servant. Australian literary scholar Anne Brewster explicitly reads these memoirs for the agency and resistance of Aboriginal women in an emergent publishing space, and takes a critical approach to the suspicion they have been met with from non-Aboriginal literary authorities. Brewster observes that while autobiographical writing has historic significance for marginalized women, it is rarely considered literary. By invoking the social and political circumstances of a text's construction, and critiquing positions from which dominant groups are able to qualify and restrain Aboriginal women's narratives, Brewster (1995, 37) highlights the enunciative conditions of these texts: both in how they continue traditions of orality, and for their articulation of Aboriginal women's lives, particularly in those instances in which colonization disrupted their connections to country, community, and culture. While some critics have focused on esthetic qualities of these texts, and on how explicitly they engage with Western narrative forms, other approaches, such as Kokatha/Mirning academic Sonja Kurtzer's reading of *Wandering Girl*, highlight the volatility with which these early publications were subject to demands of authenticity and cultural performativity from both white and Aboriginal audiences (1998, in Grossman, 2003). These narratives marked a significant shift of Aboriginal contributions away from the figure of the 'native informant', into positions of authorial power in their narratives. This is particularly significant for Aboriginal women, whose knowledge was largely ignored by anthropologists throughout the nineteenth century.

Today, however, there is a healthy diversity of Aboriginal literary expression, with some six-thousand Aboriginal authors listed in the AusLit online database of Australian Literature. In particular, the anthology or special issue emerged in the 1980s as a communal, collaborative space to demonstrate the range and vitality of Aboriginal women's writing. Some anthologies, such as *The Intervention: An Anthology* (2016), edited by Heiss and New Zealand/Australian writer Rosie Scott; and *The Stolen Children: Their Stories* (1998), edited by Australian writer Carmel Bird, combine testimony, fiction, essays and poetry to organize around social and political issues. Some center Aboriginal women's experiences and knowledges, such as *The Strength of Us As Women: Black Women Speak* (2000) edited by Wirardjuri writer Kerry Reed-Gilbert. Others, such as *Paperbark: A Collection of Black Australian Writings* (1990) edited by Australian academics Stephen Muecke, Colin Johnson, Adam Shoemaker, and Aboriginal playwright and activist Jack Davis; *Untreated: Poems by Black Writers* (2002) edited by Wardaman academic Josie Douglas, and *Message Stick: Contemporary Aboriginal Writing* (1997) also edited by Reed-Gilbert, canvas the broader range of Aboriginal writing.[1]

Perhaps as a result of its commercial viability, visual art is the most familiar form of Aboriginal self-presentation for Australian and international audiences. The descriptor of 'Aboriginal art', as it is assigned by galleries, museums, and arts organizations, is a category most often applied to twentieth and twenty-first century realia, and has been highly influenced by the aesthetics of the Papunya Western Desert art movement of the 1970s. Langton argues that two synchronized phenomena during this time challenged the 'Stone Age' mentality through which Aboriginal people were viewed and understood in the first half of the century: the avid collection and circulation of Aboriginal art throughout Europe, as opposed to the Aboriginal skulls which had been distributed over the last 100 and 50 years, and spoke to its consumers with a grand narrative of the glory of colonialism; and the agency of Aboriginal artists who responded to this demand with their supply (Langton 1994, in Grossman 2003, 81–2).

Demands for authenticity and the performance of Aboriginality discussed earlier in relation to fiction and poetry writing by Aboriginal women are present also in the curation and cultivation of Aboriginal art; leading to what Langton (1994) observes as a suspicion of innovation and experimentation in form. Contemporary art by Aboriginal women resists the same legacies of colonial inscription present in other forms of discourse and expression, but are also compelled to answer to an arts culture which has, since the late 1930s, performed its own insidious forms of colonial-capitalist exploitation of Aboriginal creative productions. Non-Aboriginal art scholars, such as Susan McCulloch, have sought to restrain contemporary artists to notions of primitivism and geographical isolation, which has been widely contested by Aboriginal curators and artists such as Lin Onus (Yorta Yorta), Hetti Perkins (Arrernte/Kalkadoon), and Fiona Foley (Badtjala) (Langton 1994, in Grossman 2003, 84–7).

Brisbane born artist Tracey Moffatt, who with Foley and others was a founder of the Boomalli Aboriginal Arts Co-operative in 1987, is a photographer and filmmaker, widely known for her short films such as *Night Cries: A Rural Tragedy* (1990), and *Nice Coloured Girls* (1987). Both films engage explicitly with colonial forms of Aboriginal women's representation. Langton, who herself starred in the film, argues that *Night Cries* is a self-conscious fictionalization, which emphasizes an aesthetics of artifice to draw the audience's attention to the inherently fictionalized nature of representation (Langton 1993, 40). The film offers an alternative ending for Australian filmmaker Charles Chauvel's 1955 film *Jedda*, itself a form of archive, in which the film's namesake does not tragically perish at the hands of the noble savage Marbuck, but survives into adulthood to care for her elderly white foster mother. As Langton observes, it is a film which both affirms and restructures the boundaries of the primitive, casting a paradigm of Aboriginal masculinity as the enemy of both white and black cultures, and the Aboriginal woman as the native belle, unable to overcome her primeval instincts and ultimately a victim of the destructive telos of Aboriginal savagery. Thus, the central critique operating in Moffatt's nightmarish revision of colonial paternalism is visualized in the former pastoral homestead, isolated and decayed in alternate and deconstructive futurity (Langton 1993, 47). *Nice Coloured Girls*, Moffatt's first short film, is similarly intertextual; weaving a narrative of contemporary young Aboriginal women on a night out in Kings Cross, taking advantage of the lecherous white men they call 'captains'; with the narration of First Fleet naval officer William Bradley's diary observations of a young Aboriginal woman being played out through unsettling, abstracted documentary-esque scenes. This entwining of both contemporary and colonial narratives inscribes agency to the historical positioning of the women through their mobilization of paternalist encounters, and establishes a generational transmission of this agency through to their descendants. *Nice Coloured Girls* demonstrates the critical potential which arises from mobilizing archival representations of Aboriginal women, and challenges assumptions of their neutrality.

These themes are performed explicitly in a recent exhibition for the inaugural Aboriginal arts festival *Yirramboi*, funded by the City of Melbourne. The exhibition *Recentre; Sisters* features work from eight Aboriginal and Torres Strait Islander women on themes of female empowerment and resistance to colonial-patriarchy, exploring Moreton-Robinson's notion of 'tactical subjectivity', through which the lives of Indigenous women are constituted by Indigenous women 'through the simultaneousness of our compliance and resistance' (Moulton 2017). Wemba Wemba/Gunditjmara artist Paola Balla's piece *And the Matriarchs Sang* (2015, in Moulton 2017) traces images of Aboriginal women across sparse white-washed boards, reflecting personally on their lives and agency with short phrases such as, 'she was too proud/to not fight/back when he/hit her', and 'May we be safe/May we be free/from harm/May we be happy'. The exhibition also features the recovery of traditional women's practices, such as weaving and cloak-making, through the work of Lee Darroch (Yorta Yorta/Boon Wurrung/Mutti Mutti), and Lorraine Connelly-Northey (Waradgerie), who use both customary materials and found objects to create their works. Presented alongside photos of both political protest and colonial caricature from artists Kimba Thompson (Wiradjuri) and Destiny Deacon (G'ua G'ua/Erub/Mer), these works are situated in ancestral legacies but also project into reclaimed futures. It is in this dynamic of past, present, and future as liberative and non-linear, Harkin tells us, that we embody and inherit future-memory, that we bring memory into futurity (5).

Conclusion: here and now

It must be recognized that Aboriginal women have invested significant amounts of intellectual and emotional labor into the articulation and safeguarding of cultural and ethical protocols around the representation of Aboriginal knowledges, experiences, and identities. Merium/Wuthathi laywer Terri Janke and Murawari playwright Jane Harrison have both produced recommendations and guidelines for the representation of Aboriginal stories and subjects in Australian film and theater. Noonuccal academic Karin L. Martin's doctoral thesis *Please Knock Before You Enter: Aboriginal Regulation of Outsiders and the Implications for Researchers* (2008) is an enormously comprehensive study of ethical procedure in the engagement, research, and publication of information pertaining to Aboriginal communities. In 2016, Wiradjuri academic and poet Jeanine Leane wrote on the politics of non-Aboriginal novelists telling 'other people's stories', and the various challenges which contemporary Aboriginal writing presents to established traditions of the settler canon for literary journal *Overland*. In the same year, Waanyi novelist Alexis Wright articulated the material and political stakes of outsiders telling the stories of marginalized and vulnerable communities, with examples regarding the Northern Territory Intervention and Don Dale Youth Detention Centre for *Meanjin*. These works perform the power and authority of Aboriginal matriarchal womanhood, and demonstrate Huggin's assertion that the increase in Aboriginal publishing from the 1990s acts to reclaim place and history in Australian society, by taking agency and demanding responsibility in the narratives produced by and about Aboriginal lives.

For Aboriginal woman, 'the spectres of the archive do not rest' (Harkin 4). The works discussed in this essay both haunt, and are haunted by colonial visions. This article has aimed to articulate the extensive history and diversity of Aboriginal women's expressions against colonial representations of their lands, cultures, and womanhood, as an offering not just for the many voices which have been raised in resistance, but also for the many who have been silenced. These commentaries, reflections, and re-creations are enabled by another field of Aboriginal women's resistance: that of Aboriginal women working in education, academia and research. These acts, along with the work taking place beyond institutionalized academia in multiple spaces and disciplines each day which remain unrecognized by the general public, are necessary interventions into the networks of misrepresentation and misunderstanding which continue to shape colonial constructions of Aboriginal women, but more importantly, they offer for their own communities self-presentations and self-images which are responsible and recognizable in the face of ongoing vilification by settlers. By meeting work which enters into colonial archives to document and challenge these inscriptions with the work Aboriginal women do every day to resist, rewrite, and reclaim their identities, we create a space in which to listen to the extensive work which has been done by Aboriginal women to heal these legacies.

Note

1. While the emergence of Aboriginal publishing houses, Aboriginal editors, and Aboriginal writing initiatives have significantly expanded opportunities for Aboriginal writers, as I have written elsewhere, there are still inherent issues in the reception and intellectual engagement with the field of Aboriginal literature (EA Corr 2016).

Disclosure statement

No potential conflict of interest was reported by the author.

References

Behrendt, L. 2016. *Finding Eliza: Power and Colonial Storytelling*. Queensland: University of Queensland Press.

Bird, C. 1998. *The Stolen Children: Their Stories*. North Sydney, NSW: Random House Australia.

Bowd, D. G. 1979. *Macquarie Country: A History of the Hawkesbury*. Rev ed. Sydney: Library of Australian History.

Brewster, A. 1995. *Literary Formations: Post-Colonialism, Nationalism, Globalism*. Melbourne: Melbourne University Press.

Conor, L. 2016. *Skin Deep: Settler Impressions of Aboriginal Women*. Western Australia: University of Western Australia Publishing.

Corr, B. 2016. "Pondering the Abyss: The Language of Settlement on the Hawkesbury Nepean Rivers." http://www.nangarra.com.au/docs/pta_all.pdf.

Corr, E. A. 2016. "Shame and Contemporary Australian Poetics." *Rabbit Poetry Journal* 21: 117–127.

Davis, J., S. Muecke, M. Narogin (Colin Johnson), and A. Shoemaker. 1990. *Paperbark: A Collection of Black Australian Writing*. Brisbane, QLD: University of Queensland Press.

Derrida, J., and E. Prenowitz. (trans). 1995. "Archive Fever: A Freudian Impression." *Diacritics* 25 (2): 9–63. doi:10.2307/465144.

Douglas, J. 2002. *Untreated: Poems by Black Writers*. Alice Springs, NT: IAD Press.

Fletcher, J. J. 1989. *Clean, Clad, and Courteous: A History of Aboriginal Education in New South Wales*. Carlton, NSW: J. Fletcher.

Grossman, M. (Ed). 2003. *Blacklines: Contemporary Critical Writing by Indigenous Australians*. Victoria: Melbourne University Press.

Harkin, N. 2014. "The Poetics of (Re)Mapping Archives: Memory in the Blood." *JASAL: Journal of the Association of Australian Literature* 14 (3): 1–14.

Heiss, A., and P. Minter. 2008. *Macquarie Pen Anthology of Aboriginal Literature*. Sydney: Allen and Unwin.

Heiss, A., and R. Scott. 2016. *The Intervention: An Anthology*. Kensington, NSW: University of New South Wales Press.

Huggins, J. 1993. "Always Was Always Will Be."*Australian Historical Studies* 25 (100): 459–464.

Jameson, F. 1981. *The Political Unconscious: Narrative as a Socially Symbolic Act*. New York, NY: Cornell University Press.

Kahaleole Hall, L. 2009. "Navigating Our Own 'Sea of Islands': Remapping a Theoretical Space for Hawaiian Women and Indigenous Feminism." *Wicazo Sa Review* 24 (2): 15–38. doi:10.1353/wic.0.0038.

Langton, M. 1993. *'Well, I Heard It on the Radio and Saw It on the Television…': An Essay for the Australian Film Commission on the Politics and Aesthetics of Film-Making by and about Indigenous People and Things*. Sydney: Screen Australia.

Martin, K. L. 2008. *Please Knock before You Enter: Aboriginal Regulation of Outsiders and the Implications for Researchers*. Flaxton, QLD: Post Pressed.

Martiniello, J. 2002. "Voids, Voices and Story without End." *Southerly* 62 (2): 91–97.

Moffatt, T. 1987. *Nice Coloured Girls*. Film. Australia.

Moffatt, T. 1990. *Night Cries: A Rural Tragedy*. Film. Sydney: Australian Film Commission.

Moreton-Robinson, A. 2000. *Talkin' up to the White Woman: Indigenous Women and Feminism*. Queensland: University of Queensland Press.

Moulton, K. 2017. *Recentre; Sisters*. Exhibition Catalogue. Melbourne: City Gallery, for Yirramboi Festival.

Reed-Gilbert, K. 1997. *Message Stick: Contemporary Aboriginal Writing*. Compiled by Kerry Reed-Gilbert. Alice Springs, NT: IAD Press.

Reed-Gilbert, K. 2000. *The Strength Of Us as Women: Black Women Speak*. Belconnen, Canberra: Ginninderra Press.

Russell, L. 2002. *A Little Bird Told Me*. New South Wales: Allen & Unwin.

Russell, L. 2013. "Indigenous Knowledge and the Archives: Accessing Hidden History and Understandings." *Australian Academic & Research Libraries* 36 (2): 161–171. doi:10.1080/00048623.2005.10721256.

Said, E. 1993. *Culture and Imperialism*. London: Vintage.

van Toorn, P. 2006. *Writing Never Arrives Naked: Early Aboriginal Cultures of Writing in Australia*. Canberra: Aboriginal Studies Press.

Wright, A. 2002. "Politics of Writing." *Southerly* 62 (2): 10–20.

Wright, A. 2013. *The Swan Book*. Sydney: Giramondo.

The shape of free speech: rethinking liberal free speech theory

Anshuman A. Mondal

ABSTRACT

Noting the apparent inconsistency in attitudes towards free speech with respect to anti-Semitism and Islamophobia in western liberal democracies, this article works through the problem of inconsistency within liberal free speech theory, arguing that this symptomatically reveals an *aporia* that exposes the inability of liberal free speech theory to account for the ways in which free speech actually operates in liberal social orders. Liberal free speech theory conceptualizes liberty as smooth, continuous, homogeneous, indivisible and extendable without interruption until it reaches the outer limits. This makes it difficult for liberal free speech theory to account for restrictions that lie within those outer limits, and therefore for the ways in which restraints, restrictions and closures are always already at work within the lived experience of liberty, for it is these – and the inconsistencies they give rise to – that give freedom its particular texture and timbre in any given social and cultural context. The article concludes with an alternative 'liquid' theory of free speech, which accounts for the 'shaping' of liberty by social forces, culture and institutional practices.

Abbreviations: UK: United Kingdom; MP: Member of Parliament.

In the spring and summer of 2016, the UK Labour Party was engulfed in controversy surrounding the tolerance or otherwise of anti-Semitism within its membership. The suspension of Naz Shah MP, then a parliamentary aide to the Shadow Chancellor, for anti-semitic postings on her Facebook page during the height of the Gaza crisis in 2014 – prior to her election as an MP – precipitated ongoing media coverage, and the ensuing furore led the leader of the party, Jeremy Corbyn – someone well known for his pro-Palestinian politics and long-standing criticisms of Israel's policies towards its Occupied Territories – to establish an independent enquiry and commission; in turn, the UK Parliament Home Affairs Select Committee also established a separate enquiry into the scope and extent of anti-Semitism within British political parties (Stewart 2016; Home Affairs Committee 2016). Both the extent of the controversy and the subsequent commissions of enquiry were a signal of the intolerability of anti-Semitism within British political and public discourse. This can be contrasted with the ways in which Islamophobia merits no such urgent attention; indeed, the former Conservative cabinet minister and now incisive and trenchant critic of government policy towards the UK's Muslim communities, Baronness Sayeeda Warsi, has gone so far as to suggest that Islamophobia is not only tolerable within British public and political life, it has become so normalized within both political and civil society that it has 'passed the dinner party test' (Batty 2011).

The question posed by this contrast between the intolerability of anti-Semitism and the tolerance, even normalization, of Islamophobia is why the former falls under the rubric of 'hate speech' and the latter does not, or, to put it another way, why the former is not protected by the rubric of freedom of expression, whilst the other does indeed appear to be. Indeed, the intolerability of expressions of anti-semitic sentiment has been intensified by the UK government's recent adoption of the International Holocaust Remembrance Alliance's definition of anti-Semitism, which suggests that 'over-sweeping condemnation' of Israel would be a form of anti-Semitism, as would any criticisms of its policies as a state if those were conceived in relation to Israel as 'a Jewish collectivity' (Walker 2016). This potentially expands the legal proscriptions against expressions of anti-semitic sentiment from 'hate speech' to certain forms of political criticism, not just of the state of Israel but Zionism as a political movement and ideology more generally, on the grounds that 'Zionism, at its core, is the belief based on the state of Israel to exist [...] connection to Israel is a key part of Jewish identity' (Weisfeld 2016). It is this connection between Jewish identity and the state of Israel that potentially makes criticisms of Israel and Zionism anti-semitic and therefore a form of hate speech that warrants no protection on the grounds of freedom of expression. On the other hand, Muslim protests against the ways in which the Prophet has been portrayed have consistently failed to muster any support on the grounds that restrictions on such portrayals would constitute an intolerable infringement of the right to free speech even though there is arguably a deeper connection between the Prophet and Muslim identity than that between Israel/Zionism and Jewish identity since the latter predated both the state of Israel and political Zionism, whereas the Prophet is the foundational figure of the Muslim faith: without him, there is no Muslim identity as such.

Whilst it is notable that many of the public figures, politicians and intellectual figures who vociferously supported the exposure of and clampdown on contemporary expressions of anti-Semitism *also* vociferously opposed Muslim arguments for protection from freedom of speech, my purpose in this article will not be to explore any arguments concerning hypocrisy, cognitive dissonance, double standards and so on, but rather to take this discrepancy as a point of departure for examining the question of inconsistency and discrepancy within contemporary and historical liberal theorizations of freedom of expression, insofar as these theorizations are the most dominant frames through which issues and controversies concerning freedom of expression are approached. This question is particularly pertinent because it compels us to critique liberal free speech theory, which, since its modern formulation by John Stuart Mill in *On Liberty* ([1859] 2011), has been structured around a binary opposition between free expression and censorship that is precisely the reason why any inconsistency in the manifestation of liberty in actually existing liberal social orders is itself such a symptomatic *aporia* that generates confusion and anxiety among liberal free speech advocates and, most of all, stimulates an urgent compulsion on their part to straighten the crooked timber of liberty as and when they can. Through a symptomatic reading of this attitude towards inconsistency, I will argue that such an aporia in fact exposes the inability of liberal free speech theory to theorize adequately the ways in which free speech actually operates in liberal social orders. In turn, this illuminates the inadequacies of liberalism's theorization of freedom more generally, precisely because liberal thought is constituted by an opposition between freedom and power (which gathers under its rubric all the other antitheses to liberty such as tyranny, oppression, censorship and so on) that does not, in fact, hold and which leads, therefore, to an under-theorization of the ways in which power itself structures and shapes what is experienced as 'freedom'.

The antipathy towards inconsistency in liberal thought is registered in various tropes and styles of argument within liberal free speech discourse. '[O]ne of the weaknesses of free speech rhetoric', writes Lee (1990, 34), 'has been the tendency to stretch support all the way from political speech to pornographic expression, under the mistaken belief that arguments for one must apply to the other'. As I have noted elsewhere, this involves a logic of substitutability that renders context meaningless and superfluous, a logic that can trace its pedigree all the way back to Mill (Mondal 2014, 36). As Haworth (1998, 27) has noted, Mill rests his general arguments for freedom of expression on what Mill himself calls his 'prioritisation of thought and discussion', which means that he (Mill) assumes that the case for 'that way of collectively striving for the truth and the case for other freedoms such as the "absolute liberty of expressing and publishing opinions" *are equivalent*' (emphasis in original). In other words, the freedom appropriate to what Haworth calls 'the seminar room' is, by extension, applicable to all other contexts until it reaches the point where liberty may legitimately be curtailed; conversely, any disturbance or discontinuity of this smooth extensibility is deemed an inappropriate infringement of liberty. In order to extend the continuity of liberty on which his argument rests to the greatest possible extent, Mill is compelled to extend it as far as possible, to the outer limits where the law may legitimately intervene (in his case, the famous example of direct incitement of a mob standing outside a corn dealer's house).

Mill thus introduces into modern liberal free speech theory a notion of liberty that exists as if on a single plane: smooth, continuous, homogeneous, indivisible and extendable without interruption until it reaches the outer limits. The dominant governing metaphor here is that of the horizon, the point beyond which freedom no longer obtains – hence the binary opposition between freedom of expression and censorship. The nature of freedom is unidimensional, reducible to the single aspect of its reach, its extension. From this perspective, only the outer limits signify as legitimate restraints upon liberty; every restriction or regulation within these limits are aberrations because there can and should not be any irregularity, distortion, heterogeneity, discontinuity or inconsistency. This is why the 'slippery slope' argument plays such an important role in liberal free speech advocacy, for its rhetorical function is to keep the horizon at bay, to raise the spectre that its encroachment signals a dimunition of liberty *across the board* precisely because the logic of smooth, planar continuity necessitates that any encroachment at one point signals an encroachment at *all* points – visually speaking, one might see it as the conjuring of a circle being narrowed. It is telling, moreover, that the trope works by introducing an element of verticality (the slope) that upsets what should otherwise be a smooth, horizontal plane.

In liberal free speech theory – and indeed, in liberal theory generally – freedom is defined by the outer limits in *quantitative* terms as 'scope' and 'extent', which are terms that feature regularly in liberal discourses on freedom of expression. *Qualitative* discussions of liberty, including ethical questions about the moral rights and wrongs of exercising one's freedom of expression, insofar as they feature at all, appear in liberal arguments only as an adjunct or corollary to the quantitative need to expand the reach of freedom as far as possible. Thus, for example, whilst Mill does indeed talk about positive liberty, by far the greater emphasis in *On Liberty* is on negative liberty. Indeed, his 'very simple principle' that is the foundation of his entire argument is a conception of liberty that is negative:

> The object of this Essay is to assert one very simple principle [...] that the sole end for which mankind are warranted, individually or collectively, in interfering with the liberty of action of any of their number is self-protection. That the only purpose for which power can be rightfully exercised over any member of a civilized community, against his will, is to prevent harm. (Mill [1859] 2011, 14)

Tellingly, when Mill does discuss positive liberty, he calls it 'development' rather than liberty, and he tends to position it as exterior to liberty itself,

> [t]hese are cases in which the reasons against interference do not turn upon the principle of liberty: the question is not about restraining the actions of individuals but helping them [...] These are not questions of liberty, and are connected with that subject only by remote tendencies; but they are questions of development. (Mill [1859] 2011, 122–23)

For Mill, liberty involves establishing the conditions in which it is possible for individuals to pursue as many 'experiments in living' as possible so as to contribute to the progressive development of humankind; each individual's capacity for development can and should be nurtured, but this principally involves leaving them alone as far as possible to get on with it. The positive liberty to which Mill turns as the justification of his argument for liberty thereby rests on a predicate, the negative liberty that enables the conditions in which it can develop and flourish. More recently, Mill's typically nine-teenth-century moral register has been eschewed by liberal discourse on free expression, which has adopted a strictly legalistic approach that concerns itself with where the horizon line curtailing the right to freedom of expression should be drawn, leaving aside all the ethical questions germane to the exercise of one's freedom as what might be termed a 'moral remainder' (Mondal 2014, 3). Such an approach, by definition, emphasizes negative liberty and is grounded more in the anti-consequentialist liberal tradition that emerged precisely in order to address some of the weaknesses of Mill's consequentialist, utilitarian approach (Rawls 2005). However, in grounding free speech in the discourse of 'natural' rights so as to avoid Mill's consequentialism, this tradition of liberal thought in fact accentuates and intensifies Mill's 'planar' model because it is even more rigidly binary in terms of the constitutive distinction between freedom and its other and therefore stronger in its emphasis on negative liberty: as a natural right, freedom of expression can only be limited by other rights. Without the backup, as it were, of consequentialism's 'goal' or 'purpose', which might justify limits on free expression *within* the horizon of liberty, any restrictions that *do* appear within that horizon as part of everyday lived experience become all the more magnified as an intolerable incursion into the empire of liberty. This may be why contemporary free speech advocates, especially the more absolutist of them, draw so heavily on anti-consequentialist arguments in their rhetoric even as they simultaneously (and contradictorily) deploy Millian arguments as well (Mondal 2014).[1]

This emphasis on negative liberty, then, both generates and is of a piece with the binarism that is so typical of liberal thought. Liberal conceptions of freedom work in terms of a binary between freedom and its other, be it oppression, suppression, censorship, regulation and so on, these antithetical terms being generally substitutable. Again, one can turn to Mill as the exemplar if not the source of this structure of thinking within modern liberalism. *On Liberty* draws a series of sharp distinctions in order to scaffold its argument, the principal one being that between an autonomous and sovereign individual, on the one hand, and society (often figured pejoratively as a 'mass'), on the other. As Alan Ryan notes, even other liberals have found Mill's arguments in *On Liberty* to be 'excessively individualistic', but although many of them may have softened the edges of the opposition, they have always upheld it since the sovereign individual is at the core of liberalism: it makes it what it is (Ryan, 'Introduction' in Mill [1859] 2011, xxii). Much depends on the difference between what Mill calls 'the external relations of the individual' and 'all that portion of a person's life which affects only himself' (18). From this opposition, Mill proposes that the latter is

> [...] the appropriate region of human liberty [which] comprises, first, the inward domain of consciousness; demanding liberty of conscience, *in the most comprehensive sense*; liberty of thought and feeling; *absolute* freedom of opinion and sentiment on all subjects, practical or speculative, scientific, moral, or theological. (Mill [1859] 2011, my emphasis)

He then goes on to suggest that

> [t]he liberty of expressing and publishing opinions may seem to fall under a different principle, since it belongs to that part of the conduct of an individual which concerns other people; but, being almost of as much importance as the liberty of thought itself, and resting in great part on the same reasons, is practically inseparable from it.

It is worth dwelling at some length on this because, having established an opposition between 'that portion of a person's life which affects only himself' and 'the external relations of the individual', he then goes on to suggest that with regard to liberty of conscience and the liberty to express and publish opinions, this distinction does not in fact hold, that the latter is in fact 'practically inseparable' from the former even though it 'may seem to fall under a different principle, since it belongs to that part of the conduct of an individual which concerns other people'. This auto-deconstruction of the fundamental premises of his argument is highly significant and has profound implications on how we might conceptualize not just freedom of expression but also freedom more generally and the question of the individual/subject in relation to them, which I will discuss in due course. But for now it suffices that we should note that with respect to freedom of expression, Mill's sleight of hand enables him to transfer that which is properly internal to the individual to the world of external relations and thereby endow upon that latter world – of expressing and publishing opinions – all the properties of the former. That is, it enables Mill to *extend* the 'absolute' freedom of opinion, which is proper to the interiority of individual conscience, to the external world of publishing and expression, and thereby continue that extension along the singular plane of liberty so conceived right out to the outer limits.

It is precisely because the external world of publishing and expression should mirror, by extension, the internal world of the conscience – the autonomous mind which should be allowed to entertain 'all subjects' – that Mill's arguments for 'liberty of thought and discussion' in the second chapter of *On Liberty* turn on the opposition between openness and closure. Since the absolute sovereignty of the conscience is carried over into the external world of expressing and publishing opinions, Mill argues that the 'lists' should be kept perpetually 'open' (28) so that any individual can access any and all possible ideas even though this does, in fact, stand in tension with his other argument that freedom of expression is necessary in order to enable the 'truth' to be ascertained (comprising his famous 'infallibility', 'testing' and 'partiality' arguments). His martial metaphors – e.g. 'both teachers and learners go to sleep at their post, as soon as there is no enemy in the field' (50) – when used as a vehicle for this epistemological argument, would suggest that the truth vanquishes falsehood. But if this is the case, then the trope of infinite and perpetual openness to all possible ideas must, by the very process of arriving at the truth, involve a form of closure that Mill would otherwise suggest is an intolerable infringement of liberty. He thus admits that '[w]rong opinions and practices gradually yield to fact and argument' and that

> As mankind improve [sic], the number of doctrines which are no longer disputed or doubted will be constantly on the increase: and the well-being of mankind may almost be measured by the number and gravity of the truths which have reached the point of being uncontested. The cessation, on one question after another, of serious controversy, is one of the necessary incidents of the consolidation of opinion; a consolidation as salutary in the case of true opinions, as it is dangerous and noxious when the opinions are erroneous.

Perhaps realizing, however, what the implications are for his insistence on infinite and perpetual openness, he then goes on to suggest that

> though this gradual narrowing of the bounds of diversity of opinion is necessary in both senses of the term, being at once inevitable and indispensable, we are not therefore obliged to conclude that all its consequences must be beneficial. The loss of so important an aid to the intelligent and living apprehension of a truth, as is afforded by the necessity of explaining it to, or defending it against, opponents, though not sufficient to outweigh, is no trifling drawback from, the benefit of its universal recognition. Where this advantage can no longer be had, I confess I should like to see the teachers of mankind endeavouring to provide a substitute for it; some contrivance for making the difficulties of the question as present to the learner's consciousness, as if they were pressed upon him by a dissentient champion, eager for his conversion. (51)

Having so vigorously argued that the reason freedom of expression is necessary is to enable the truth to emerge, Mill is here confronted with the implacable implications of that logic in the form of an admission that if freedom of expression is a means to an end (truth), that end will itself restrict the very freedom he argues is required to get there. He is forced, then, to invent a rather lame artificial simulacrum of freedom ('some contrivance') concocted by the 'teachers of mankind' in order to sustain that which is, on the one hand, absolutely necessary to human 'development' but is, on the other, oriented eventually towards the cessation of both 'development' and the need for freedom. Against this, Mill is forced to assert that the lists should somehow be kept open even though it is at odds with his argument about truth in order to keep at bay the auto-deconstructive implications, namely, that *the logic of closure secretly inhabits the fabric of freedom because it is not its antithesis or its 'other' but its necessary supplement, on which the concept of freedom depends.*

In the next section of this article, I will attempt to show how this supplementarity is at work in 'free' societies, but for now, it is worth re-stating that if, in the course of both his argument that establishes the premises of liberty and the subsequent discussion of applications and practical consequences, Mill is compelled to blur the lines of the sharp distinctions he draws in order to establish his 'very simple principle', those distinctions are nevertheless the structural foundations of his view of liberty and this bequeaths to subsequent liberal thought a note of regret concerning any exceptions that might necessarily arise in the translation of liberal theory into lived experience. Even the most pragmatic of liberals see restraints on freedom as a regrettable but unavoidable necessity, thus suggesting that restraint (or closure) is inimical to freedom and antithetical to it. While many contemporary thinkers writing within the broad liberal tradition have addressed liberal free speech theory's limitations with respect to hate speech with some, like Jeremy Waldron and the critical race theorists, demonstrating that Mill's 'harm principle' extends to forms of speech beyond direct incitement (Waldron 2012; Matsuda et al. 1993), and others addressing the tension that consequently arises between liberty and equality (Levin 2010; Saunders 2011), I would suggest that we should go further and deconstruct the constitutive oppositions of liberalism in order to attend to the restraints, restrictions and closures that are always already at work within the lived experience of liberty, for it is these – and the inconsistencies they give rise to – that give freedom its particular texture and timbre in any given social and cultural context.

Discursive liquidity: shaping freedom of speech

In contrast to the liberal conception of freedom as 'planar' and unidimensional, I would like to amplify and substantiate Talal Asad's (2011, 6763 [Kindle]) intuition that social forces, culture and institutional practices 'shape' freedom, especially freedom of expression, in particular, context-specific and historically determined ways. Rather than visualizing freedom in terms of its scope and extent, across a flat and uniform social space that is emptied of context, I suggest we conceptualize liberty in terms of forces and flows channelled by and through an irregular and uneven terrain. From this perspective, as regards freedom of expression in particular, discourse can be conceptualized as elemental, as 'liquid'; it will follow whatever channels it can and fill the available space.[2] The freedom of discourse, then, is not one of being or not being free, of having or not having free speech. In so far as discourse is plastic, malleable, freedom of discourse is channelled, shaped, sculpted, and, like flows of liquid, may in turn channel and sculpt. Some of the forces that shape free speech are dense, have great mass and, like the earth itself, are only slowly and incrementally modified: these are the great institutional bulwarks, law, the state, the bureaucratic machinery; others are like shoals of sand, as much shaped by as shaping the currents: civil society, culture, ideology, moral norms and values. The social terrain within which liberty is lived is, then, something like that represented by an ordnance survey map marked by contours indicating gradients and degrees of resistance and obstruction.

If we were to illustrate the ways in which this conception of free expression is at work in actually existing free societies, we might first point to the institutional landmarks that mark the terrain through which it flows, in particular, the legal statutes and provisions through which the power of the state to shape freedom is enforced. In relation to the discrepancy with which I began this article, one might point to the ways in which the flow of anti-semitic expression is intensely obstructed by the incitement to racial hatred provisions of the Public Order Act 1986 which encompasses 'racialised' religious groups such as Sikhs and Jews but does not cover other religious groups such as Muslims, Hindus and Christians, although the UK's blasphemy laws would have performed an adjacent function with respect to Christians until their abolition in 2008. In contrast, although the Racial and Religious Hatred Act 2006 (RRHA) was framed as an extension of the protection against incitement to hatred enjoyed by Jews and Sikhs to other religious groups, its passage into law was itself shaped by cultural and ideological forces that took great pains to ensure that the extensive protections afforded racialized groups against hate speech in the 1986 Public Order Act were *not* carried over into the new Act (Mondal 2014, 185–192).

These attenuating forces accepted the existing bulwarks on free expression – by, for example, accepting the need for limitations on freedom of expression with regard to certain classes of hate speech – but mobilized on behalf of particular conceptions of 'free speech' in order to ensure that the terrain of free expression was not altered so as to materially obstruct free expression with respect to other, non-racialized religious identities. Consequently, the Racial and Religious Hatred Act 2006 was effectively rendered a 'dead letter'. This partially explains, then, the inconsistency in the UK with regard to anti-semitic and Islamophobic expression, but it must be borne in mind that this is itself part of a wider terrain shaping free expression in the UK, which includes legal statutes that restrict expression with regard to the right to protest; copyright; the restriction of access to forms of expression based on age; the prohibition of certain forms of expression because of their exploitation and abuse of other persons; laws on libel, slander, privacy and so on. All these legal provisions constitute a jagged patchwork of restrictions and restraints that channel speech and expression, with varying degrees of intensity and force.

However, such legal landmarks are but one dimension of the ways in which expression is shaped. As the above example of the RRHA demonstrates, if the terrain through which expression flows is sculpted and shaped by ideological and cultural forces that are themselves articulated by forms of expression that are channelled by and through it, then the lie of the land, so to speak, is itself complexly determined by the dialectic between what is expressed and the limits to expression. If the Public Order and Racial and Religious Hatred Acts constitute two particular legal landmarks which channel understandings of permissible and impermissible speech with respect to religious identity, then these are themselves shaped by cultural and ideological framings of 'religion' 'race' and identity. As Meer (2008) has noted, wider understandings about religion and race as 'voluntary' and 'involuntary' identities, respectively, are at work within contemporary British society, and I have argued at length elsewhere how these wider understandings fed into the specific debates that surrounded the introduction of the RRHA in ways that decisively shaped and attenuated the form in which it eventually arrived onto the statute books (Mondal 2014, 186–188). Beyond these are more general ideological configurations impalpably and imperceptibly shaping, for example, perceptions and prejudices pertaining to particular religious identities such as Muslims and Jews.

Liberal free speech theory finds it acutely difficult to account for the ways in which culture and ideology predetermine the shape and flow of free expression principally because, following Mill, there is an aversion to closure. Moreover, there is little recognition of the ways in which closure – that is, the ways in which all possible ideas are *not* always and perpetually available to any given individual – relates to *foreclosure*, those predetermined and pre-inscribed limits not just to *expression* but also *thought*. This is principally because, on the one hand, liberal theory's reliance on the sovereign individual relies on an abjuring of any substantive theory of subjectivity as, for example, has developed in various non-liberal accounts such as Marxism, psychoanalysis, structuralism and post-structuralism and, on the other, because the individual's sovereignty would be inevitably and always already compromised by any theory that presupposes not only that this individual's autonomy is not a pre-given axiom but, in fact, is impossible.

Mill does, in fact, come close to acknowledging something akin to a theory of hegemony; indeed, it is paradoxically central to the argument of *On Liberty*, as is evident in the above quotation about 'the truths which have reached the point of being uncontested' being the consequence of an 'inevitable and indispensable' process. His principal concern is not with political tyranny, as such, although, like every liberal he is of course opposed to it; rather, in *On Liberty*, he is more concerned with the 'moral coercion' exerted by society on individuals to conform to certain expected norms of thought and behaviour. It is on the grounds of resisting this social pressure that he makes his case for liberty of conscience, of thought and expression and of pursuing one's own course in life as long as one does not harm or interfere with the life and liberty of others. At times, he explicitly suggests that the effect of this is to foreclose what might be thought or even perceived by any given individual: 'In our times', he writes,

> from the highest class of society down to the lowest, every one lives as under the eye of a hostile and dreaded censorship …. I do not mean that they choose what is customary, in preference to what suits their own inclination. *It does not occur to them to have any inclination, except for what is customary*. (Mill [1859] 2011, 70, my emphasis)

This seems to be very closely aligned to a Gramscian theory of hegemony, but if this is the effect of social coercion, such that an individual appears to consent to their own oppression, then this not only undermines the individual's autonomy of thought, but also forecloses any possibility of thinking otherwise: '[a]nd thus is kept up a state of things very satisfactory to some minds, because, without the unpleasant process of fining or imprisoning anybody, it maintains all prevailing opinions outwardly undisturbed' (39). Again Mill here threatens to undermine his own argument, so he is compelled to state that '[o]ur merely social intolerance kills no one, roots out no opinions, but induces men to disguise them, or to abstain from any active effort for their diffusion' (ibid.). If social coercion 'roots out no opinions', then this suggests that in the minds of men all possibilities are always infinitely open, but the effect of the coercion is simply to keep a lid on the expression of them. This notion of closure is more congenial to Mill than the implied foreclosure he admits elsewhere because, as we have seen, one of the structuring oppositions upholding his argument is the one between openness and closure; foreclosure, on the other hand, undercuts this opposition and compromises the autonomy of the individual. If the individual is not autonomous, if what s/he thinks is not a matter of rational choice, but an effect of power, of structural relations in society, of unconscious and irrational motivations, then s/he is not and cannot possibly be the 'sole author' (Smith 2012) of themselves and of what they say: they are, instead, subject to pressures external to themselves – thereby undercutting the basis of Mill's 'very simple principle'.

It is, for this reason, that Mill turns Marxian conceptions of power and ideology on their head: Mill is concerned with the social 'tyranny' of the majority over an embattled minority, whereas the Marxian tradition is concerned with the ways in which ideology enables and sustains the hegemony of a minority over a majority. This minoritarian emphasis in Mill is a strand of liberal thought that resonates particularly strongly in contemporary free speech advocates who portray themselves as an embattled minority defending enlightenment rationalism (and, *sotto voce*, male white privilege) from the tyranny of 'political correctness'. And just as Mill's pressing need to quarantine the rationally autonomous and sovereign individual from social tyranny blinded him to the pressure of structural forces he is elsewhere forced to admit but nonetheless keep at bay, so too does contemporary liberal thought continue to find difficulty in accounting for the effect of power relations and structural forces, nowhere more so than in the circulation and flow of ideas, opinions, and forms of discourse. 'All the political changes of the age promote [social conformism and mass mediocrity]', writes Mill in chapter two of *On Liberty*:

> since they all tend to raise the low and to lower the high. Every extension of education promotes it, because education brings people under common influences, and gives them access to the general stock of facts and sentiments. Improvements in the means of communication promote it, by bringing the inhabitants of distant places into personal contact, and keeping up a rapid flow of changes of residence between one place and another. The increase of commerce and manufactures promotes it, by diffusing more widely the advantages of easy circumstances, and opening all objects of ambition, even the highest, to general competition, whereby the desire of rising becomes no longer the character of a particular class, but of all classes. A more powerful agency than even all these, in bringing about a general similarity among mankind, is the complete establishment, in this and other free countries, of the ascendancy of public opinion in the State [...] [which ensures] there ceases to be any social support for nonconformity – any ... protection [of] opinions and tendencies at variance with those of the public. (83)

It is difficult to see how under conditions of such extensive material pressure it could ever be possible for the 'diversity of opinion' that gives rise to individuality to remain perpetually and infinitely open, especially given that he concludes here by saying that the greatest effect of such material pressure is on the conformism of 'public opinion' and its effect on government. What Mill is doing here is what he does elsewhere too: gesturing beyond closure towards an understanding of foreclosure not merely as an effect of political suppression or even psychological coercion but as something that *materially* structures 'free' societies.

Politics and the shaping of free speech

There is also another way in which freedom of expression is channelled and shaped by social forces, and this is by what I have elsewhere termed the 'politics of free speech' (Mondal 2014). This politics is, of course, most visible during public controversies over free speech itself, but by far the most significant way in which the politics of free speech shapes and channels the flow of social discourse and circulation of ideas is through what might be termed a vernacular politics of free speech, which encompasses the everyday regulation and negotiation, on the one hand, of speech codes in the workplace and other public spaces, all of which intersect with legal, institutional, cultural and ideological frameworks and, on the other hand, the more informal testing and contesting of the limits of speech proprieties in various other social spaces. Moreover, the modalities of such politics can encompass both the singular and discrete acts of particular individuals and the public mobilization of groups and organizations within civil society – and any position in between.

Take, for example, the circulation of knowledge in institutions of learning such as schools and universities. Debates and disputes about curriculum and canon selection (the two are, of course, intimately related) are not often framed in terms of freedom of expression; on the other hand, it has long been acknowledged that there are deeply political concerns at work in the selection of a curriculum and the formation of a pedagogic or cultural canon, including questions about power, authority and exclusion. These inevitably intersect with and impinge upon the flow of discourse, but perhaps one reason concerns about freedom of expression are seldom raised is because most people accept that there needs to be some kind of closure in any curriculum, that not everything can be taught within it, and therefore a process of selection and exclusion must inevitably take place. As a result, in most discussions and debates about curricula, the politics of knowledge rarely intersects with the politics of free speech because these debates are rarely – if ever – framed in terms of censorship, and they are rarely framed in terms of censorship because the censorship remains largely invisible – although, as I shall argue, whether to even call it censorship is problematic. When the politics of free speech involved in the practice, policy and policing of education *does* become visible, such questions *are* raised, but they are broached in such ways as to invite further examination of the inadequacy of prevailing conceptions of free speech in accounting for them.

In the United States, the adoption of public (that is, state) school textbooks, and therefore the content and structure of the curriculum, has long been the arena for political contestation between liberals and conservatives (Taylor 2017). Christian pressure concerning the content of school textbooks in the United States can be traced back to the mid-nineteenth century, but it is only since the advent of the Civil Rights and Women's Movements from the 1960s – and the subsequent 'New Right' reaction on behalf of Christian fundamentalist groups – that the politics of education has become a prominent and highly visible frontline in the 'culture wars' (13–16). The existing research literature on these efforts to shape the textbooks being procured on behalf of schools in the United States, which is largely conducted from within a liberal paradigm, does frame them in terms of 'censorship' but it does so either solely in relation to conservative efforts – thereby assuming that 'liberal' or 'progressive' efforts to shape the curriculum do not warrant consideration under the censorship rubric – or they dismiss both liberal and conservative efforts from the Olympian height of an idealist commitment to infinite and perpetual openness, 'treating both as irksome distractions from the true purpose of education' (26). Either way, an opposition is set up between openness and closure and this in turn enables the construction of a subsequent opposition between liberal shaping as 'inclusive' and conservative efforts as 'exclusionary'. While the latter is aligned with 'censorship', the former is identified as 'selection':

> While censorship involves approaching literature with the intent of weeding out what is objectionable, selection involves approaching literature with the intent of finding that which is most excellent. Censorship seeks to exclude where selection seeks to include; selection prioritizes the right of the reader to read, while censorship prioritizes the protection of the reader from the presumed effects of reading. (7)

Taylor (2017) notes, however, that 'humanist' pressure on publishers and school boards in the wake of the Civil Rights and Women's movements initially proceeded with regard to 'the eradication of racist and sexist language' as well as the 'inclusion of material by and about racial minorities and women in the curriculum' (28). This being the case, it is clear that the opposition set up by liberal observers of this particular form of politics between conservative 'censorship' and liberal 'selection/inclusion' (with its connotations of openness) does not entirely hold. This is evident in the terminology employed to characterize the process, which ranges from 'pre-publication censorship' to 'proactive censorship' to 'silent editing' (6). The last term in particular illuminates the extent to which any sharp distinctions cannot be sustained for the adjective is clearly redundant – all editing is silent and invisible unless specifically flagged up in order to draw attention to itself (as in scholarly editions) – and the term's emergence as a 'by-product' of James J. Lynch and Bertrand Evans' 1963 survey of literature anthologies, grammar and composition books, during which they discovered that 'pages were removed and works were cut to fit the available space' (24) merely underscores the point: all editors wrestle with these considerations on a daily basis; this does not make them censors because censorship is not the appropriate term to be applied here.

Taylor is right to suggest that 'content analysis' of textbooks that have been subject to 'expurgation' may reveal the 'internal logic of the censoring bodies more clearly than does an examination of straightforward banning. While the removal of an entire book from the curriculum […] sends a clear message as to the intolerability of the views it expresses[…]it is not clear what aspects of the book are most intolerable; however, a 'line-by-line comparison of an expurgated text with its source text illuminates exactly which words in which contexts and combinations are found objectionable' (21). She pursues this analysis to great effect, but the point I am making is that this is only the visible tip of a very large iceberg which, in these instances, can with some justification and rigorous analysis be aligned with 'censorship' but which, in most cases, cannot because the line between editing and expurgation is not as clear as liberal theories of free speech and censorship would have us believe. Indeed, the same lack of distinction is also operative with respect to 'selection'. The 'removal' of a work *may* be due to censorship but there are other reasons why works might be removed from the curriculum, reasons which undercut the alignment of 'removal' with 'censorship' and, conversely, 'selection' with 'inclusion'. First, since curricula are limited in all sorts of ways – by time, principally – the idea that 'selection' can be simply a 'broadening of the scope of material presented to students' (28) such that 'inclusion' does not have to be accompanied by an accompanying 'exclusion' is a fallacy that speaks to the liberal trope of infinite and perpetual openness. Second, any removal of a text may not, in fact, be tantamount to a great act of excision but rather a pragmatic decision based on the suitability of that particular text to the learning criteria and outcomes of that particular curriculum. These can intersect with all sorts of other material factors that bear down on the selection and deselection of learning materials, as anyone with pedagogic experience will know. And behind all this, informing and shaping all these factors, are moral considerations with respect to the instructors' relation to the material he or she is teaching. This is clearly part of the textbook adoption scenarios Taylor and others have examined, but they are equally germane to individual tutors who make morally informed personal choices as to what to present to their students; to align these moral choices with 'censorship' is to reduce the complexity of syllabus formation into the 'flat' and one-dimensional consideration of liberty that I have discussed earlier: in some cases it is, indeed, appropriate to talk of the effect of these choices in terms of 'censorship' but, conceptually speaking, it is not possible to draw a sharp distinction between them and these other considerations – ultimately, at a conceptual level, the question of whether what has not been adopted has therefore been 'banned' or 'prohibited' is a tricky one that is in fact undecidable in advance. The same is perhaps less true of texts that have been expurgated, where the term censorship might indeed be appropriate, but expurgation is also an extreme form of editing, and there is a continuum in the editing process whereby some forms of editing may be more indistinct and where the term 'censorship' might be too clear-cut a term to be really precise.

There are further considerations that need to be accounted for here, all of which shape freedom of discourse at a vernacular level, and on an everyday basis, in ways that cannot be encompassed by the sharp distinction of freedom and censorship. Principal among these are the commercial and economic factors that are largely invisible but which have a profoundly important effect on the kinds of discourse that is made available in the 'marketplace of ideas', to use a key liberal metaphor. One of the great advantages of examining textbook adoption processes – and here Taylor's research is exemplary – is the way in which it reveals the extent to which commercial considerations decisively shape the terrain of discourse in free societies. In the United States, the school textbook marketplace is unlike a 'normal' market insofar as it is more akin to government procurement conducted by 'elected officials who need to satisfy their constituents in order to retain their positions' – hence the politicization of the process (Taylor 2017, 16). In these conditions, 'publishers must go to great expense to develop new series of texts without any guarantee that they will be approved … It is therefore in the publishers' interests to produce material that will be considered non-controversial by the widest range of readers' (16–17). The result is that publishers produce 'complex lists of content guidelines to assist book editors in their attempt to toe the narrow line' between what liberal and conservative protestors deem acceptable (16). As a result, the flow of discourse is profoundly shaped by rather mechanistic accommodations and negotiations that are, ultimately, as much rooted in mundane – banal, even – considerations of profit and loss as the moral sensitivies of the respective political antagonists. While these particular circumstances are peculiar to the United States, the wider point is generalizable to other societies.

Conclusion

What I have tried to do in this article is to outline the ways in which the shaping of freedom, and of freedom of expression in particular, both constitutes and is constituted by the dynamic of hegemony and counter-hegemony, the shifting of closures and foreclosures that define the limits of freedom within and without the bounds of the law in liberal social orders. The multidimensionality of this complex process stands in stark contrast to the 'planar' model of liberty that operates within liberal free speech theory. Shifting the terms of debate on freedom of expression within liberal social orders is such an urgent and vital task, because the dominant ways in which it is conceptualized are all rooted in the liberal free speech tradition, which does not accord with and is inadequate to account for how freedom of expression actually works as a lived practice as opposed to an abstract theoretical principle. Moreover, liberal free speech theory is itself not logically consistent even when it tries to suggest that consistency is precisely what freedom requires. This, in turn, is rooted in a structure of thinking that conceptualizes freedom in terms of its antithesis and freedom of expression in terms of the opposition between openness and closure. If, on the other hand, I have insisted on dismantling these oppositions, it is because they simply cannot be sustained either theoretically or in relation to social life. We will never grasp what freedom is if we continue to view it only by the shadow cast by tyranny, by the other which alone gives freedom its form and substance in many liberal imaginings. We need instead to see it as a complex and subtle web of relations, subject to pressures and forces that not only provide the context for liberty as a lived practice but its content as well. In short, liberty is the sum of a whole series of calibrations and compromises, such that to speak disparagingly and regretfully of one's freedom being 'compromised' is to spectacularly misunderstand the very nature of freedom itself.

Notes

1. Indeed, with respect to free speech, the divergence between Mill and anti-consequentialism may not, in fact, be as great as it might at first appear. It could be argued that anti-consequentialist liberal arguments take issue not so much with Mill's theorization of free speech but his wider arguments for liberty. That is, in pushing his case to the 'outer limits' within which free speech should be virtually unlimited, Mill presses his argument for free speech – but not liberty per se – as far towards an anti-consequentialist position as his wider consequentialism will allow, such that liberal anti-consequentialism could be read as an attempt to address (and close) the *gap* between Mill's theorization of free speech and his more avowedly utilitarian arguments for liberty in general.
2. I echo here Zygmunt Bauman's work on liquid modernity and also work on liquid racism (Bauman 2013; Weaver 2011; Werbner 2013).

Disclosure statement

No potential conflict of interest was reported by the author.

References

Asad, T. 2011. "Freedom of Speech and Religious Limitations." In *Rethinking Secularism*, edited by C. Calhoun, M. Juergensmeyer, and J. van Antwerpen, 282–297. New York: Oxford University Press (Kindle edition).

Batty, D. 2011. "Lady Warsi Claims Islamophobia Is Now Socially Acceptable in Britain." *The Guardian* 20. Jan. https://www.theguardian.com/uk/2011/jan/20/lady-warsi-islamophobia-muslims-prejudice.

Bauman, Z. 2013. *Liquid Modernity*. London: Polity.

Haworth, A. 1998. *Free Speech*. London: Routledge.

Home Affairs Committee. 2016. *Antisemitism in the UK*. London: UK Parliament.

Lee, S. 1990. *The Cost of Free Speech*. London: Faber.

Levin, A. 2010. *The Cost of Free Speech: Pornography, Hate Speech and Their Challenge to Liberalism*. Basingstoke: Palgrave Macmillan.

Matsuda, M., C. Lawrence, R. Delgado, K. Crenshaw, and K. Crenshaw. 1993. *Words That Wound: Critical Race Theory, Assaultive Speech, and the First Amendment*. Boulder, CO: Avalon Publishing.

Meer, N. 2008. "The Politics of Voluntary and Involuntary Identities: Are Muslims in Britain an Ethnic, Racial or Religious Minority?" *Patterns of Prejudice* 42 (1): 61–81. doi:10.1080/00313220701805901.

Mill, J. S. [1859] 2011. *On Liberty*. London: Penguin. Kindle edition.

Mondal, A. A. 2014. *Islam and Controversy: The Politics of Free Speech after Rushdie*. Basingstoke: Palgrave.

Rawls, J. 2005. *A Theory of Justice*. Cambridge and London: Harvard University Press.

Saunders, K. 2011. *Degradation: What the History of Obscenity Tells Us about Hate Speech*. New York: NYU Press.

Smith, Z. 2012. *NW*. London and New York: Hamish Hamilton.

Stewart, H. 2016. "Naz Shah Suspended by Labour Party Amid Antisemitism Row." *The Guardian*, April 27. https://www.theguardian.com/politics/2016/apr/27/naz-shah-suspended-labour-party-antisemitism-row.

Taylor, S. 2017. We Don't Need No Education: Belief, and the Expurgation of US Public School Literature Texts in Response to Activist Beliefs. PhD thesis, School of Literature, Drama and Creative Writing, University of East Anglia.

Waldron, J. 2012. *The Harm in Hate Speech*. Cambridge: Harvard University Press.

Walker, P. 2016. "UK Adopts Antisemitism Definition to Combat Hate Crime against Jews." *The Guardian*, December 12. https://www.theguardian.com/society/2016/dec/12/antisemitism-definition-government-combat-hate-crime-jews-israel?CMP=Share_iOSApp_Other.

Weaver, S. 2011. "Liquid Racism and the Ambiguity of Ali G." *European Journal of Cultural Studies* 14 (3): 249. doi:10.1177/1367549410396004.

Weisfeld, H. 2016. "What Hope the Fight against Antisemitism When Malia Bouattia Leads the NUS?" *The Guardian*, April 22. https://www.theguardian.com/commentisfree/2016/apr/22/antisemitism-malia-bouattia-nus-muslim-anti-zionist.

Werbner, P. 2013. "Folk Devils and Racist Imaginaries in a Global Prism: Islamophobia and Anti-Semitism in the Twenty-First Century." *Ethnic & Racial Studies* 36 (3): 450–467. doi:10.1080/01419870.2013.734384.

In a different voice: 'a letter from Manus Island' as poetic manifesto

Anne Surma (iD)

ABSTRACT

On 9 December 2017, *The Saturday Paper* published 'A Letter from Manus Island', an essay and manifesto written by Behrouz Boochani, a Kurdish journalist and refugee being held on Manus Island with hundreds of other men. Boochani writes in a radical, 'poetic' voice that makes the ordinary strange again, as he talks of love, the interdependence of human beings, and the strength to be derived from acts of solidarity. He challenges not only the prevailing vituperative tenor of contemporary public rhetoric, but also the dehumanising discourses within which humanitarian practices in Australia, and in the west more broadly, operate. This paper is written as a letter, in direct reply to Boochani's own. It is inspired by Lilie Chouliaraki's critique of contemporary practices of humanitarianism and the ways in which politics, the market and technology have transformed 'the moral dispositions of our public life'. It explores the unsettling effects and provocative insights presented by Boochani's poetic voice – the refugee as human subject and agent rather than victim or object of pity (or hate). The paper thus reflects on our conventional responses to the ethical call to solidarity from vulnerable subjects and imagines how we might respond otherwise.

Dear Behrouz

Heartfelt thanks for your letter from Manus Island, your manifesto 'for humanity and love', published in *The Saturday Paper* on 9 December 2017.[1] I have read your words and I have listened to them again and again.[2] They are haunting; they speak to me in a different voice.[3]

And after reading and listening, I felt the need to respond to you somehow, but I wasn't sure how.[4] I decided I must write to you, rather than merely write something about what you have written. Perhaps that's presumptuous, since I don't know you, although, of course, I have known *of* you for a very long time, as one of the so-called 'illegals', 'irregular maritime arrivals', 'economic migrants', 'boat people' and 'queue jumpers' who, travelling by boat, have tried to seek refuge on Australian shores in the last few years.[5] In other words, as I said, in truth I don't know you very well at all.

Nonetheless, you have tried to help us get to know you, as you have been writing, and writing for some time, whether via Twitter or through other publishing platforms.[6] I have read your tweets, your longer pieces for *The Guardian* and your poems as rejoinders to the attempts of various institutions and individuals to dehumanize you or to rationalize you out of existence.[7] However, your manifesto takes another significant step, as I read it, in boldly challenging the logic, the rhetoric and the discourses constituting our humanitarian practices in Australia and in the west more broadly, which have been operating for some time now.[8] Even though your situation, and that of your fellow refugees, is not, in Australia at least, widely understood as demanding a humanitarian response, blurred as it is by mischievous challenges to the legitimacy of your claims to protection,[9] you make an extended, critical and performative intervention into this territory by rearticulating humanitarianism as an ethical encounter and social practice, rather than as an expedient, instrumentalist strategy. And what is also striking to me is that your manifesto[10] makes this intervention in a different (poetic) voice, a subjective voice that recasts language as offering rather than missile, and as solidary rather than self-serving. That is to say, as a refugee and long-term prisoner on Manus Island, your writing voice, your agency and your suffering dramatize a profound commitment to responsibility for the other, to the ethics of care: to human (and animal) interdependence, to

Feelings of friendship.
Feelings of compassion.
Feelings of companionship.
Feelings of justice.
And feelings of love.

In this way, then, in your manifesto you manage to do (at least) two very important things: you disrupt the contemporary discourse of humanitarianism and the neoliberal foundations on which it largely depends;[11] and you achieve this disruption on altered grounds, as your voice, your agency and your use of language (as insistently social) enact your subjectivity and your humanity.

Before exploring these ideas further, though, can I just say that your words touched me deeply, in particular your assertion of the primacy of love, and its refrain through the manifesto. Love! I'd heard about it two days before your letter was published. It was 7 December 2017 and the Australian Government was in carnival mood: celebrating love. What a day for love, Mr Turnbull said, in a Parliament that seemed briefly to forget itself and its habitual mode of doing politics. MPs from all sides of the House cheered and cried and clapped and hugged each other; and they sang 'We are one and we are many'. Everyone was smiling and it felt spectacularly good, for those MPs and for those of us watching too. And it was indeed an historic day when the same-sex marriage bill was passed in Australia by an overwhelming majority.[12]

As I mentioned, you too talk about love in your letter. You use the language that is (7 December excepted) largely taboo in our public discussions about others, whether gay, poor, unemployed or refugee, for example. But for people in your situation or, I should say, for people in our situation, your talk of love – which, as you use it, suggests an imaginative openness to and embrace of the other – is particularly risky, even radical. So while our acceptance of homosexual love has now been legally and (broadly) culturally sanctioned, through the passing of the same-sex marriage bill, there are still certain kinds of love that are out of bounds, delegitimized or regarded as politically and economically reckless: in fact, un-Australian. A case in point: the trolls on Twitter respond to your assertions about love, humanity and care with what cannot be described as anything other than hate and venom.[13] But it's perhaps even worse than that. For now, it seems, that a vituperative rhetoric, one boasting its volume, strike and reach and gleeful in its muting of other voices may more readily raise the public's cheers than their hackles (or heckles). Thus, some of us find it quite acceptable to denigrate asylum seekers and refugees, people like you. We don't flinch when Mr Dutton, Minister for Home Affairs, says of asylum seekers held in offshore detention: 'Some people have even gone to the extent of self-harming, and people have self-immolated in an effort to get to Australia'.[14] Or, of those refugees departing Australia having been accepted for settlement in the USA:

There are a lot of people that haven't come out of war-ravaged areas, they're economic refugees – they got on a boat, paid a people smuggler a lot of money … Somebody once said to me that the world's biggest collection of Armani jeans and handbags [is] up on Nauru waiting for people to collect when they depart.[15]

Dutton's comments illustrate how the scripts of a powerful state figure, which insistently rehearse the alleged scheming of suspect (albeit non-specific) others, become established as a form of colloquial indictment; such commentary about marginalised others is now commonplace in Australian government rhetoric.

Therefore, I have wondered at your courage and your patience in continuing to write about what you witness, knowing that these days such writing, from a position of precarity, is not for the faint-hearted. The manifesto, in which you communicate your 'humanitarian message to Australian society and beyond', tells of the three weeks (23 days, to be exact), from 31 October to 23 November 2017, during which you and your 600 fellow prisoners staged a protest against your continued imprisonment on Manus island, a protest against the Australian Government's attempts to transfer you to one of three new 'transit centres' on Manus, a place where you feel unsafe and unwanted, rather than expedite your resettlement in a third country. Paradoxically, the closure of Delta prison presented you with a cruel parody of freedom, as the gates were opened and the security personnel departed. In response, you chose to exercise a real freedom: freedom in the practice of collective resistance.

> The refugees have established that they desire to exist only as free individuals. They desire only an honourable existence. They have established this in confrontation with the proliferation of violence in the detention centre, one that is implemented by a mighty power structure. Up against the determination of this monolith, the refugees have, ultimately, vindicated themselves.

Because you refused to leave on 31 October, the Government stopped supplies of water, food and medicine to the facility (though friends and supporters managed to smuggle in supplies over the next three weeks). You describe how you persevered during this period by relying on one another and by staying 'true to the principles of love, friendship and brotherhood'. Indeed, you write of the close collaboration between the refugees themselves and between the refugees and supporters outside Delta prison, including Manusians and specific groups in Australia, with whom you formed 'an important partnership', and who staged protests on Manus and in different Australian cities in support of your struggle. Your manifesto goes on to describe 'the messages' you tried to convey by your three-week staging of a peaceful resistance, which, as you make clear, is expressly carried out in contradistinction to the violence inflicted on the refugees in Manus prison over the period of your incarceration. In so doing, you confidently affirm 'the personhood', which we have (both deliberately and indirectly) repeatedly denied you, while you also make clear that such personhood entails a relationship with others: not only human, but animal and environmental too:[16]

> All this violence designed in government spaces and targeted against us has driven our lives towards nature.
> towards the natural environment,
> towards the animal world,
> towards the ecosystem.

In the manifesto, you challenge us to pause, reflect on and reconsider our stance on humanitarianism and on the refugee; on how we understand the *human* in *humanity* and respond to the call to *solidarity* from one another, and in particular human beings in extreme vulnerability; why we respond as we do; and how we might do so differently: in ways that motivate what you call 'feelings of justice'. You are also forthright, as you remind 'a majority of the Australian public' that although 'they have only ever imagined that their democracy and freedom has [sic] been created on the basis of principles of humanity', this is not borne out in their treatment of refugees. And, consequently, 'our resistance is the spirit that haunts Australia'. Clearly, therefore, you are under no illusions that writing against the grain means writing into an overwhelmingly hostile space, in which refugees like you, who have been compelled to flee your homes and who have arrived by boat, are considered by the government and by many people of this country as unworthy, as inauthentic, as not in need of our measured benevolence and calculable support (for this is how we typically and efficiently understand our role as humanitarians), let alone our loving embrace. You write knowing that you are regarded suspiciously by those who think you are up to no good, who scorn your desire for refuge as unjustified, who believe you are untrustworthy and even criminal.

Perhaps we should pause here, briefly, to consider how it has come to this. A concerted and exorbitantly costly effort has been expended, over nearly two decades now, through various discursive means – government, media, legal and policy – to help shape citizens' understanding of and responses to asylum seekers and refugees.[17] These include our suspicions of the vulnerable other and our reactive protection of ourselves and our own; our hyper-alertness to threats of global terror, and the consequent 'border militarisation and securitisation', as you put it, designed to ward off such threats; and our hunkering down and inwards to hold on fiercely to what (material goods) we've got. Moreover, the censoring of media coverage of the incarceration of refugees offshore, the restrictions imposed on medical professionals from disclosing their experience of visiting the camps and treating refugees, and the prohibiting of employees and former employees of the contractors charged with running the camps from discussing what they have witnessed have all served to produce refugees as shadowy faceless figures, quantitative not qualitative, onto which we may cast our own fears and insecurities. Concomitantly, our national borders have been strengthened as they increasingly serve as the point of risk calculation for the negative difference between you and us.[18]

In this climate in Australia, then, our political leaders – and we – too frequently indulge in unabashed relishing of the abject powerlessness of refugees, particularly since you have been held up (even in your forced invisibility) as the very symbols and objects of deterrence. You and your fellow refugees are treated as legitimate targets of humiliation. You are goaded, not only by Twitter trolls, whose wanton verbal abuse and relentlessly outrageous othering is a symptomatic and shameful magnification of the effects of consecutive Australian governments' agenda-setting, but also by populist political and media elites, including so-called shock-jocks and high-profile commentators, with a ready base of public support via mainstream and social media platforms.[19] So pervasive and insistent are these voices that even the patient advocacy in support of you by prominent individuals and institutions, including the church, business, government, law, medicine and the arts struggles to gain rhetorical traction in the maelstrom.

Our immunity to flinching, even when we hear or watch the terrible things that you and your friends have endured or witnessed, and captured on your phones for us to see or to read, reminds me of Franz Kafka's short story, 'Description of a Struggle'.[20] Have you read it? It's a nightmare-like narrative, in which the characters witness violence or do violence to one another as if it is completely ordinary, natural or obvious. The characters are indifferent to one another, or speak at one another without ever conversing with one another. They also fail to name their experiences of the world for what they are.[21]

In the same way, our capacity to imagine our interdependence with you and our part in your plight has therefore been progressively obscured. If we are honest, this obscurity also suits us because we are made uncomfortable when, as in your manifesto, you trouble our ethically complacent understandings of humanity, and of humanitarianism. You provoke us to see each of them anew.

Take humanity, which folds in two key meanings: the collective of human beings, or humankind, on the one hand, and the extension of compassion in recognition of that shared membership, on the other. Humanity thus describes, in general terms, not only the world's people and what it means to be human, but the at-once ethical and emotional ties that bind us to one another. Through your practices of resistance, in the manifesto's recurrent reference to the refugees as human beings and to your half-naked bodies (bodies not covered in things, but evidently not nothing), you press us to think again about what constitutes the human, to consider it as meaning something other than, to put it crudely, someone who has stuff or status.[22] Thus, you push us to question the very norms by which we have come to make the human intelligible.[23] In your alternative rendering, the human is embodied and relational, in defiance of its neoliberal expression, which reduces the human to an atomistic, essentially economic unit. Similarly, the repeated references to humanity in your letter call up the tensions between such relational and positivist dispositions. However, through your collocation of humanity with the 'principles of love, friendship and brotherhood', you show how the vital meaning of humanity is effectively instantiated in its socially situated enactment, in concert with others.

And take humanitarianism. So often, our humanitarian energies are directed to satisfying ourselves, as we offer financial support to causes or campaigns that will, we are told, empower others who are aspiring to be like us. Or we pity those, in far-off places, who stand in imagined orderly queues, waiting patiently (and often forever) to escape misery, fear and trauma. Or we are seen donating to those who (thankfully!) do their suffering in their own (preferably distant) backyards, rather than ungraciously 'trespassing' into ours.[24]

By contrast, you transform and render humanitarianism into practices of solidarity and care, as you describe the acts of compassion and protection you extended to the sick refugees and to the dogs in the camp, as well as to the 'important partnership' that developed between the refugees and your supporters on Manus and in Australia. And during your three-week period of resistance you describe poignantly what emerged from this experience of interdependence:

> We learnt that humans have no sanctuary except within other human beings. Humans have no felicitous way to live their lives other than to trust in other humans, and the hearts of other humans, and the warmth within the hearts of other humans.

You show us how our vulnerability (the vulnerability of all of us) need not mean passivity or victim-hood but, rather, how it actually animates our humanity and what it means to be human. In so doing, you also proffer an alternative way of understanding humanitarianism and our relationship as human beings to others. And you urge us to think again about the particular bonds and connections that constitute the very foundation, purpose and ethical texture of our lives, the private and public relation-ships that those different ties enable and the experiences they make meaningful. Oddly enough, this is now an extraordinary way of thinking, especially since a successful contemporary life in the west is generally promoted as one predicated on individual autonomy, on individualism, on competition and on economic 'improvement'. This renders largely invisible and worthless the interdependence which, as you describe, not only nourishes us deeply and gives us joy but is also our lifeblood. From the way you convey this, you encourage me to remember that this is true not only for the survival of refugees, but of us all.

Similarly, throughout your manifesto, by refocalising our business-as-usual perspective on vulnera-ble people, as you transform the refugee into an individual human subject and agent, you manage to make the obvious strange again. You also challenge us to see and understand things otherwise, or to question what has become (culturally validated as) ordinary. As we have seen, for example, you undercut our ordinary use and understanding of the terms and practices of humanity and humanitarianism, and you invoke love as the basis for forging ties of solidarity and friendship. In so doing, you overturn our now all-too ordinary expressions of indifference, ill-will and even enmity for the refugees whom the government holds in detention.

These are powerful acts of resistance and, as you say, they usher in 'a kind of political poetics', and 'a particular style of poetic resistance'. What is the poetic, after all, if not a making strange (calling into ethical question) and imaginative and emotional transformation of the vernacular?[25] Moreover, this is you, *your* voice speaking and writing to us. Not a celebrity advocate, standing between you and us, and speaking on your behalf. Not a sophisticated, slick social media campaign, at once dazzling and disfiguring, disturbing and comforting in its manicured design, its familiar language and register. And not a government spokesperson whose, as you put it, 'ridiculous fabrications' aim to reinforce your alleged undeserving otherness. Your voice in the manifesto both undercuts and throws into relief all such as those.

You move through different voices in the manifesto – shifting from the *they*[26] through to the *I* and the *We*. In these different positions, you demonstrate for us not only how practised you are in speaking and being spoken about in the third-person, whether singular or plural,[27] but also how the first-person voice humanizes you. Actually, you favour the *we*, as you talk of solidarity, of camaraderie – the *we* that pulls you and your fellow prisoners together. By turning *them* into *we* and *I*, you have offered us a gift: the chance to listen to you,[28] to respond to you.

We can also see this transformation in powerful passages such as the following, when you write about the ways in which

> the detention regime wanted to manufacture a particular kind of refugee with a particular kind of response. However, the refugees were able to regain their identity, regain their rights, regain their dignity. In fact, what has occurred is essentially a new form of identification, which asserts that we are human beings.

Here, you show the construction of the figure of the refugee, as stereotype, by 'the detention regime'. You then counter this positioning as other by using a third-person voice[29] to affirm and present to us the reality of refugees as embodied and collectively active subjects in the world, as you tell how 'the refugees were able to regain their identity, regain their rights, regain their dignity'. And finally, you voice your collective agency as speaking subjects, when you affirm, in the first-person plural voice, that 'we are human beings'.

As well, and as you go on to explain, you and your fellow refugees never gave up 'to become mere bodies subject to politics', but claimed bodies asserting a different kind of politics – 'a kind of political poetics'. In other words, you perform a resistance to the attempts of formidable state and populist forces to elide your humanity, to reduce it to the status of 'mere bodies'.[30] Where other refugees, through hunger strikes or lip-sewing, have protested the state's dehumanising control of the refugee,[31] you have turned to writing as a radical political and ethical move,[32] reminding us, the Australian public, 'what it has lost or what it is in the process of losing': our belief in our own plural humanity. In defiance of this imminent loss, you declare that the refugees on Manus 'have been able to reconfigure the images of themselves as passive actors and weak subjects into active agents and fierce resistors'.[33] It seems to me that through your manifesto, you strive – audaciously, some would have it – to document, make visible and intelligible not only a different voice but also a different language, by reinscribing the refugee as both relational, writing subject and as resisting, embodied agent. In your every utterance, and in the vivid depiction of the refugee as vital and interdependent human being, you thereby unsettle the borders that the Australian government spends so much money on trying to maintain between us, between you and me, I mean.[34]

I referred above to what some may consider your audaciousness at your refreshingly categorical and declarative (rather than submissive and deferential) style in the manifesto. You seem proud of the way in which your resistance has enabled 'the refugees to refashion the image of themselves' in order that you 'now present the real face of refugees for a democratic Australia to discern'. Nonetheless, your awareness of the precarity of your position, as you offer 'poetic resistance' to 'the real politics of the day' is acute:

> Refugees pushed back
> Risking their lives and bodies
> Just fragile humans risking everything.
> Risking everything that is beautiful.

Your letter of resistance from Manus Island, impassioned and considered, cuts through the abstract tangle of dog-whistle or, increasingly, vindictive rhetoric, which many of our narratives, commentaries and debates have become. In response to such texts, the poetry you speak of, and the poetry you speak, seems to offer some hope or even 'Possibility', as the poet Emily Dickinson suggests, when favourably comparing poetry to prose.[35] You instantiate another mode of writing and speaking by puncturing what has, even in its brazen efforts to defile you, now become banal. You speak to us directly in an alternative register, so that we can stop, read and listen carefully, and perhaps learn to respond and relate to you otherwise.

From your letter, I understand completely why you wouldn't want to be 'like us'. Instead, you have asked me – asked us – to be different, and to consider the possibilities of writing and speaking differently.

Thank you so much for writing, Behrouz. I hope to hear from you again very soon.

Notes

1. Boochani (2017a).
2. On the same day that 'A Letter from Manus Island' was published in *The Saturday Paper*, writer and slam poet Maxine Beneba Clarke performed the manifesto at the Malthouse Theatre, Melbourne (https://soundcloud.com/the-saturday-paper/a-letter-from-manus-island).
3. The echo with Carol Gilligan's now-classic (1982) text *In a Different Voice*, in which the idea of 'the ethic of care' is first developed, is intended. In her influential work, Gilligan proposes the gendered difference between the respective voices of 'justice' and of 'care'. Over subsequent decades, this work has given rise to significant and sophisticated developments in feminist care ethics, in which the responsibilities for and practices of care are understood as central to human life, in both private and public spheres, and in cultural, social and political domains.
4. The focus of my response to Boochani's letter is also inspired by the incisive work of Lillie Chouliaraki, particularly in *The Ironic Spectator* (2013). Chouliaraki analyses practices of humanitarianism and, as she calls its contemporary manifestation, post-humanitarianism. She traces the institutional, political and technological changes that have together instrumentalized the aid and development 'market', so that rather than orienting ourselves to the suffering

of vulnerable others and to taking action on their behalf, we are now motivated to engage in humanitarian practices for consumerist and self-serving ends. I am interested in what happens when the suffering subject, in this case Behrouz Boochani, himself directly challenges the norms, hierarchies and relationships that constitute contemporary humanitarian practice.

5. In 2001, John Howard's Liberal–National Coalition Government launched the policy of offshore processing (the Pacific Solution) in an attempt to stop asylum seekers arriving by boat in Australia. In 1992, the Paul Keating (Labor) Government introduced the policy of mandatory detention for people arriving in Australia without a valid visa. Subsequent governments have variously developed and extended these policies, so that today anyone attempting to arrive by boat will not only be held and processed offshore, but will never be allowed to settle in Australia. For an overview of the history and current practices relating to Australia's treatment of asylum seekers arriving by boat, see McAdam and Chong (2014); Australian Human Rights Commission (2017).

6. For an account of Boochani's use of social media as journalist and witness, see Rae, Holman, and Nethery (2017).

7. See Boochani's Twitter account: @BehrouzBoochani. Boochani has also written a number of articles that have been published by *The Guardian* since early 2016. See, for example, Boochani (2016a, 2017b, 2017c). For a sample of Boochani's poetry, see Boochani (2016b).

8. See, for example, Chouliaraki (2013); Kurasawa (2013); Little and Vaughan-Williams (2017).

9. To seek protection as an asylum seeker is not illegal, 'but rather the right of every individual under international law' (McAdam and Chong 2014, 52).

10. The word manifesto comes from the Latin, *manifestare*, meaning 'to make public'; and from *manifestus*, meaning 'obvious'.

11. In this paper, I understand neoliberalism as a 'distinctive form of reason' (Brown 2015, 35), which has progressively effected 'the disenchantment of politics by economics' (Davies 2014, 4). Under neoliberalism, the human subject is instrumentalized, normatively understood as *homo economicus*, a rational and competitive market actor; and all domains (social, governmental, private and public) are reconceived as markets (Brown 2015, 35–45).

12. See Parliament of Australia (2018).

13. See tweets in response to Boochani's tweet about 'A Letter from Manus Island' (@BehrouzBoochani, December 8 2017).

14. McIlroy (2016).

15. Koziol (2017).

16. For a related discussion on dispossession and 'the differential allocation of humanness: the perpetually shifting and variably positioned boundary between those who are rendered properly human and those who are not, those who are entitled to a long life and those relegated to slow death', see Butler and Athanasiou (2013, 31–32; see also 32–37).

17. For a sample of critical perspectives see Hodge (2015); McAdam (2013); Surma (2016).

18. See the website of the Australian Border Force for an account of the state border as the site of risk calculation (https://www.homeaffairs.gov.au/australian-border-force-abf).

19. Prominent Australian commentators who regularly feature the 'problem' of asylum seekers and refugees held in detention include Sydney Radio 2 GB's Ray Hadley ('The Ray Hadley Morning Show': https://www.2gb.com/show/ray-hadley-morning-show/); Alan Jones ('The Alan Jones Breakfast Show': https://www.2gb.com/show/the-alan-jones-breakfast-show/); and Andrew Bolt ('Andrew Bolt Blog' for the *Herald Sun*, Melbourne's biggest circulation print and digital daily: http://www.heraldsun.com.au/blogs/andrew-bolt).

20. Kafka ([1912] 1971).

21. Butler offers an incisive reading of this story, pointing out how it exposes the 'very gap between what has become ordinary and the destructive aims it covers over and conveys'. In so doing, the text also propels the reader 'into ethical responsiveness and alert' (2014, 26).

22. Compare Athanasiou's discussion of the conventional ways in which the category of the 'proper' human is differentially allocated, and 'its presumed self-evidence as a predicate to a man with property and propriety' (Butler and Athanasiou 2013, 32).

23. Butler claims that 'the term and the practice of 'civilization' work to produce the human differentially by offering a culturally limited norm for what the human is supposed to be. It is not just that some humans are treated as humans, and others are dehumanized; it is rather that dehumanization becomes the condition for the production of the human to the extent that a 'Western' civilization defines itself over and against a population understood as, by definition, illegitimate, if not dubiously human' (2006, 91).

24. See also Chouliaraki 2013, 58–60).

25. In other words, poetry's disruption of conventional language (whether through its voice, graphics, grammar, word use, rhythm or rhyme, for example) both takes the reader aback (distances her) *and* takes her in (brings her close) to the richness, precision and ambivalence of poetic meaning. The distancing provides a critical space for working out how language works, and how and what the voice that utters it might mean. The bringing close enacts the communicative, social and interactive potential of language, as we capture and are captured by the meanings it evokes.

26. However, and as I show below, the use of the third-person voice does not necessarily relegate a subject to otherness.

27. See Chouliaraki and Zaborowski's (2017) discussion of the 2015 refugee crisis in Europe, and how refugees 'speak' in the news.
28. See Fiona Robinson's (2011) critique, from a feminist ethics of care perspective, of the notion of ethics as a dialogue between human beings as equals.
29. Thus, as stated above, the third-person voice does not always relegate a subject to otherness but, as here, may be used to declare, performatively, their real, material existence for recognition by others.
30. This idea resonates with Giorgio Agamben's notion of 'bare life': human life understood in terms only of its biological dimension, rather than in terms of how it is lived – its social and political potential or possibility. Agamben argues that Western politics is built and thus depends on the exclusion of biological life from politics: 'in Western politics, bare life has the peculiar privilege of being that whose exclusion founds the city of men' (1998, 7). However, as Boochani shows, a bare life, consisting in 'mere bodies', must be refused by the refugees in order that they may formulate an alternative politics of resistance.
31. Patricia Owens notes that these acts of protest consist in 'a re-enactment of sovereign power's production of bare life on the body of the refugee' (Owens 2009, 573). However, note that Owens (drawing on Hannah Arendt to critique Agamben's position) also argues that an act of protest, such as lip sewing, 'can form the basis of a new politics if it is acted upon and talked about over and over again; if, in other words, bare life is repudiated and a new worldly community is formed around resistance to injustice' (Owens 2009, 577–78).
32. Athanasiou claims that 'in the domain of dispossession, ethics and politics are not (or should not be) mutually exclusive' (Butler and Athanasiou 2013, 108).
33. Rancière remarks that political activity 'makes visible what had no business being seen, and makes heard a discourse where once there was only place for noise; it makes understood as discourse what was once only heard as noise' (1999, 30).
34. The Australian Border Force represents a very specific understanding of the border as a commercial and competitive space and therefore, as suggested above, a space of risk: 'Our mission is to protect our border and manage the movement of people and goods across it and, by doing so, we aim to make Australia safer and more prosperous'. See https://www.homeaffairs.gov.au/australian-border-force-abf/protecting.
35. Emily Dickinson, 'I dwell in Possibility' (466). https://www.poetryfoundation.org/poems/52197/i-dwell-in-possibility-466

Disclosure statement

No potential conflict of interest was reported by the author.

ORCID

Anne Surma (iD) http://orcid.org/0000-0001-5634-7714

References

Agamben, Giorgio. 1998. *Homo Sacer: Sovereign Power and Bare Life*. Translated by Daniel Heller-Roazen. Stanford, CA: Stanford University Press.
Australian Human Rights Commission. 2017. *Asylum Seekers, Refugees and Human Rights: Snapshot Report*. 2nd ed. Sydney: Australian Human Rights Commission.
Boochani, Behrouz. 2016a. "It's Hard for Me to Leave Manus Island without Justice: Behrouz Boochani on the US Refugee Deal." *The Guardian*, November 13. https://www.theguardian.com/australia-news/2016/nov/13/its-hard-for-me-to-leave-manus-island-without-justice-behrouz-boochani-on-the-us-refugee-deal.
Boochani, Behrouz. 2016b. "Behrouz Boochani." Poems. *Writing through Fences*. http://writingthroughfences.org/2016/01/behrouz-boochani/.

Boochani, Behrouz. 2017a. "A Letter from Manus Island." *The Saturday Paper*, December 9–15. https://www.thesaturdaypaper. com.au/news/politics/2017/12/09/letter-manus-island/15127380005617.

Boochani, Behrouz. 2017b. "I Write from Manus Island as a Duty to History." *The Guardian*, December 6. https://www. theguardian.com/commentisfree/2017/dec/06/i-write-from-manus-island-as-a-duty-to-history.

Boochani, Behrouz. 2017c. "All We Want is Freedom – Not Another Prison Camp." *The Guardian*, November 13. https://www. theguardian.com/commentisfree/2017/nov/13/all-we-want-is-freedom-not-another-prison-camp.

Brown, Wendy. 2015. *Undoing the Demos: Neoliberalism's Stealth Revolution*. New York: Zone Books.

Butler, Judith. 2006. *Precarious Life: The Powers of Mourning and Violence*. London and New York: Verso.

Butler, Judith. 2014. "Ordinary, Incredulous." In *The Humanities and Public Life*, edited by Peter Brooks and Hilary Jewett, 15–38. New York: Fordham University Press.

Butler, Judith, and Athena Athanasiou. 2013. *Dispossession: The Performative in the Political*. Cambridge: Polity Press.

Chouliaraki, Lilie. 2013. *The Ironic Spectator: Solidarity in the Age of Post-Humanitarianism*. Cambridge: Polity Press.

Chouliaraki, Lilie, and Rafal Zaborowski. 2017. "Voice and Community in the 2015 Refugee Crisis: AContent Analysis of News Coverage in Eight European Countries." *International Communication Gazette* 79 (6–7): 613–635.

Davies, William. 2014. *The Limits of Neoliberalism: Authority, Sovereignty and the Logic of Competition*. London: Sage.

Gilligan, Carol. 1982. *In a Different Voice: Psychological Theory and Women's Development*. Cambridge, MA: Harvard University Press.

Hodge, Paul. 2015. "A Grievable Life? The Criminalisation and Securing of Asylum Seeker Bodies in the 'Violent Frames' of Australia's Operation Sovereign Borders." *Geoforum* 58: 122–131.

Kafka, Franz. (1912) 1971. "Description of a Struggle." In *The Complete Stories*. Translated by Edwin Willa, Muir Tania and James Stern, 25–73. New York: Schocken Books.

Koziol, Michael. 2017. "'Armani Refugees': Peter Dutton Accused of Undermining US Deal with 'Extraordinarily Irresponsible' Critique." *Sydney Morning Herald*, September 29. http://www.smh.com.au/federal-politics/political-news/armani-refugees-peter-dutton-accused-of-undermining-us-deal-with-extraordinarily-irresponsible-critique-20170928-gyqidd. html.

Kurasawa, Fuyuki. 2013. "The Sentimentalist Paradox: On the Normative and Visual Foundations of Humanitarianism." *Journal of Global Ethics* 9 (2): 201–214.

Little, Adrian, and Nick Vaughan-Williams. 2017. "Stopping Boats, Saving Lives, Securing Subjects: Humanitarian Borders in Europe and Australia." *European Journal of International Relations* 23 (3): 533–556.

McAdam, Jane. 2013. "Australia and Asylum Seekers." *International Journal of Refugee Law* 25 (3): 435–448.

McAdam, Jane, and Fiona Chong. 2014. *Refugees: Why Asylum Seeking is Legal and Australia's Policies Are Not*. Sydney: UNSW Press.

McIlroy, Tom. 2016. "'Asylum Seekers Have Self-Immolated to Get to Australia': Peter Dutton." *Sydney Morning Herald*, August 8. http://www.smh.com.au/federal-politics/political-news/asylum-seekers-have-selfimmolated-to-get-to-australia-peter-dutton-20160811-gqq48 f.html.

Owens, Patricia. 2009. "Reclaiming 'Bare Life': Against Agamben on Refugees." *International Relations* 23 (4): 567–582.

Parliament of Australia. 2018. "Marriage Amendment (Definition and Religious Freedoms) Bill 2017." *Parliament of Australia*. https://www.aph.gov.au/Parliamentary_Business/Bills_Legislation/Bills_Search_Results/Result?bId=s1099.

Rae, Maria, Rosa Holman, and Amy Nethery. 2017. "Self-Represented Witnessing: The Use of Social Media by Asylum Seekers in Australia's Offshore Immigration Detention Centres." *Media, Culture and Society* 40 (4): 479–495.

Rancière, Jacques. 1999. *Dis-Agreement: Politics and Philosophy*. Translated by Julie Rose. Minneapolis, MN: University of Minnesota Press.

Robinson, Fiona. 2011. "Stop Talking and Listen: Discourse Ethics and Feminist Care Ethics in International Political Theory." *Millennium: Journal of International Studies* 39 (3): 845–860.

Surma, Anne. 2016. "Pushing Boundaries: A Critical Cosmopolitan Orientation to Public Relations." In *Routledge Handbook of Critical Public Relations*, edited by Jacquie L'Etang, David McKie, Nancy Snow and Jordi Xifra, 393–404. London: Routledge.

Manus prison poetics/our voice: revisiting 'A Letter From Manus Island', a reply to Anne Surma

Behrouz Boochani

Even if there were only one person reading my writings beyond this island, I would continue writing for that one reader.

Dear Anne,

This here is a pledge, a personal commitment. I made this pact with myself five years ago, during a time when no one knew where Manus Prison was. And now, after five years, I honestly cannot hide my feelings of joy. I cannot contain the satisfaction and pleasure it gives me to know that there are people in the public sphere and among intellectual circles who critically analyse what Australia is doing on Manus Island (Papua New Guinea) and the Republic of Nauru (Repubrikin Naoero) from philosophical and historical perspectives. After numerous years of writing from Manus Prison, my work has slowly entered public discourse and scholarly debate. I have discovered people who draw on these writings as foundations for serious academic research, and for me, this is the beginning of new initiatives and future approaches.

On the 23 November 2017, a few buses entered the new prison camp in East Lorengau, the largest town on Manus Island. This camp is thirty-five kilometres from the prison at Lombrum Naval Base, the one that had incarcerated refugees for four and a half years. The arrival of the buses at East Lorengau marked the crushing end of our twenty-three day resistance.[1] The government suppressed the prisoners' stand-off, and the refugees could no longer avoid forced removal.

The scene was like a battlefield.
Dozens of individuals with wounded and bloodied faces and bodies.
Distressed.
Subjugated.

The prisoners disembarked from the buses. The refugees formed a queue. Each one received a package containing a bedsheet, soap and other essentials. This scene affected me profoundly. It was the day after police officers violently hauled me away from the Lombrum Naval Base.

I sit on the balcony of the new prison camp. I light my cigarette and proceed to write a manifesto, 'A Letter From Manus Island'.[2]

I felt that our historic stand in the face of oppression was lacking something: it had to be documented in the form of a manifesto. I described the space and the circumstances by reaching deep down, projecting the very depths of what you refer to in your letter, Anne, as a 'different voice'. This manifesto was written in the midst of a tragedy and bears witness to an epic. The words stand like soldiers in a ritual of mourning, weeping over the masses who have fallen. Refugees put their bodies on the line and rose up for twenty-three days. The manifesto reflects the resistance of the refugees, bringing together the genres of epic, political discourse and poetry, and in a peculiar way, embodies a time when the refugees themselves belonged to the realms of epic, political thought and poetry. This 'different voice' is the voice of the defiant refugees, conditioned by the threat of forced transfer from one prison to another, and the tragic circumstances that ensued. Even the author of the manifesto could not contain this voice: it is the voice of a different author. Only the genre of poetry could express the intensity and volume of the message. In these times, when the world has become so compartmenta-lized, mechanical and mundane, only poetry can convey what that protest at the Lombrum Naval Base prison meant. Poetry: a form of expression that dismantles all these structures.

In your letter, you criticize Western human rights and humanitarian practices, and examine the bureaucratization of advocacy. Bureaucracy pertains to the very *essence* of a prison such as Manus. To critically examine this phenomenon, I use a concept that I call *The Kyriarchal System*.[3] It refers to the total experience of Manus Prison and all its internal and external dimensions. The Kyriarchal System is a complex set of structures that subject imprisoned refugees to relentless and pervasive practices of micro-control and macro-control. Refugees are tortured using perverse and targeted rules and regulations; the system transforms prisoners into machines, erasing their human identities, and stripping individuals of autonomy and selfhood. But I imagine that the place I have been calling Manus Prison is a replica of thousands of other constructions that control Western societies: universities, schools, army barracks, governments. All of them, in their own particular ways, participate in The Kyriarchal System that defines Manus Prison.

The Kyriarchal System controls human rights organizations. Through the production of com-plex and perverse bureaucratic structures, they become harmless, non-confrontational entities that are easily regulated and tempered. My conclusions are based on years of experience working with these organizations. Contemporary human rights advocacy is a global phenom-enon that is based on certain predetermined universalist moral principles, and human rights organizations are either direct products of The Kyriarchal System that gives rise to Manus Prison, or are modelled on its characteristics. They confront the ideology spawned by The Kyriarchal System by using the same terminology and concepts devised by the system; that is, they replicate and reinforce discourses that, in many ways, legitimize borders and control of movement.

Media organizations conform to the same terminology constructed by the government – in your letter, you unpack this issue so well. After all these years, the media still calls the prisons on Manus Island and Nauru 'offshore processing centres'. For us, these sites are harsher and more brutal than prison. Meanwhile, the issues that the media and human rights organiza-tions neglect are those of living-well and freedom. The incarceration of a child in these prisons is an issue worthy of less moral outrage than the suitability of the kind of food provided to that same child. This is Kyriarchal logic and it is truly remarkable. In Australia, imprisoning innocent people has become acceptable, and the notion of imprisoning people for a whole lifetime has become normalized. And this is the reason behind the misguided interpretation of the media, including the 'pervasive and insistent' shock-jocks and commentators that you describe, regarding the actions of the refugees during those twenty-three days under siege.

One must not reduce refugees to a general category as the Australian media has so often done. Indeed, they must not be reduced to a vague notion such as 'refugee'. Their existence as unique persons must not be fragmented or eroded, something that The Kyriarchal System has always tied to do – a system whose objective is to render refugees using a simple, one-dimensional code. *Refugees...* and nothing more. The manifesto is nothing other than an attempt to reclaim our personhood. It claims that we are unique human beings in opposition to a system and culture that has instrumentalized us, and our sense of selfhood, for political ends. The manifesto stands against a system that identifies refugees as numbers, that atomizes each situation as a calculable equation and that tries to change people into machines. A system that diminishes human beings.

The manifesto speaks of the *human* in *humanity*. It expresses a language of empower-ment and emancipation: they are part of the refugees' core message to the world. And for this reason, the different voice presented in this manifesto – in reality, the voice of the refugees under siege – is consolidated by a shared experience of humanity.

Humanity.
Freedom.
Justice.
Love.
It was resistance...
it was pure...
it was true...
... it was beautifully human. It was a bond with nature. It was connected to the land, in communication with the animal world.
The animals, what magnificent allies.

This vision and these values occupy a salient role in the struggle. They are powerful not only because they bring human beings and animals into harmony with each other. They position the worth of animals over and above human beings. And this is a simple philosophy we live by here: One who does not love animals cannot love humans. The realm of nature is a landscape from which we draw power and become inspired to challenge The Kyriarchal System. It is by engaging with the ecosystem that we can oppose regulating structures and experience the exhilaration of freedom – even if only for a short period of time.

You elaborate on my use of this *we*. Solidarity in our community was motivated by a common form of expression empowered by notions of humanity, justice, freedom and love. The solidarity amongst the refugees was essentially based on a simple philosophy that we might pose as a question: Do humans have any sanctuary except within other human beings? During those days of struggle, the refugees had nowhere to retreat except within the brotherhood of their fellow-prisoners. What we felt was mutual affliction.

Justice.
Freedom.
Humanity….
And love.

Justice, freedom, humanity and love transcend anything that can be imagined, whether by someone living in a village in Kurdistan, in a city such as Sydney, or in a community inside the jungles of Manus Island. *We* refers to all the refugees and encompasses all who participated in acts of solidarity with the refugees during those days. *We* is inspired by a solidarity beyond borders. Everyone in the prison, everyone outside the prison acting in solidarity and understanding: I consider them all as one. A profound experience. Those outside the prison are not engaged simply in gestures of compassion. They share in this profound experience by taking a principled stance with us. Human beings form identity interdependent with one another through love and by striving for justice.

You consider me a brave person. In response, I would like to say that I never consider myself to be a brave person. Actually, this is a confession: the thing that gives my writings and actions courage is merely the fact that I have no choice but to fight, and no option but to resist. I can do nothing but stand up to the manipulative politicians and commentators (as you appropriately describe them), no choice but to stand up against a system that has distorted and degraded my identity.

Finally, this manifesto is a part of Australia's forgotten history, Australia's hidden history, a history excluded from official accounts. In order to understand Australia's role in constructing prisons on Manus Island and Nauru, it is crucial to seek out perspectives that do not corroborate the dominant voices in Australian government and media.

Seek out the human perspective.
Seek out humanity
Seek out the human story…
Human beings, and the affliction they endure.

Notes

1. See '"This is hell out here": how Behrouz Boochani's diaries expose Australia's refugee shame', Behrouz Boochani, trans. M. Mansoubi and O. Tofighian, *The Guardian*, 4 December 2017.
2. 'A Letter From Manus Island', Behrouz Boochani, trans. O. Tofighian, *The Saturday Paper*, December 9–15, 2017.
3. *System-e hākem* in Farsi. This is described comprehensively in Behrouz Boochani, trans. O. Tofighian, *No Friend but The Mountains: Writing From Manus Prison* (2018, Picador, Sydney).

Behrouz Boochani and the Manus Prison narratives: merging translation with philosophical reading

Omid Tofighian

ABSTRACT

No Friend but the Mountains: Writing From Manus Prison is a literary work typed using mobile phone text messaging and produced after five years of indefinite detention in the Australian-run immigration detention centre on Manus Island, Papua New Guinea. Behrouz Boochani's Manus Prison narratives represent the fusion of journalism, political commentary and philosophical reflection with myth, epic, poetry and folklore. By experimenting with multiple genres he creates a new literary framework for his uncanny and penetrating reflections on exile to Manus Island and the prison experience from the standpoint of an Indigenous Kurdish writer. In addition, the narratives he constructs function as political and philosophical critique and expose the phenomenon of Manus Prison as a modern manifestation of systematic torture. Drawing on scholarship from social epistemology, this article emphasises the situated nature of Boochani's writing and the interdependent way of knowing uniquely characteristic of his positionality. This study also demonstrates, from the perspective of the translator, the interdisciplinary nature of the translation process and indicates how a particular philosophical reading was required, particularly in order to communicate the work's decolonial trajectory. The Manus Prison narratives depict a surreal form of horror and are best described in terms of anti-genre: the stories redefine and deconstruct categories and concepts; they resist style and tradition; and they show the limitations of established genres for articulating the physical, psychological and emotional impact of exile and indefinite detention on refugees.

'The prison had fallen into a heavy silence; the prison had fallen into heavy sleep. Only the sound of crickets; they hollowed out the depths of silence even further. The very great weight of the silence had infused the moaning with a destructive power.

My god, prison is so horrific. Prison is so oppressive. Prison is so merciless. (Boochani 2017a, 97)[1]

Behrouz Boochani's *No Friend but the Mountains: Writing From Manus Prison* (forthcoming 2018a) is a book that merges various genres and, paradoxically, deconstructs them at the same time. The author employs the journalism skills and political analysis we are familiar with from his reports from Manus Prison, in addition to incorporating special elements of the edifying and lyrical voice that speaks through his poetic manifesto 'A

Letter From Manus Island' (Boochani 2017b; see also, Boochani 2018b, 2017a, Boochani 2017c). We are also introduced to Boochani's philosophical ruminations, his psycho-analytic examinations and his vivid description of dream states – sometimes glorious, sometimes romantic, at times humorous, often horrific. The book also incorporates styles of writing that are best understood as epic and mythic. *No Friend but the Mountains* is a novel – rather, more than a novel, it is an anti-genre.

Reflecting on the phenomenon of mixing and manipulating genres, Boochani explains different forms of expression and their relationship with knowledge production. When telling me about the conditions he endured when writing his manifesto, he examines how he intertwined three genres: epic, political commentary and poetry:

> This is what is so fascinating about the text. It brings all these together with a particular philosophical trajectory. I learned so much from the process, and then from looking over what I had written. I realised that one can bring together all these forms of expression and make them work successfully. Reconstructing voice taught me something special… both employing and deconstructing writing structures taught me more about the prison. (Behrouz Boochani, personal correspondence)[2]

In the book's supplementary essay, 'No Friend but the Mountains: Translator's Reflections', I suggest that, considering the burgeoning cultural industry around refugee stories (part of the broader 'refugee industry'), it is misleading to reduce Boochani's book to refugee memoir or other forms of refugee writing. The work is better positioned within a range of collections, such as clandestine philosophical literature, prison narratives, philosophical fiction, Australian dissident writing, Iranian political art, transnational literature, decolonial writing and the Kurdish literary tradition (Tofighian, forthcoming 2018b). In the same essay, I draw on scholarship from social epistemology and narrative studies to examine the treatment of refugees by states and divergent elements within their constituent societies; of course, with a focus on Australia. In particular, I define what Boochani and I see as the *pro-refugee/anti-refugee disposition* and what we call *The Kyriarchal System*, or *system-e hākem* in Farsi. In this essay, I will also use concepts and theories from the same scholarship to explore issues pertaining to the reception and the book's philosophical underpinnings. In the translator's note (Tofighian, forthcoming 2018a), I describe the translation project as a shared philosophical activity. This particular process of translation – a form of collective knowledge production – developed new knowledge; translation enabled a way of knowing distinctly different to what I would have acquired from a deep reading. This essay shares aspects from my insights and continues to develop what Boochani and I describe as *Manus Prison Theory*.

Manus Prison, Narrative and Knowing

As a location, a system and an ideology, Manus Prison creates tortuous conditions that affect all forms of interaction between the incarcerated refugees and their oppressors, whether they are staff employed by the system, politicians or Australian citizens. Manus Prison is constructed on one of Australia's former colonies, an extrajudicial site where men seeking asylum are warehoused. But the oppressive circumstances and cruel political strategy have also created conditions where many of the imprisoned refugees have formed unique and methodical ways of thinking and produced particularly savvy analyses of the political situation and the ways it determines their fates.

In my conversations with Boochani, he builds on revelations acquired from resisting through the 23 day siege (beginning 31 October, 2017) to re-examine significant parts of his book. After being forcibly removed from the original prison and transferred to a new prison camp, he meditates on factors, such as space and time:

> Now that I'm no longer there I cannot write about what I endured and what I saw. The siege has ended, and the brutality and affliction particular to the four and a half years leading up to it are different during this current phase of incarceration. For instance, in the book I write about queuing as a technique of torture – how can I describe this now that I no longer have to wait in those same lines? I can't. In the book I write about the destructive psychological and physical effect that queuing has on people, I detail the horrible encounters and sights. At the moment I'm not furious and resentful in the same way. But back then I wrote exactly as I was lining up – I wrote exactly what I was feeling. It would be really difficult to write about that experience now. I can write about it… it would just turn out differently. But writing back then and from there? In the book you really get a sense of what it is like being in the prison. That's what emerges when you write from the inside. (Behrouz Boochani, personal correspondence)

I became friends with Boochani and began working with him from the beginning of 2016 and I soon became acutely aware of many features related to his physical environment, intellectual perspectives, cultural background and literary methods. This intensified once I began translating *No Friend but the Mountains*. Positionality and context determine what one knows and how one knows it, and Boochani's circumstances are so remarkably distinct and extraordinarily horrific that radically new sets of concepts, methods and criteria are required for interpretation. Since knowing is intertwined with cultural values and social positioning, I realized throughout the translation process that any attempts to understand Boochani's philosophical views will always remain limited when applying available theories of knowledge. Also, reinscribing certain stereotypes and tropes about refugees is unavoidable if the specific literary, philosophical and political features pertaining to Boochani's identity and vision are not factored into interpretations of his creative work.

Gaile Pohlhaus (2012) uses the term *wilful hermeneutical ignorance* to describe situations where people from the dominant socio-cultural group continue to oppress marginalized peoples as they engage in collective acts of epistemic resistance.[3] Epistemic domination occurs when privileged knowers misunderstand and misinterpret those who resist epistemic oppression and, in addition, do not take appropriate measures to establish equity in their interactions and transform society overall.[4] In order to create and apply remedies to epistemic injustice, one must recognize the nature of socio-political hierarchies and oppressive knowledge systems, and identify the epistemic agents positioned throughout. Rather than posit a non-social epistemic agent – the generic and self-sufficient knower characteristic of classical epistemology – Pohlhaus explains that we must recognize the *situatednesss* and *interdependent* aspects of knowers; that is, the significance of social positioning and the collective nature of their inquiry into the world (Pohlhaus 2012: 717–723).

Boochani's cultural background, education, intellectual and literary influences define the style, form and techniques employed in the book. In addition, the rhetorical appeals and emotional and psychological themes are derived from the frustration and fury of 5 years of incarceration, 5 years of systematic torture and degradation. In our conversations during the process, Boochani shared his concerns regarding the book's potential to expose the details and extent of the torture planned and orchestrated within Manus Prison, and the capacity of readers to grasp the depths of what he is trying to reveal.

> Do you think Australians will get it, do you think those who read this book will hear the message?
>
> Of course, it's a brilliant piece of literature, especially the way you fuse genres, the tropes you introduce, the multiple literary techniques you apply, the spaces you create…
>
> OK, but regardless of its literary qualities… what about torture? Does it describe the torture? What do you understand about torture when you read it?

No Friend but the Mountains is an account not only of what Boochani has come to know as a result of these ongoing 5 years, but also an expression of *how* he knows. That is, the book conveys a particular way of knowing, a critical standpoint (Pohlhaus 2012: 720, 730–31; Harding 1991), exclusively linked to his time locked-up in Manus Prison and his endurance experienced together with the community of refugees.

Dismantling Damaging Tropes

The exclusionary and violent ideologies constructed and perpetuated by nation-state border regimes are racialized and militarized in ways that impact our epistemic resources and how we apply and modify them. In addition to Nauru and the other immigration detention centres, Manus Prison has become such an integral part of Australian political discourse and global attention that it is inseparable from contemporary forms of racial thinking in and about Australia. It is also intertwined with other major discussions: the possibilities of communication technology, complicity, censorship, media images and responsible reporting, the economy and environmental policies. Any theorizing of borders and migration in Australian universities now requires a deep consideration of the phenomenon of Manus Prison. Therefore, our experience of the border in Australia, and citizenship in general, has become imbedded within systems of connected practices, concepts and theoretical approaches pertaining to the island prison. *No Friend but the Mountains* speaks back to all views on the political spectrum: for readers in Australia and abroad, the book allows for a distinct way of knowing and feeling, and it conveys critical positions unique to the narratives Boochani creates.

There exist a number of tropes regarding displaced and exiled peoples that Boochani challenges with the very act of cultural production and the individual stories he constructs. This kind of critical commentary is made possible by the power of his unique form of literature. It is worth reintroducing the tropes I list in the book's supplementary essay in order to develop frameworks and interpretative tools that resist similar kinds of essentialism:

- Caged person – escape to the West
- Desperate supplicant
- Struggling overcomer – the battler
- Tragic and miserable victim
- Broken human being
- Mystic sage – quirky and mysterious, a trickster

The damaging effects of standard, easy tropes restrict efforts to imagine criteria that amplify resistance and work to empower the oppressed. Interpretation needs to be a transnational, intersectional and anti-colonial political project led by the subjugated identity and plight of the author (Dhamoon 2015; Denzin and Lincoln 2014). There is an element of responsibility suggested here: learning about the epistemic resources of subjugated knowers requires an engaged political commitment to their lived situation (Pohlhaus 2012: 721). Support and empowerment in the form of transformed epistemic resources involves respect for expressions of defiance and engaging with the epistemologies that drive the activism of oppressed epistemic agents.

The following passage from *No Friend but the Mountains* foregrounds resistance and empowerment and centres issues related to colonialism and the defence of homeland. The relationship between affect, knowledge and place function within the narrative to construct a uniquely situated view of the Kurdish experience during the war between Iran and Iraq (1980–1988). The memory of war acts as a culturally and politically specific trope that works to convey something distinct about the oppressive conditions and the subjugated position of the knower; it also amplifies many of the features I introduce as interpretative reference points in the following section on a situated schema for reading. Boochani's flashback (analepsis) dream vision occurs in the darkness of night while lying atop one of the containers in Manus Prison, looking for the source of moaning sounds. The scene occurs just moments prior to witnessing a brutal beating of a refugee by guards:

> Animosities had reached climax and teeth were gnashing from extreme hate. Old wounds were opened and blades of battle tapped into the cesspool of history, the history of hate, and disseminated its loathing, spread across what once were fields of goodwill; our vivid, green and bounteous homeland. A putrid smell came over the whole place. Enemy also didn't recognise enemy. On one side, corps with steely determination whose objective was to fight in the name of religion. On the other side, corps who also fought in the name of religion. On one side, Iraqi Ba'athists would empty their rounds. On the other side, Iranians with religious devotion would open fire. In the middle were our homes – our homes left desolate. Two grand war elephants – administering nothing but a lot of hurt.

> The Peshmerga also battled from within the mountains. Their slogan represented defence of homeland and dignity. It was a war for no end, like all the other wars of history. A war with roots in earlier wars. And those wars had roots in other wars. A chain of wars born out of the nether regions of history. And so it was a seed of resentment that blossomed after centuries with the colour of blood once again.

> It was these very mountains that witnessed the spectacle; it was these ancient chestnuts that lamented.

> I was born in the cauldron of this war. (Boochani 2017a, 103)

A Situated Schema For Reading

For most of us, our epistemic resources and affective encounters are far-removed from the horrific, ever-changing and twisted experience of imprisonment on Manus Island. Trying to find conceptual tools, literary frames and examples, points of reference and the appropriate constellation of symbols for interpretation is hindered or blocked if interaction with the author or informed consultation and guidance is unavailable. Pohlhaus' explanation regarding the limits of our evaluation of the world in a stratified society provides perspective here: 'The right standards for knowing the world well will be determined by what is salient in the experienced world itself, and what is salient in the experienced world itself will depend upon *situatedness*: what do I/we need to know (or care to know) and why?' (Pohlhaus 2012: 718, emphasis in original). To arrive at *what we need to know and why* will require an intellectual rupture and aesthetic shift – a move toward altering instituted social imaginaries (Dotson 2014: 119). Such ruptures and shifts are particularly necessary regarding our shared meanings and concepts pertaining to forced migration, border politics, displacement and exile. This is possible by first engaging with features that constitute the identity and situation of the author and the culturally specific forms and symbols that work to build narratives (Coupe 2006).

In the supplementary essay to *No Friend but the Mountains*, I list a set of themes that helped formulate a multifaceted and nuanced understanding of Boochani's various narrative techniques. These themes enable a richer encounter with his feelings, thoughts and activism, and my conceptualization of them was developed during the translation process. They are not exhaustive nor are they meant to function as criteria. I include the following features here – and subsequent comments – as a schema to foster a closer and more dynamic literary encounter with the text and form more emancipatory and culturally fluid, rather than normative, criteria necessary for intimate and ethically transformative engagement:

- Indigenous Kurdish presence
- Evocation
- Self-determination
- Custodianship
- Decolonization and liberation
- Intersectional and transnational rhetoric
- Horrific surrealism
- New knowledges

The intricacies of these themes are subject for another more focused study. For the purposes of this article, it is important to indicate Boochani's complex and multidimensional connection to Kurdish language, heritage and an Indigenous Kurdish knowledge system – elements that contribute both to structuring the book and characterizing its content. He has shared with me issues pertaining to his Indigenous Kurdish identity and his thoughts on aspects of modern Western culture:

> Consider my indigeneity and my connection to the land. My voice in this book is not limited to my Indigenous identity. My views are also deeply influenced by modern Western thought and culture. I am both a proud Indigenous Kurdish man and an intensely modern individual. I see the power of these influences projected through my love of music – I generally only listen to two forms. I listen to Western classical music, I listen to Beethoven, I enjoy Vivaldi. But I also listen to *Houreh*. This could be one of the oldest forms of song still performed today, the Kurds have preserved it from ancient times. Its history goes back so far that not many people today are really able to engage with *Houreh*, there are very few people in Kurdistan who listen to it now. So I listen to one of the most significant forms of Indigenous music that is quickly losing its place in Kurdish society, and I also have a taste for Western music, mostly from the modern period. You can see these kinds of elements featured in my book. My encounters with people and understanding of the human condition are felt and theorised using modern Western approaches and Indigenous

knowledge. I am constantly grappling with these different aspects of who I am. (Behrouz
Boochani, personal correspondence)

Attention to the above list of features also helps to foreground the visceral feelings and
psychological trauma that result from systematic torture and exile. Decoloniality is a
salient factor throughout the book's political and philosophical dimensions, especially
the nuanced and emotive connections to land; the attention Boochani gives to ecolo-
gical destruction; and the complex social and political ways labour exploitation is
depicted in relation to Manusians (Boochani 2017a; Boochani 2017d).

The Standpoint from Manus Prison: A Thought Experiment

In his analysis of segregation and the epistemic standpoint of the black community
described in W.E.B. Du Bois' *Souls of Black Folk* (1903), Charles Mills explains the
contempt Du Bois has for the white cognitive world that excludes him. Entering this
world would mean living in a permanent state of 'double-consciousness'; that is, seeing
himself through the cognitive lens of white supremacy, seeing himself as a problem, the
subject of contempt and pity (Mills 2017: 107).[5] For Du Bois and Mills, black communities
in America have a *meta-perspective*. They have the potential for 'second-sight' or to see
through the misconceptions, manipulations and machinations of white communities in
America and acquire an epistemically privileged position. In this situation, it is the
dominant culture that is disadvantaged and blind to the functions of racism and to
the structures and operations of a socio-political world divided on racial grounds. Mills
argues that there is no possibility for reconciliation of epistemologies here: total resistance is the only approach when up against white supremacy (Mills 2017: 106–107; see
also Medina 2012).

Mills also discusses Du Bois' modification of Plato's Allegory of the Cave (Du Bois uses
the metaphor of the veil). Du Bois situates those kept in the darkness, black Americans,
as people with access to the social truth, and white Americans as ignorant even though
they dwell in the light (Mills 2017: 108). In the supplementary essay accompanying *No
Friend but the Mountains*, I begin with a short philosophical narrative inspired by Mills'
contextualization of Du Bois' account within the epistemic injustice discourse. I want to
end this essay by repeating the thought experiment, a narrative that helps illuminate the
uniquely situated and interdependent philosophical thrust of Behrouz's book:

*There is an island isolated in a silent ocean where people are held prisoner. The people
cannot experience the world beyond the island. They cannot see the immediate society
outside the prison and they certainly do not learn about what takes place in other parts of
the world. They only see each other and hear the stories they tell one another. This is their
reality; they are frustrated by their isolation and incarceration, but they have also been
taught to accept their predicament.*

*News somehow enters the prison about another island where the mind is free to know and
create. The prisoners are given a sense of what life is like on the other island but they do not have
the capacity or experience to understand fully. The people on the other island have special insight:
they see things that the prisoners cannot, they create things that the prisoners cannot, and they
certainly know things that the prisoners cannot. Some of the prisoners resent the people on the
other island. Some simply do not understand the people there or try to undermine them. Some are*

indifferent to the other society. Some prisoners feel pity for them because they are confident that their own situation is changing for the better and will eventually provide greater freedoms.

The two islands are polar opposites. One island kills vision, creativity and knowledge – it imprisons thought. The other island fosters vision, creativity and knowledge – it is a land where the mind is free.

The first island is the settler-colonial state called Australia, and the prisoners are the settlers.

The second island contains Manus Prison, and knowledge resides there with the incarcerated refugees.

(Tofighian, forthcoming 2018b)

Behrouz Boochani's *No Friend but the Mountains: Writing From Manus Prison* (Picador) is due for release on 31 July 2018. Boochani's feature-length film *Chauka, Please Tell Us the Time* (2017), co-directed with Arash Kamali Sarvestani, is available to watch on Vimeo: https://vimeo.com/ondemand/chauka

Notes

1. This passage is from a chapter that was published separately in *Island* magazine a year prior to the book's release: Boochani, B. (2017a) 'Chanting of Crickets, Ceremonies of Cruelty. A Mythic Topography of Manus Prison'. trans. Tofighian, O. *Island* 150: 96–115.
2. Examples of personal correspondence in this article took place either through Whatsapp voice messaging or during my two visits to Manus Island in 2017 and 2018. These are my own translations from Farsi to English.
3. Pohlhaus classifies wilful hermeneutical ignorance under what Charles Mills calls *epistemology of ignorance* (1997).
4. Kristie Dotson refers to this phenomenon as *contributory injustice* (2012).
5. Samia Mehrez analyzes the relationship between the famous French writer and scholar Azouz Begag and Ahmed Beneddif. Both are from the *beur* generation; they were born in France to Algerian parents who immigrated for work. While Begag is a French citizen, Beneddif never acquired citizenship due to his father's insistence to keep his Algerian nationality. Beneddif's life, in stark contrast to the successful writer and academic, has been impacted by disadvantage and intense discrimination, crime, imprisonment and multiple instances of deportation. The two develop a problematic relationship based on writing and publishing Beheddif's story; one that Begag describes as originally based on pity for the *beur* with Algerian nationality, pity for the *clandestine* who had experienced a difficult and tortuous past (Mehrez 2002).

Disclosure statement

No potential conflict of interest was reported by the author.

References

Boochani, B. 2017a. "Chanting of Crickets, Ceremonies of Cruelty. A Mythic Topography of Manus Prison." Trans. Tofighian, O." In *Island*, 96–115. Vol. 150.

Boochani, B. 2017b. "A Letter From Manus." *The Saturday Paper*, trans. O. Tofighian Available at https://www.thesaturdaypaper.com.au/news/politics/2017/12/09/letter-manus-island /15127380005617 [9 December 2017].

Boochani, B. 2017c. "This Is Hell Out Here': Behrouz Boochani's Diaries Expose Australia's Refugee Shame." *The Guardian*, trans. M. Mansoubi and O. Tofighian Available at https://www.theguar dian.com/world/2017/dec/04/this-is-hell-behrouz-boochani-diaries-expose-australia-refugee-shame [4 December 2017].

Boochani, B. 2017d. "An Island Off Manus", *The Saturday Paper*, trans. M. Mansoubi Available at https://www.thesaturdaypaper.com.au/2017/05/06/island-manus/14939928004582 [6-12 May 2017].

Boochani, B. 2018a. *No Friend but the Mountains: Writing From Manus Prison*. forthcoming. trans. O. Tofighian, Sydney:Picador.

Boochani, B. 2018b. "Mohamed's Life Story Is a Tragedy. But It's Typical for Fathers Held on Manus", *The Guardian*, trans. O. Tofighian Available at: https://www.theguardian.com/commen tisfree/2018/mar/27/mohameds-life-story-is-a-tragedy-but-its-typical-for-fathers-held-on-manus [27 March 2018].

Coupe, L. 2006. *Myth*. London: Routledge.

Denzin, N. K., and Y. S. Lincoln. 2014. "Introduction: Critical Methodologies and Critical Inquiry." In *Handbook of Critical and Indigenous Methodologies*, eds. N. K. Denzin, Y. S. Lincoln, and L. T. Smith, 1–20. London: Sage Publication.

Dhamoon, R. 2015. "A Feminist Approach to Decolonizing Anti-Racism: Rethinking Transnationalism, Intersectionality, and Settler-Colonialism." *Feral Feminisms: Complicities, Connections, & Struggles: Critical Transnational Feminist Analysis of Settler Colonialism 4 (Electronic)*, Summer. http://www. feralfeminisms.com/rita-dhamoon/

Dotson, K. 2012. "A Cautionary Tale: On Limiting Epistemic Oppression." *Frontiers: A Journal of Women Studies* 33 (1): 24–47. doi:10.5250/fronjwomestud.33.1.0024.

Dotson, K. 2014. "Conceptualizing Epistemic Oppression." *Social Epistemology: A Journal of Knowledge, Culture and Policy* 28 (2): 115–138. doi:10.1080/02691728.2013.782585.

Harding, S. 1991. *Who's Science? Who's Knowledge?: Thinking From Women's Lives*. Ithaca, N.Y.: Cornell University Press.

Medina, J. 2012. *Epistemologies of Resistance: Gender and Racial Oppression, Epistemic Injustice, and Resistant Imaginations*. Oxford: Oxford University Press.

Mehrez, S. 2002. "Ahmed De Bourgogne": The Impossible Autobiography of a "Clandestine". *Alif: Journal of Comparative Poetics* The Language of the Self: Autobiographies and Testimonies 22:36–71.

Mills, C. 1997. *The Racial Contract*. Ithaca, N.Y.: Cornell University Press.

Mills, C. 2017. "Ideology." In *The Routledge Handbook of Epistemic Injustice*, eds. I. J. Kidd, J. Medina, and G. Pohlhaus Jr., 100–112. New York: Routledge.

Pohlhaus, G. 2012. "Relational Knowing and Epistemic Injustice: Toward a Theory of Willful Hermeneutical Ignorance." *Hypatia: A Journal of Feminist Philosophy* 27 (4, September): 715–735. doi:10.1111/hypa.2012.27.issue-4.

Tofighian, O. 2018a. Translator's Tale: A Window to the Mountains. In *No Friend but the Mountains: Writing from Manus Prison* by B. Boochani, translated by O. Tofighian. Sydney:Picador forthcoming.

Tofighian, O. 2018b. No Friend but the Mountains:Translator's Reflections. In *No Friend but the Mountains: Writing from Manus Prison* by B. Boochani, translated by O. Tofighian. Sydney:Picador forthcoming.

Afterword

Reconstructing voices and situated listening

Timothy Laurie, Tanja Dreher, Michael R. Griffiths and Omid Tofighian

We have become exhausted by debates around freedom of speech in liberal democracies. Exhausted not in the sense that these debates lack significance – indeed, they often become the locus of powerful symbolic struggles over national and political identities – but rather in the sense that, as a legalistic orientation to speech as an *act*,[1] free speech discourses have provided so little guidance in responding to the overwhelming rise in everyday hate speech and vilification as diffuse and decentered social practices. When we edited the issue of *Continuum* from which this volume emerged, we could not have imagined the vast gap between liberal frameworks for regulating speech, and the whirlwind of misinformation subtending the COVID-19 pandemic, including its appropriation by paranoid social imaginaries to further anti-immigration and xenophobic agendas (including incitements to violence). During the 2020 COVID-19 pandemic in the United States, unrelenting verbal attacks on China from President Donald Trump have been used to distract from the failure of the White House to safeguard public health, leading to corollary attacks on Asian Americans (see Kipgen 2020). In the Australian context, one-third of all racist attacks in 2020 have been linked to racialised understandings of COVID-19 transmission, and most have been perpetrated against East Asian communities (Asian Australian Alliance et al. 2020; Tan 2020). The Australian immigration detention regime – both onshore and offshore carceral sites – not only continues to detain people seeking asylum indefinitely, putting both detainees and staff in grave danger of COVID-19 infection, but the Minister for Home Affairs Peter Dutton is manoeuvring to confiscate mobile phones, which will cut off connection between those unlawfully imprisoned and the outside world. In the United Kingdom, Prime Minister Boris Johnson's quips and caricatures about Niqabs in 2018 contributed immediately to a rise in recorded hate crimes against Muslim women (see Allen 2020, 57), and contributed to a more recent political atmosphere in which Black and other racialised communities have been publicly blamed for higher rates of COVID-19 transmission (e.g. BBC News 2020), despite clear evidence that these communities have been relatively neglected by public health services (see Public Health England 2020). We group these incidents together not to argue that free speech is out of control, but rather to suggest that the political issues raised by vitriolic public speech cannot be exhausted simply by weighing up competing freedoms. More cynically, we wonder whether the perfunctory invocation of free speech talking points can obfuscate the role of everyday verbal abuse and intimidation as a structuring element in deeply hierarchical societies. To this end, we use this discussion to bring together key critical concerns about freedom of speech as a site of constant public debatability (see Lentin, this volume), and to outline some priorities

---

1 For an extensive survey of approaches to speech for legal purposes, see Solum (1988).

that might guide future analyses of public speech beyond such debates. In particular, we suggest that the contributions of marginalised voices to public platforms do not merely provide evidence that free speech is alive and well, but may actually unsettle assumptions about what these platforms intend to achieve and the communities they purport to serve.

We begin with a sideways step. This is not an argument for or against the freedom to speak either as a formative principle or as an intended outcome of regulatory frameworks. Our purpose is not to prescribe a positive framework through which speech should be governed, but to illuminate the situatedness of speech against the tendency, found in both progressive and conservative political circles, to treat speech as a metaphysical or transcendent social good. Understood from the viewpoint of negative liberty, the freedom to speak is simply the absence of limitations upon speech. However, as Stanley Fish (1994, 108) has famously argued, speech only acquires meaning within contexts and communities that, precisely through the limitations they impose, create the possibilities for shared knowledge and therefore understanding. For this reason, people rarely squabble over speech emptied of any content whatsoever ('speech for the sake of speech'), but are perfectly willing to fight over 'the regulation of speech they want heard and the regulation of speech they want silenced' (110). Free speech attracts most controversy when the relative *value* of different kinds of speech is already at issue, and political resolutions to such controversies invariably require advancing the interests of some speakers – and the communities to which they belong – over others. Against the negative liberty paradigm which has dominated 20th-century accounts of free speech (see Mondal, this volume), Gavan Titley points toward 'the lattice of constraints it neglects', including the 'political power, media access and communicative capacity that organise the meaningful distribution of expression and attention in racially-ordered capitalist societies' (2020, 9). Freedom of speech is most easily conceived as a protection for the individual to disseminate ideas without state interference, but access to platforms for dissemination is not equally distributed. Indeed, it is often those with the greatest capacity to disseminate their views that claim foul when faced with the possibility of censure.

Deplatforming controversies on Australian university campuses illuminate this tension between speech as an empty category to be protected from censorship, and the specific sites through which speech is produced or disseminated. In 2018, a proposed public talk by 'men's rights' activist Bettina Arndt at the University of Sydney was vigorously protested by students, primarily on the basis that the talk, entitled 'Is there a rape crisis on campuses?', would further promote Arndt's frequent public criticisms of sexual assault survivors and advocates. In response to the protests, conservative newsmedia columnists claimed that there was a free speech 'crisis' in Australian universities,[2] and after heated protests on the day of Arndt's speech, a string of polemics in the Sydney-based *Daily Telegraph* included 'University Fascists Stop Debate', 'Big Bad Bettina Traumatises Toddlers', and 'Teaching Universities Freedom of Speech 101'. Against the charge of censorship, we might acknowledge that students were not seeking to remove Arndt's right to disseminate her views *tout court*, but rather to withhold the symbolic value accorded to any speech disseminated within the context and community of universities. Nevertheless, worries about censorship on campus prompted an *Independent Review of Freedom of Speech in Australian Higher*

2 These events share commonalities with controversies over Milo Yiannopoulos' tour of North American university campuses in 2017. See Johnson (2019).

Education Providers funded by the Australian Federal Government, which found no evidence of a free speech crisis. However, the review did suggest that 'freedom of intellectual inquiry' be disaggregated into 'freedom of speech' and 'academic freedom' to better capture speech not belonging to research or teaching, such as employees or students criticising their own universities (see French 2019). As it happened, student organisers at the University of Sydney had been subject to student misconduct allegations that had been interpreted an indirect disincentives to cease further protests.[3] To this extent, the substantive issues around political communication cut in two different directions: on the one hand, the familiar spectre of celebrity speakers claiming that the cancellation of a speaking platform constitutes censorship; on the other hand, the indirect regulation of political speech through disciplinary measures within organisations, which in turn reflect or seek to consolidate the tacit values of that institution.[4]

This raises a more intractable problem embedded in the aforementioned 'symbolic value' of universities as platforms. While it is pragmatic to argue that universities must be committed to specialist academic speech (or 'free intellectual inquiry', in the phrase used often by the Higher Education Standards Framework 2015), the ostensible virtue of academic inquiry has often been weaponised against marginalised communities – and in particular, against Indigenous or colonised peoples. Māori scholar of education Linda Tuhiwai Smith (2013) argues that many 'researchers, academics and project workers may see the benefits of their particular research projects as serving a greater good "for mankind"', and that it becomes 'so taken for granted that many researchers simply assume they embody this ideal' (2). The symbolic status of university-funded research must be subjected to criticism from the viewpoint of diverse stakeholder communities that have historically been excluded from participation or institutional decision-making. Although free speech controversies may require strategic arguments for the value of one speaker or ideology over another, they also provide important opportunities to reflect on the values of the platforms over which such struggles are fought, and can suddenly illuminate entrenched inequalities in the ways that expertise is understood and mobilised. For this reason, we want to suggest that deplatforming debates should not begin and end with institutional codes of conduct or standards frameworks, but instead open onto a more difficult question: how might scholarly research agendas be informed by, and respond to, wider challenges to inherited hierarchies of knowledge and expertise outside the tertiary sector? '[New] forms of collaboration and consultation are necessary which remove boundaries separating academia from communities', writes Omid Tofighian, suggesting that 'new models can emerge where people with experiences of and insight into displacement and exile become influential interlocutors and producers of new knowledges' (2020, 1148). Behrouz Boochani's reflections on 'speaking differently' also underscore the significance of political voice as a way of establishing new kinds of relational knowledge beyond narrow assertive individualism (Boochani, this volume). We want to reflect on the challenges in creating space for new kinds of knowledge by considering the gap between the freedom to speak and the freedom to be understood – or heard – when speaking, especially in cases where, as Tofighian puts

---

3 These allegations were later dismissed. See Ward (2019).
4 A similar issue arose from Rugby Australia's termination of a star player's contract, Israel Folau, due to a homophobic Twitter post (see Dale 2019).

it, the 'epistemic resources' of 'subjugated knowers' may be under-represented, devalued, or simply dismissed altogether (see Tofighian, this volume, p. 144).

Respect for marginalised and stigmatised knowers must be interdependent with a commitment to developing sustainable support mechanisms, while at the same time dismantling infrastructure that disproportionately benefits power and domination. When considering issues pertaining to subjugated speech, thinking critically about the conditions for knowledge production can shift discussion and action toward the formation and configuration of empowering ecologies of knowledge. We argue that systems of oppression and domination thrive on entangled epistemic, symbolic and material components – in order to foster new anti-colonial landscapes of knowledge, a transformation must occur on all fronts. Who speaks, who is heard, who is silenced, are determined by multiplicative, intersecting structures of power, and these structures are maintained through multidimensional narratives of exclusion and disempowerment. The power to speak is vital; it is a step toward sharing stories that can impact social imaginaries. Resistance to oppression requires addressing the epistemic and aesthetic, in addition to systemic and institutional barriers; historical injustices; obstacles within organisational cultures; silencing strategies; and intersectional discrimination. Subjugated knowers (and speakers) are empowered, and therefore heard, when their historical, political and creative potential is recognised and amplified; when hierarchies and fixed notions of identity are deconstructed; and when positionality and multiplicity of experiences are respected for the different ways of knowing they narrate.

Tensions around the arrival of alternative forms of expertise and knowledge were raised by Perth-based Indigenous hip hop artist Ziggy Ramo, who was invited to appear as a speaker on current affairs panel program *Q&A*, hosted by the Australian Broadcasting Corporation (ABC). In the panel discussion, Ramo noted that he was denied permission to perform a song entitled 'April 25th', named after Anzac in Australia, which takes place on the anniversary of Australian armed forces landing at Gallipoli during World War One and broadly commemorates Australian and New Zealand military veterans. In 'April 25th', Ramo begins by repeating racist speech commonly directed toward Australian Aboriginal communities ('Fuck those wack blacks', 'I heard they get money from the government'), and then redirects this same language toward ANZACs: 'Fuck those ANZACs/Now, how fucked up is that?' By juxtaposing commonplace racist speech with entirely uncommon anti-ANZAC speech, Ramo highlights the radical inequality between heightened public concerns around the dignity of ANZACs (which includes Indigenous Australian veterans), and the relative neglect of Indigenous Australians who continue to suffer everyday indignities. Despite his highly visible credentials as a successful performer and communicator, the *Q&A* producers seemed uncertain about Ramo's capacity to autonomously control his own meanings outside of the mediated space of panel discussion. Ramo's subsequent commentary on the issue within the *Q&A* discussion is instructive:

> Having one [member of a cultural minority group] is not cultural diversity. And then, on top of that, is it cultural diversity, or is it performative cultural diversity? Because, for example, on this show today, … the song I initially was going to perform was called 'April 25th'… [and] I was basically censored in the fact that the ABC said that it was not appropriate. So, is it performative? Because me sitting on this panel ticks off a box for the ABC that is cultural diversity, but if I'm not able to express my perspective, is it performative or is it actual cultural diversity? Because, as Barnaby [Joyce] said, it's important that we have freedom of speech and freedom

of expression. So, if we have seats at the table, but then we're not able to express our lived experience, are we actually having cultural diversity, or is it performative?

In place of 'April 25th', Ramo performed the song 'Stand for Something', which directly addresses inequalities facing Indigenous Australian communities, but does not comment on hate speech or on hypocrisies in the way that dignity is accorded to some groups and not others. Ziggy Ramo's appearance on *Q&A* is notable for three reasons.

First, by employing the language of free speech – and contrasting it with the tokenism of what he calls 'performative cultural diversity' – Ramo gestures toward a possible alliance with conservative politician Barnaby Joyce, who promptly downplays his own free speech stance by deferring to the potential offence caused to veterans. Ramo activates a language intended to bring together different, otherwise disparate, members of a community around a common liberal language.[5] Setting aside Barnaby Joyce's somewhat sheepish withdrawal from the dialogue, Ramo's invocation of free speech may provide unexpected moments of affinity between radically incommensurable political projects. Second, Ramo's criticism of the ABC is directed less toward the empty category of speech than to his own *situatedness* as a speaker called upon to do the 'performative' work of showcasing the ABC's commitment to media diversity. In the context of Muslim representation within Australian mediascapes, Abdel-Fattah and Krayem (2018) make a similar observation about the media valorisation of 'moderate' Muslims, 'who are emptied of their politics, their dissent, their resistance' (433). Formal permission to speak does not guarantee freedom to speak outside the parameters of the speech *expected* from the speaker, and minoritised speakers are particularly subject to scrutiny and misinterpretation from (often hostile) majorities.

This raises a third issue around the dialogic aspects of speaking and listening. Shared background literacy is always required in some minimal way for communication to be effective. If the punchline to a joke is delivered in Cantonese to a Spanish-speaking audience that does not understand, we do not say that the free speech of the comedian has been compromised. And yet, the capacity to speak has been constrained due to the absence of a shared language. When powerful social groups refuse to acquire the minimal cultural or 'racial literacy' (see Nash et al. 2018) needed to understand marginalised groups, the miscommunications that result can serve to reinforce existing social hierarchies. As Poppy de Souza (2018) notes in her commentary on ex-AFL player Adam Goodes, audiences may 'willfully mishear' Indigenous voices as mere provocations or emotional outbursts (460), rather than as expressions of perspectives and worldviews that differ from those ordinarily privileged within Australian society. In the case of *Q&A*, the ABC had felt comfortable enough to host a panel discussion about the 'April 15th' lyrics,[6] but not to allow Ziggy Ramo to present the same lyrics in a musical performance. 'There's a lot of context… to understand where that comes from', host Hamish McDonald had suggested, 'but without context, there may be issues…' Chief among these issues may have been the program's lack of trust in its audience to hear 'April 25th' without misconstruing the meaning as an attack on ANZACs, and not a commentary on the dignity denied to Indigenous Australian communities.

---

5 We could also compare this 'opportunistic' use of liberal ideologies to Elizabeth Povinelli's pragmatic account of neoliberalism: 'neoliberalism is not a thing but a pragmatic concept – a tool – in a field of multiple manoeuvres among those who support and benefit from it, those who support and suffer from it, and those who oppose it and benefit from it nevertheless' (2011, 19).

6 See *Q&A*, 17 August 2020, www.abc.net.au/qanda/2020-17-08/12550138

These problems cannot necessarily be remedied by fortifying media broadcasters' commitments to freedom of speech. Once we acknowledge that shared racial literacies are cumulative and dialogic, speech can better be understood as an affordance of a community of listeners, which in turn requires sustained practices of public pedagogy. As Jill Stauffer (2015) argues, not being heard can itself be an injustice, compounding traumatic injustices that go unacknowledged to produce 'ethical loneliness'. The ABC's caution around Ziggy Ramo's prospective performance on *Q&A* speaks to a longer history of dialogic failure, wherein audiences have refused to hear the intended meaning behind political speech from marginalised or under-represented communities. Consider the following two examples. In late April 2020, as the COVID-19 pandemic escalated in Australia, the Victorian Deputy Chief Health Officer faced calls to be stood down after a tweet that likened Captain Cook to the coronavirus on the 250th anniversary of his arrival into Botany Bay (McMahon 2020). Dr Annaliese van Diemen tweeted:

> Sudden arrival of an invader from another land, decimating populations, creating terror. Forces the population to make enormous sacrifices & completely change how they live in order to survive. COVID19 or Cook 1770?

The comment circulated just before the pandemic forced the cancellation of a state-funded 're-enactment' voyage in which a replica of Cook's HMS Endeavour would circum-navigate Australia – a voyage that did not actually take place (Williams 2020). Calls for Dr van Diemen's resignation from the Home Affairs Minister and others echoed the attacks on ABC commentator and former Young Australian of the Year, Yassmin Abdel-Magied, in 2017. As noted in Abdel-Fattah and Krayem (this volume), Abdel-Magied faced months of bullying and backlash after tweeting 'Lest. We. Forget (Manus, Nauru, Syria, Palestine …)', in reference to Anzac Day. After enormous backlash from conservative media outlets, Abdel-Magied subsequently relocated to the United Kingdom, giving a complex account of her decision in an important piece entitled 'Leaving for Good' (2017).

These public controversies demonstrate not only the recurring policing of speech by precisely those actors who most loudly proclaim a commitment to free speech, but also the recurring refusal to listen when talk turns to the founding and ongoing violence of colonisation and the racial carceral state. To borrow from Patrick Wolfe (2006), we might argue that this silencing of speech and the refusal to hear is not simply an event, but rather a structure that is deeply fundamental to the settler colonial project, which has long involved a foundational investment in maintaining colonial relations of speaking and listening. This became acutely evident during the Black Lives Matter uprising following the death of George Floyd in police custody in Minneapolis in 2020. An Australian news journalist reporting from Los Angeles drew criticism for asking what a protester meant when he said 'the country was built on violence', concluding the interview with: 'I really appreciate you giving your perspective because people in Australia doesn't [sic] have the understanding of the history of police killings here' (Smith 2020). The reporter was quickly called out for ignoring the continuing high rates of Indigenous over-incarceration, deaths in custody, over-policing and police brutality in Australia, which were brought to public attention more than 25 years ago by the landmark Royal Commission into Aboriginal Deaths in Custody. The systemic racism, over-policing and over-incarceration documented by the Royal Commission have been at the centre of the First Nations media agenda, and of First Nations activism and advocacy throughout the intervening decades (Thomas et al. 2020).

That this reporter received such rapid criticism is a possible sign of growing awareness around the importance of racial literacy, but also points to an enduring assumption, at least within newsmedia organisations, that no specific expertise is required to talk about race-based discrimination or the experiences of subjugated communities.

While the Australian journalist was unable to make the connections to racist violence and white supremacy in her own country, the death of George Floyd did prompt unprecedented mass demonstrations and public debate on Aboriginal deaths in custody in Australia. Family and advocates highlighted the connections with the story of Dunghutti man David Dungay Jr, who died in jail after saying 12 times 'I can't breathe' while restrained by corrections officers attempting to prevent him from eating a packet of biscuits. First Nations activists, advocates, media, policy leaders and numerous other commentators called for an end to the enduring silence on institutionalised colonial violence against Indigenous people (including Coe 2020, Moon 2020, McQuire 2020, Whittaker 2020, Williams 2020). For example, Gomeroi poet, lawyer and essayist Alison Whittaker's piece, 'Despite 432 Indigenous deaths in custody since 1991, no one has ever been convicted. Racist silence and complicity are to blame' (2020) and Darumbal/South Sea Islander journalist and researcher Amy McQuire, 'When Aboriginal people die in custody, there is a national silence' (2020). But despite growing public awareness around both the circumstances of Dungay's death and its place within a long history of Aboriginal deaths in custody, *Croakey* social journalism for health noted the resounding silence of governments and peak medical organisations in Australia in response to the Black Lives Matter movement (see McGlade 2020). In stark contrast to public statements at the United Nations, the American Public Health Association and in leading international scientific journals that joined their voices to the call of #BlackLivesMatter, the Australian Prime Minister, federal Health Minister and Chief Medical Officer have not used their authority to name and address the systemic racism and over-incarceration that contributes to poorer healthcare. In a somewhat perplexing response, the government has focused on criticising protesters. In July 2020, Prime Minister Scott Morrison called for the arrest of protesters gathering in support of the Dungay family's call for justice, citing public health concerns, even as football stadiums were reopened to large crowds. Beyond the high-profile free speech debates on racist cartoons and shock jock provocations lies a deeply entrenched and continually reinforced silence on the structural violence of the settler colony.

We have journeyed from the thickets of free speech controversies to the ethical problem of *situated* listening – that is, learning to listen in a particular time and place, within a network of relations that sustain both the speaker and ourselves. We might consider the absence of listening, or the absence of being heard in the face of consistent and persistent voice, as an active refusal rather than a simple accident (see Dreher 2009). Here again, First Nations knowledges in the settler colony can provoke and guide. In *Living on Stolen Land*, a 'call and guide to action' by Ambelin Kwaymullina, the section on Pathways begins with poems on 'Humility' and then 'Listening'. Listening, writes Kwaymullina, 'means listening to the sound of settler-colonialism inside your head and all around you so that you can hear past it and understand our voices on our own terms' (2020, 55–56). Listening in Kwaymullina's account also means listening for 'no', or refusal, listening for boundaries and for accountabilities: a stark contrast to the violent assertions of 'free speech' that characterise the most public of debates.

What might a future engendered through new ways of listening sound like? In the field of law and policy, the landmark Uluru Statement from the Heart (2017) demands Voice, Treaty and Truth-telling as the fundamental claims for First Nations justice in so-called Australia. Lead author of the statement, Professor Megan Davis, explains that the demand for a First Nations Voice would 'enshrine a norm of listening' in the Constitution (2018), grounded in the 'Right to Be Heard' as recognised in international law (2017). The Uluru Statement has not been universally lauded within Aboriginal communities: Tony Birch observed that for some who attended the summit at Uluru, the statement 'did not provide a legitimate and authoritative role for Aboriginal representation in parliament, and largely ignored the demand for a discussion of treaties' (2017).[7] Nevertheless, given its modest and (to some) largely symbolic force, it is notable that even the Uluru Statement's proposal for First Nations Voice to parliament was casually dismissed by the then-Prime Minister Malcolm Turnbull (see Grehan 2018) Political philosopher Duncan Iverson (2019) argues that assertive Indigenous sovereignty and the Uluru Statement is a challenge for liberalism to take up, adapt and change – even in cases where, as the critics of the Uluru Statement have noted, the assertion of sovereignty is carefully framed within the liberal language of dialogue and democracy. Wiradjuri man, author and journalist Stan Grant (2020) takes up this work to ask, 'Can liberal democracy meet the demands of First Nations' people?'. Grant argues that 'the blindfolds of liberalism' would need to be lifted, while Morgan Brigg and Mary Graham (2020) argue the need to embrace Aboriginal Ethics. Responding to Grant, Brigg and Graham state that

> The dominant political ideas that underpin and guide the Australian political order are thus inadequate to the task of protecting Indigenous sites or lives, or of recasting the relationship between Indigenous and Settler Australia. Liberalism has had long enough to redeem itself and has already generated far too much Indigenous suffering.

Where liberalism relegates questions of ethics to individual choice, according to Brigg and Graham, Indigenous political concepts offer an emphasis on relationality, responsibility and care:

> A powerful way to reform Australia's politico-conceptual architecture is by engaging with Indigenous political concepts. In contrast to liberalism's approach to ethics, Indigenous political thought tends to see ethics as a normal part of human development that is bound with a custodial ethic of caring for Country (sentient landscape), and thus as a pursuit that everyone enacts as part of their being and the overall ordering of society. Ethics is not a choice, but is part of *being human*. One's humanness and thus ethical conduct is continually affirmed and managed through relations with Country, kin, and ancestor figures.

Listening, responsiveness, witnessing, receptivity and responsibility all require shifting or yielding on the part of the dominant. Across the *Unsettled Voices* volume and our closing discussion, we have attempted to extend beyond the free speech debates, foregrounding turning attention to the politics of 'ethical responsiveness', including listening and witnessing (Dreher and Mondal 2018). Contributions in this volume from Boochani and Tofighian demonstrate the crucial importance of seeking out different voices to support

---

7 Commenting on the emergence of the SEED Indigenous Youth Climate Network and Warriors of Aboriginal Resistance (WAR), which both pivot away from campaigns oriented toward symbolic constitutional recognition, Birch (2017) concludes by suggesting that 'As Aboriginal people, we must refuse the invitation to sit at the big table where, ultimately, we are made fools of'.

and sustain interdependent ways of knowing. These are calls for 'new' forms of translation, reading and listening, and point toward ways of 'reconstructing voice' by 'both employing and deconstructing writing structures' and developing translation as collective knowledge production (Boochani, quoted in Tofighian, this volume, p. 157). 'Support and empowerment in the form of transformed epistemic resources', writes Tofighian, 'involves respect for expressions of defiance and engaging with the epistemologies that drive the activism of oppressed epistemic agents' (536). In this context, this volume has sought to centre decolonial and critical race knowledges, and to privilege writing from the inside – inside prisons and inside settler colonial and orientalist structures. Rather than urging progressive thinkers to adopt a strong position on free speech as a principle or logic, we encourage instead a shift in the conditions of audibility: a shift, a change, a nudge, a transformation in the practices of listening, which are then the possibilities for being heard. 'Ultimately, if we are to sustain the connections between all life that in turn sustain all of us', write Ambelin Kwaymullina and Blaze Kwaymullina (2010, 206), 'we must all learn how to read the signs, to listen to country, and to escape the fixed binaries of colonisation'.

References

Abdel-Fattah, R., and M. Krayem. (2018) 'Off script and indefensible: The failure of the "moderate Muslim"'. *Continuum: Journal of Media & Cultural Studies* 32 (4): 429–443.

Abdel-Magied, J. (2017). 'Leaving for good'. *Meanjin* 76 (4): 30–33.

Allen, C. (2020). *Reconfiguring Islamophobia: A Radical Rethinking of a Contested Concept*. Cham: Palgrave Pivot.

Asian Australian Alliance, O. Chiu, and P. Chuang. (2020). *COVID-10 Coronavirus Racism Incident Report*. (Penrith, Australia). https://asianaustralianalliance.net/wp-content/uploads/2020/07/COVID-19-racism-incident-report-preliminary.pdf.

BBC News. (2020). 'Craig Whittaker: MP defends saying some Muslims not taking COVID seriously'. *BBC News*, 31 July 2020. www.bbc.com/news/uk-politics-53612230.

Birch, T. (2017). 'On sovereignty'. *Overland*, 229. https://overland.org.au/previous-issues/issue-229/column-tony-birch/.

Brigg, M., and M. Graham. (2020). 'The ongoing destruction of Indigenous Australia demonstrates the need for Aboriginal ethics'. *ABC Religion and Ethics*. Available at www.abc.net.au/religion/stop-destroying-indigenous-sites-and-lives-morgan-brigg-and-mar/12355284. Accessed 25 November 20202.

Coe, L. J. (2020). 'This is black liberation in Australia – the time is here to be on the right side of history'. *The Guardian Australia*. Retrieved from www.theguardian.com/commentisfree/2020/jun/08/this-is-black-liberation-in-australia-the-time-is-here-to-be-on-the-right-side-of-history. Accessed 25 November 2020.

Dale, A. (2019). 'Employment: Losing my religion, losing my job?' *LSJ: Law Society of NSW Journal* 58: 36–39.

de Souza, P. (2018). 'What does racial (in) justice sound like? On listening, acoustic violence and the booing of Adam Goodes'. *Continuum: Journal of Media & Cultural Studies* 32 (4): 459–473.

Dreher, T. (2009). 'Listening across difference: Media and multiculturalism beyond the politics of voice'. *Continuum: Journal of Media & Cultural Studies*, 23 (4): 445–458.

Dreher, T., and A. A. Mondal. (Eds.). (2018). Ethical Responsiveness and the Politics of Difference. Cham, Switzerland: Palgrave MacMillan.

Fish, S. (1994). 'There's no such thing as free speech, and it's a good thing, too'. In *There's No Such Thing as Free Speech*, 102–119. New York and Oxford: Oxford University Press.

French, R. (2019). *Report of the Independent Review of Freedom of Speech in Australian Higher Education Providers*. Department of Education and Training (Australia).

Grant, S. (2020). 'Three years on from Uluru, we must lift the blindfolds of liberalism to make progress'. *The Conversation*. Available at https://theconversation.com/three-years-on-from-uluru-we-must-lift-the-blindfolds-of-liberalism-to-make-progress-138930. Accessed 26 November 2020.

Grehan, H. (2018). 'First Nations politics in a climate of refusal: Speaking and listening but failing to hear'. *Performance Research* 23 (3): 7–12.

Higher Education Standards Framework (Threshold Standards). (2015). The Australian Government.

Johnson, J. (2019). 'When hate circulates on campus to uphold free speech'. In *Studies in Law, Politics, and Society*, edited by A. Sarat, 113–130. Bingley, UK: Emerald Publishing Limited.

Ivison, D. (2020). *Can Liberal States Accommodate Indigenous Peoples?* UK: Polity Press.

Kipgen, N. (2020). 'COVID-19 pandemic and racism in the United States and India'. *Economic and Political Weekly* 55 (23): 21.

Kwaymullina, A. 2020. *Living on Stolen Land*. Broome, Western Australia: Magabala Books.

Kwaymullina, A., and B. Kwaymullina. (2010). 'Learning to read the signs: Law in an Indigenous reality'. *Journal of Australian Studies* 34 (2): 195–208.

McGlade, H. 2020. 'Calling for urgent pandemic action to prevent more deaths in custody'. *Croakey*, April 20.

McMahon, A. (2020) 'Coronavirus: Victorian health officer's 'Captain Cook or virus' tweet sparks outrage'. *news.com.au*. Available at: www.news.com.au/national/victoria/politics/coronavirus-victorian-health-officers-captain-cook-or-virus-tweet-sparks-outrage/news-story/f3a545406b8515bc8bf23ff982402d76. Accessed 25 November 2020.

McQuire, A. (2020). 'There cannot be 432 victims and no perpetrators'. *The Saturday Paper*. Retrieved from www.thesaturdaypaper.com.au/news/law-crime/2020/06/06/there-cannot-be-432-victims-and-no-perpetrators/15913656009926. Accessed 25 November 2020.

Mondal, A. A. (2018). 'The shape of free speech: Rethinking liberal free speech theory'. *Continuum: Journal of Media & Cultural Studies* 32 (4): 503–517.

Moon, H. (2020). 'Australia must stop turning a blind eye to our own black deaths'. *Junkee*. Retrieved from https://junkee.com/black-deaths-in-custody-australia/. Accessed 25 November 2020.

Nash, K., J. Howard, E. Miller, G. Boutte, G. Johnson, and L. Reid. (2018). 'Critical racial literacy in homes, schools, and communities: Propositions for early childhood contexts'. *Contemporary Issues in Early Childhood* 19 (3): 256–273.

Povinelli, E. (2011). *Economies of Abandonment: Social Belonging and Endurance in Late Liberalism*. Durham, NC: Duke University Press.

Public Health England. (2020). *Beyond the Data: Understanding the Impact of COVID-19 on BAME Groups*. London: PHE Publications.

Smith, D. (2020). 'Nine reporter called out for 'ignorance' on Australian black history'. *NITV*. Available at www.sbs.com.au/nitv/article/2020/06/01/nine-reporter-called-out-ignorance-australian-black-history. Accessed 25 November 2020.

Smith, L. T. (2013). *Decolonizing methodologies: Research and indigenous peoples*. London: Zed Books Ltd.

Solum, L. B. (1988). 'Freedom of communicative action: A theory of the first amendment freedom of speech'. *Northwestern University Law Review* 83 (1–2): 54–135.

Stauffer, J. (2015). *Ethical Loneliness: The Injustice of Not Being Heard*. New York: Columbia University Press.

Tan, C. (2020). 'COVID19 has prompted a spike in racist attacks. We need to track them better'. *ABC News*, 9 May.

Thomas, A., A. Jakubowicz, and H. Norman. (2020). *Does the Media Fail Aboriginal Political Aspirations? 45 Years of News Media Reporting of Key Political Moments*. New South Wales: Aboriginal Studies Press.

Titley, G. (2020). *Is Free Speech Racist?* London: Polity.

Tofighian, O. (2020). 'Introducing Manus prison theory: Knowing border violence'. *Globalizations* 17 (7): 1138–1156.

Uluru Statement from the Heart. (2017). Retrieved from https://ulurustatement.org/

Ward, M. (2019). 'The issue of free speech at the University of Sydney is not what you think'. *Overland*, 23 July.

Whittaker, A. (2020). 'Despite 432 Indigenous deaths in custody since 1991, no one has ever been convicted. Racist silence and complicity are to blame'. *The Conversation*. Retrieved from https://theconversation.com/despite-432-indigenous-deaths-in-custody-since-1991-no-one-has-ever-been-convicted-racist-silence-and-complicity-are-to-blame-139873. Accessed 25 November 2020.

Williams, C. (2020). 'Scott Morrison Is Spending $60m To 'Reenact' A Voyage That Never Happened' *The Huffington Post*. Available at www.huffingtonpost.com.au/entry/january-26-events-that-arent-captain-cook-related_au_5e1d1c50c5b6640ec3d9b3e6. Accessed 25 November 2020.

Wolfe, P. (2006). 'Settler colonialism and the elimination of the native'. *Journal of Genocide Research* 8 (4): 387–409.

Index

Note: **bold** page references indicate tables and the suffix 'n' indicates a note.

ABC (Australian Broadcasting Corporation) 2–3, 39, 40, 41, 78, 97, 152–153, 154
Abdel-Fattah, Randa 5, 6, 38–52, 153, 154
Abdel-Magied, Yassmin 2–3, 5, 39, 40–41, 43, 44, 46, 47, 50, 154
Abetz, Eric 40–41
Aborigines: Aboriginal Ethics 156; child removal 60–61, 98, 106, 107; incarceration of 2, 5, 30, 31, 53–67, 154, 155; and the national anthem 4, 24–26, **25**, 33n5, 78; and offensive language 5, 28–31, **30**, **31**, 71, 72, 152–153; representation of 2, 68–69, 96–111; women 6, 60, 96–111; *see also* Blackfullas; Cheetham, Deborah; Goodes, Adam; Indigenous peoples
Abu Hamdan, Lawrence 74–75
acoustic violence 6, 68–80
African Americans 26, 33n4, 63, 73–74, 79n8, 102
Agamben, Giorgio 134n30
Ahmad, F. 42
Ahmed, Sara 18, 75
Akermanis, Jason 70, 71
Aly, Waleed 43, 47, 73, 75
Anderson, Benedict 98
Angelou, Maya 26
animal world 128, 129, 130–131, 138
Anthony, T. 30, 62
anti-colonialism 26, 144, 152
anti-racism 15, 16, 17–19
anti-Semitism 18, 88, 112, 113, 118–119
ANZAC Day 2, 40, 152–153, 154
Araluen Corr, Evelyn 6, 62, 96–111
archive, colonial 6, 96–111
Arendt, H. 55, 134n31
Arndt, Bettina 150
Arthur, Mary Ann and Walter George 101, 105
Asad, Talal 7, 118
asylum seekers 3, 5, 7, 8, 11, 15, 19, 54–60, 128, 129; *see also* immigration; refugees
Atkinson, Judy 97
Attwood, Bain 98
Austin, Lena 106

Australia 1, 4–8, 17, 99; and COVID-19 149, 154; free speech in 2–3, 4–5, 24–37, **30**, **31**, 49–50, 70, 71, 97, 150–151, 152–153; national anthem 4, 24–25, 78, 79n8; racism in 2, 3, 5–6, 10, 57, 60, 68–79, 97, 123, 149, 152, 154–155; as *terra nullius* 25–26, 31, 33n5, 78; 'un-Australians' 45, 53, 69, 128; White Australia policy 56, 57; *see also* Aborigines
'Australia Day' 3, 26, 65

Balla, Paola 108
Barati, Reza 58–59, 64–65
'bare life' 61, 134n30, 134n31
Behrendt, Larissa 6, 69, 98, 99, 103
Bengaroo, Lloyd 29
Benjamin, Walter 91–92
Bennelong 101
Bernardi, Cory 71
Bessie Flower 103
Beswick, Katie 19
Bickford, S. 70
bigot, right to be a 2, 5, 29, 31, 71
Billig, M. 18
Birch, Tony 59, 156
Bird, Carmel 107
Birmingham, Simon 46
Bishop, Julie 40, 41
Black Lives Matter 154, 155
blackface 10
Blackfullas 4–5, 24–37, **30**, **31**; *see also* Aborigines
Blum, L. 13, 14, 15, 16
Bolt, Andrew 2, 29, 71
Bond, Chelsea 4–5, 24–37, 97
Boochani, Behrouz 7–8, 127–132, 136–139, 140–147, 151, 156–157
booing 2, 5–6, 24, 68–69, 72, 73, 75, 76
borders 2, 7–8, 40, 55, 56, 58, 93, 129–130, 132, 134n31, 137, 143
Bowd, D. G. 101
Brandis, George 29, 61, 62, 71
Brangy, Kitty and Edith 106
Brewster, Anne 106

Brexit 16
Brigg, Morgan 156
Bringing Them Home Report 60–61
Bromberg, Justice 29
Butcher, T. 69
Butler, J. 72, 73, 77, 133n21

Canada 27, 32, 60, 99
Canagarajah, Suresh 84
capitalism 20, 57, 90, 104, 107, 150
cartoons 1, 2, 3, 62, 90, 97, 99
censorship 18, 43–44, 113, 114, 115–116,
   120, 122–124, 130, 143, 150–151, 152; self-
   censorship 16, 18, 43–44; *see also* silencing of
   marginalised voices
Centres for Disease Control and
   Prevention (US) 3
Césaire, Aimé 26
Charleston church shooting 10
Charlie Hebdo 1, 3, 88
Charlottesville 1, 9
Chauvel, Charles 108
Cheetham, Deborah 4–5, 24–25, 26, 27,
   31, 71, 78
Chikowero, M. 26
Chouliaraki, Lillie 132n4
Christensen, George 41
Christianity 34n10, 118–119, 122
Clarke, John 56
Clarke, Maxine Beneba 7, 69, 132n2
class 19, 20, 56, 64, 75, 90, 121
closure of free speech 117, 118, 119–120,
   122, 124
Coghill, Shane 4–5, 24–37
colonialism 6, 72, 79, 85, 89, 96, 97–98, 100, 102,
   107, 144, 154; *see also* settler colonies
Connelly-Northey, Lorraine 108
Conor, Liz 98, 99, 103
consequentialism 115
Continuum 62, 149
Cooper, W. 26
Corbyn, Jeremy 112
COVID-19 1, 149, 154
Crime and Misconduct Commission
   (CMC) 30–31
Cripps, Kylie 97
critical race analyses 1, 13, 102, 118, 157
curricula 122–124

Darling, Governor 101, 105
Darroch, Lee 108
Darwin, Charles 101–102
Davis, A. 25, 32
Davis, Jack 107
Davis, Megan 97, 156
Dawe, Bryan 56
De Lint, W. 55
de Souza, Poppy 5–6, 68–82, 153
Deacon, Destiny 108

decolonisation 1, 28, 73, 84–85, 141, 145, 146
denial 4, 9–21
Denmark 1, 90
deplatforming 150, 151
Derrida, J. 25, 96
detention: of Indigenous peoples 60–63, 109; of
   juveniles 2, 62; of migrants 3, 7, 55, 57–58, 59,
   65, 127–132, 136–139, 140–147, 149
Dickinson, Emily 132
Dieudonne M'Bala 87
Dinnison, Melissa 97
domestic violence 43, 47–48
Douglas, Josie 107
Draper, Hal 88
Dreher, Tanja 1–8, 50, 70, 85, 149–159
D'Souza, D. 13
Du Bois, W. E. B. 19, 33n4, 146
Dunbar, Paul 26
Dungay, David Jr 155
Dunn, K. 12
Dutton, Peter 40–41, 55, 128, 149

Eatock, Pat 29
Eddo-Lodge, R. 38
'embodied ear' 73–74
ethics, Aboriginal 156
ethics of care 128, 134n28
Evans, Bertrand 123

Fanon, F. 27, 28, 84, 90
Farbman, J. 15
Farquharson, K. 42
Farrar, Salim 39, 46
Ferguson, W. 26
Fields, B. and K. 15
Fields, James Alex Jr 9
Finsbury Park Mosque 10
First Nations peoples 3, 4, 5, 8, 27, 60, 75; in
   Australia 2, 27, 28, 154, 155, 156; *see also*
   Aborigines; Indigenous peoples
Fish, Stanley 150
Fletcher, J. J. 98
Floyd, George 154, 155
Folau, Israel 151n4
Foley, Fiona 107–108
Ford motors 83
foreclosures 119–120, 121, 124
France 1, 3, 27, 87–88
Frankenberg, R. 39
Fraser, Eliza 99, 103
free speech 1–8, 24–37, 83–95, 112–126,
   149–151, 155; in Australia 2–3, 4–5, 24–37,
   30, **31**, 49–50, 70, 71, 97, 150–151, 152–
   153; and Blackfullas 24–37; and closure
   117, 118, 119–120; and Muslims 4–5, 6, 85,
   86, 87, 92, 93, 113; politics of 121–124; as
   privilege 49–50; right to be a bigot 2, 5, 29,
   31, 71; right to vilify 1, 2, 3, 28–29, 71; *see
   also* hate speech

freedom/liberty 3, 4–5, 7, 8, 26–27, 88, 113–114, 127, 129, 138–139; 'liquid' flows 7, 118; and Mill 7, 114, 115, 116–118; negative 7, 115–116, 150; planar model of 7, 118, 123–124; restraints on 114, 118, 119

Garcia, J. 12–13, 14, 15, 17
Gay, Roxanne 40
Gaza 87, 112
Giannacopoulos, M. 55, 64
Gilroy, Paul 17, 18
Goldberg, David 20
Gooda, Mick 60
Goodes, Adam 2, 5–6, 24, 68–82, 153
Goodhart, David 16–17, 20
Graham, Mary 156
Grant, Stan 72, 75, 76, 156
Green, Margaret 106
Greer, Germaine 40
Griffiths, Michael R. 1–8, 53–67, 85, 149–159

Hage, G. 40, 49, 56, 57, 59, 60
Hall, Stuart 90, 91
Hammill, Janet 97
Hanna, Hekmat Alqus 59
Hanson, Pauline 2, 45, 98
Harkin, Natalie 6, 98, 99–100, 104, 105, 109
Harrison, Jane 109
hate speech 2, 87, 113, 118, 119, 149
Haworth, A. 114
hearing racism 6, 73, 75–77
hegemony, theories of 120–121, 124
Heiss, Anita 105, 107
Hervik, Peter 90
Hesse, B. 12
Heyer, Heather D. 9
Hitchens, C. 86–87, 91
Hizb ut-Tahrir 46–47
Holiday, Billie 26–27
Honeyford, Ray 17–18, 19
hooks, bell 102
Howard, John 133n5
Howson, Peter 98
Huggins, Jackie 97, 98, 109
human rights 2, 7, 74, 97, 137, 138
humanitarianism 7, 127–128, 129, 130–131, 132n4, 137
humanity 7, 57, 127, 128, 129, 130, 131, 132, 138, 156
Hurley, Chris 29
Hurstville Boys, Sydney 45
'hurt feelings' 69–70, 71

'I know why the caged bird sings' 26–29
Ihram, Silma 43
immigration 2, 10, 16–18, 19, 20, 56, 57, 149; see also asylum seekers; refugees
incarceration 53–67; of Indigenous peoples in Australia 2, 5, 31, 40, 61–62, 154, 155; see also detention

Indian Wells tennis tournament 76
Indigenous peoples 11, 54, 60, 61, 64, 90, 99, 102, 103–104, 145–146, 151; in Australia 2, 3, 4, 26, 30–31, 32, 59–63, 64, 68–69, 71, 72, 75, 78, 97–98, 108, 152–153, 154–155, 156; Indigenous sovereignty 69, 77, 78, 156; see also Aborigines; First Nations peoples
inquiries 5, 28, 53–67, 97
Iran/Iranians 58, 59, 141, 144
Iraq/Iraqis 19, 57, 59, 88, 89, 144
ISIS (Islamic State of Iraq and Syria) 88, 89
Islam 2–3, 6, 39–50, 85, 86, 87, 91, 92, 93, 113, 118–119; see also Muslims
Islamist, as term 6, 84–85, 86, 91, 92, 93
Islamophobia 10, 16, 39, 41–44, 45, 46–47, 48, 49, 88, 89, 112–113, 119, 149
Israel 6, 17, 65n1, 70–71, 74, 112, 113
Iverson, Duncan 156

Jackson, Ray 59
Jameson, Frederic 103–104
Janke, Terri 109
Johnson, Boris 149
Johnson, Colin 107
Jones, Tony 39
Joyce, Barnaby 153
Judd, B. 69

Kafka, Franz 130
Kahaleole Hall, Lisa 97
Kaufman, Eric 16–17
Kelly, Ruth 10
Kennett, Jeff 69
Khiabany, G. 87–88, 90
King, Martin Luther Jr. 26
knowledge production 141, 152, 157
Knox, Roger 32
Kramer, Holly 40
Krayem, Ghena 39, 46
Krayem, Mehal 5, 6, 38–52, 153, 154
Kundnani, Arun 41–42, 90
Kurds/Kurdish culture 141, 144, 145–146
Kurtzer, Sonja 106–107
Kwaymullina, Ambelin and Blaze 155, 157
Kyriarchal System 7–8, 137–138, 141

Lambie, Jacquie 40
Langton, M. 30, 97, 98, 100, 107, 108
Latham, Mark 46
Laurie, Timothy 1–8, 149–159
Leak, Bill 2, 28, 62, 97, 99
Leane, Jeanine 109
Lee, S. 114
Lentin, Alana 4, 9–23, 90, 149–150
Leyonhjelm, David 11, 71
liberal free speech theory 112–126
liberalism 4, 6–7, 8, 84, 86, 88, 90, 91, 93, 113–114, 116, 156; late 1–8, 53, 60, 61, 62–63, 64; settler colonial 5, 54

liberty *see* freedom/liberty
liberty of conscience 116, 120
listening 4, 8, 49, 68–79, 85, 153, 154, 155–157;
    see also hearing racism
Lock, Maria 6, 101, 105
Lorde, Audre 75–76, 102
Losurdo, Domenico 90
love, primacy of 128, 129, 131, 139
Lynch, James J. 123

Makela, Richard 87
Malhotra, S. 77
Maltilina, Rebecca 106
Manne, R. 55, 57
Manus Island, Papua New Guinea 2, 7–8, 40, 58,
    127–135, 136–139, 140–147
Marley, Bob 26, 27
Marmo, M. 55
Marsalis, W. 27
Martin, Karin L. 109
Martiniello, Jennifer Kemarre 103
Marxism 88, 120, 121
McCulloch, Susan 107–108
McDonald, Annie 103
McDonald, Hamish 153
McGinty, A. 42, 46
McGuire, Eddie 69
McKenzie, Lisa 19, 20
McQuire, Amy 97, 155
Meer, N. 119
migrants 10, 11, 18, 54, 64; detention of 3, 7,
    55, 57–58, 59, 65, 127–132, 136–139, 140–
    147, 149; *see also* asylum seekers; refugees
Mill, John Stuart 7, 113, 114, 115, 116–118,
    120–121
Mills, Charles 25, 28, 31, 146
minorities 5, 14, 19, 20, 28, 31, 49, 71, 83, 93
Minter, Peter 105
Mobourne, Maggie 105
'moderate' Muslims 3, 5, 6, 8, 38–52, 153
Modood, T. 42
Moffatt, Tracey 108
Mondal, Anshuman A. 6–7, 112–126, 150
moral injury 70, 71
Moreton-Robinson, Aileen 26, 33, 39, 64, 100, 102
Morgan, Sally 106
Morrison, Scott 155
Morsi, Yassir 6, 41, 48, 83–95
mourning 5, 54, 61, 99–100
Muecke, Stephen 107
Mukandi, Bryan 4–5, 24–37
Mulrunji 29–30, 61, 62
multiculturalism 16, 19, 39, 40, 41, 42, 49, 64
Mundine, Ngunggai Warren 97
Muslims 10, 11, 16, 84–85, 90; in Australia 2, 3,
    39–50, 153; and free speech 4–5, 6, 85, 86, 87,
    92, 93, 113; 'moderate' 3, 5, 6, 8, 38–52, 153;
    see also Islam; Islamophobia
Myers, Kevin 18

Native Americans 27, 33n5
Nauru 2, 8, 40, 58, 136, 137, 139, 143
Neale, T. D. 63
negative freedom 7, 115–116, 150
Nelson, J. 12
neoliberalism 62, 128, 130, 153n5
New Zealand 99, 152; *see also* ANZAC day
Ngo, Helen 34n9
No Friend But The Mountains (Boochani) 8,
    140–147
Noonuccal, Oodgeroo 106
'not racism' 1, 2, 4, 5–6, 9–23, 69–70

offensive language charges 5, 30–31, **30, 31**
Omi, M. 12
Orientalism 85, 93–94
Osborne, Darren 10
other, the 1, 3, 40, 59, 83–84, 89, 90, 128, 146–
    147; and Islam 39, 43, 85–86, 89, 90, 91, 92, 93;
    and racism 12, 75, 76, 77, 97; refugees as
    130, 131

Pacific Solution 55
Palestine/Palestinians 6, 40, 59, 70–71, 74, 87,
    88, 112
Palm Island 35n18, 61, 62
Paradies, Y. 12
Patten, J. T. 26
Peris, Nova 71
Pitcher, Ben 18
planar model of freedom 7, 118, 123–124
Plato's Allegory of the Cave 146
poetry/poets 7, 26, 75, 77, 98, 99, 100, 103, 104,
    105, 106, 107, 109, 127–132, 137, 141, 155
Pohlhaus, Gaile 142, 144–145
Povinelli, E. A. 62–63, 153n5
Powell, Enoch 18
Power, Katrina Ngaityalya 2
Price, Bess Nungarrayi 2
public nuisance charges 29–31, **30, 31**
Public Order Act 1986 118–119

Racial and Religious Hatred Act 2006 (RRHA) 119
racial contract 25, 28, 29, 31
Racial Discrimination Act 1975 2, 3, 28, 49, 71;
    Section 18C 2, 3, 28–29, 49, 71–72, 97
racial literacies 153, 154, 155
racial self-interest 16–17, 20
racism 4, 64, 88, 89, 90, 92, 93, 97, 146; anti-
    racism 15, 16, 17–19; in Australia 2, 3, 5–6,
    10, 57, 60, 68–79, 97, 123, 149, 152, 154–155;
    definition 10, 11–15, 16–17, 18, 19–20, 57;
    hearing 6, 73, 75–77; as morality 11, 12–
    15, 20; 'not racism' 1, 2, 4, 5–6, 9–23, 69–70;
    rationality of 16, 18, 20; sound of 68–80; as
    'unhelpful' 4, 12, 15, 16–17, 19, 20; in United
    States 1, 6, 9, 10, 13, 14, 16, 76, 154, 155
Ramo, Ziggy 152–153, 154
Rankine, Claudia 77

Reed-Gilbert, Kerry 107
refugees 5, 7, 53–60, 61, 64–65, 127–132,
    136–139, 140–147; *see also* asylum seekers;
    immigration
representation 6, 44, 46, 97–98, 99, 100–103,
    108, 109
Rifi, Jamal 43
riots 58, 61, 62–64
Roof, Dylann 10
Rowe, A. C. 77
Royal Commission into Aboriginal Deaths in
    Custody (RCIADIC) 30, 60, 154
Royal Commission into the Protection and
    Detention of Children in the Northern
    Territory (RCPDCNT) 60
Ruediger, Dorothea 106
Rushdie, Salman 1
Russell, Lynette 100
Ryan, Alan 116

Sahhar, Micaela 5, 53–67
Said, Edward 34n13, 93, 102
The Saturday Paper 7, 127
Sayyid, Salman 88
Scott, Rosie 107
settler colonies 1, 2, 3, 4, 5, 26, 28, 53–67, 72, 75,
    78–79, 97, 98, 99, 147, 154, 155
Seyit, Kuranda 45
Shah, Naz 112
sharia law 39, 46
Shelby, Tommie 13–14, 15
Shoemaker, Adam 107
silence: choosing 77–78; resistance to 97,
    98, 155
silencing of marginalised voices 1, 3, 4, 6, 7, 8,
    31, 39, 43–44, 53, 88, 101, 150, 152, 154; *see
    also* censorship
Simone, Nina 26–27
Simpson, Audra 61
Sinclair, Douglas 83
Sine, Maurice 88
situatedness 142, 145, 150, 153, 155
slavery 2, 27, 90, 105
Smith, Dick 10, 11, 45
Smith, Linda Tuhiwai 84–85, 151
social media 9, 19, 43, 44, 47, 78, 87, 127, 128,
    130, 131, 151n4
Sohrabi, H. 42
solidarity 4, 7, 8, 44, 130–131, 138–139
Song, Miri 11, 13, 15, 16
sonic warfare 70–71, 74–75
sovereignty 5, 54–60, 70; Indigenous 69, 77,
    78, 156
Spillers, H. J. 63
Spivak, Gayatri Chakravorty 100
Stanner, W. E. H. 101
Stauffer, Jill 154
Sterling, Donald 18
Stoever, J. 73–74

subjectivity 3, 89, 98, 108, 120, 128
subjugated knowers 144, 151–152
Suleiman, Sheikh Shady 43
Surma, Anne 7, 127–135, 136–139
Switzerland 45
Syria 57, 88

Taylor, Louise 97
Taylor, S. 123, 124
terra nullius 25–26, 31, 33n5, 78
terrorism 6, 42, 43, 48, 55, 84, 86, 89–91, 94
textbooks 122, 123, 124
Thill, Cate 77
Thompson, Kimba 108
Tiddas (Aboriginal folk group) 25, 26, 27
Tietze, T. 15
Titley, Gavan 10, 90, 150
Tofighian, Omid 8, 140–148, 149–159
Torres Strait Islander peoples 33n1, 60–61, 108
Trad, Keysar 45
translation process 140–147, 157
Trump, Donald 1, 3, 9, 16, 18, 149
Turnbull, Malcolm 2, 28, 41, 72, 128, 156
Twitter 19, 127, 128, 130, 151n4

Uluru Statement 2, 156
United Kingdom (UK) 10, 16, 17–18, 19, 87, 112–
    113, 119, 149, 154
United Nations 155
United States (US) 3, 27, 32, 128; African
    Americans 26, 33n4, 63, 73–74, 79n8, 102; and
    COVID-19 1, 149; Muslims in 42, 46; racism
    in 1, 6, 9, 10, 13, 14, 16, 76, 154, 155; school
    textbook marketplace 122–124; *see also*
    Trump, Donald
universities 46, 137, 150–151; *see also* curricula

van Diemen, Dr Annaliese 154
Van Dijk, T. A. 39
van Toorn, Penny 102, 103, 106
Veiszadeh, Mariam 43, 47
vilify, freedom to 1, 2, 3, 28–29, 71
Voller, Dylan 2, 60, 61, 62

Waldron, Jeremy 118
War on Terror 42, 43, 48, 55, 84, 89–91, 94
Ward, Glenyse 106
Warrior in Chains (Knox) 31–32
Warsi, Sayeeda 112–113
Weizman, E. 56
West Bank 6, 70–71, 74
White Australia policy 56, 57, 59
white ear 6, 69, 70, 75, 78
white gaze 77, 84
White, Richard 91, 92
white supremacy 4, 9, 10, 11, 26–27, 146, 155
Whitefellas 27, 28, 29
Whiteness 4, 5, 11, 17, 28, 38, 39–40, 41, 42, 43,
    45, 50, 54, 60, 77

Whittaker, Alison 155
Who Let The Dogs Out? 29–31
wilful hermeneutical ignorance 142
Williams, Patricia 83, 84, 94
Williams, Serena 76–77
Williams, Venus 76
Williamson, M. 87–88, 90
Winant, H. 12
Wolfe, Patrick 98, 101, 154

Wotton, Lex 62
Wright, A. 104–105, 109
Writing Never Arrives Naked: Early Aboriginal cultures of writing in Australia (van Toom) 103

Younge, Gary 10

Zionism 113

For Product Safety Concerns and Information please contact our
EU representative GPSR@taylorandfrancis.com Taylor & Francis
Verlag GmbH, Kaufingerstraße 24, 80331 München, Germany